Yesterday, Today, Tomorrow

Yesterday, Today, Tomorrow

My Life

SOPHIA LOREN

**SIMON &
SCHUSTER**

London · New York · Sydney · Toronto · New Delhi

A CBS COMPANY

First published in Great Britain by Simon & Schuster UK Ltd, 2014
A CBS COMPANY

Copyright © 2014 by RCS Libri S.p.A

Originally published as *Ieri, oggi, domani* in 2014 in Italy by RCS Libri.

For illustration and photography credits, see pages 331-332.

1 3 5 7 9 10 8 6 4 2

Simon & Schuster UK Ltd
1st Floor
222 Gray's Inn Road
London WC1X 8HB

www.simonandschuster.co.uk

Simon & Schuster Australia, Sydney
Simon & Schuster India, New Delhi

A CIP catalogue record for this book
is available from the British Library

English language translation by Sylvia Adrian Notini

ISBN: 978-1-47114-072-3
Trade Paperback ISBN: 978-1-47114-073-0
Ebook ISBN: 978-1-47114-075-4

Printed and bound by CPI Group (UK) Ltd, Croydon, CR0 4YY

To my four grandchildren,
the great miracle of my life

Contents

Yesterday, Today, Tomorrow

Prologue

The doorbell to my apartment keeps ringing while I finish kneading the last of the *struffoli*, our traditional Neapolitan Christmas pastry. I leave the dough to rest and hurry to open the door, my hands covered in flour, wiping them as best I can on my apron.

The florist, behind a huge poinsettia, hints at a smile.

"For you, Signora Loren. Can I get your autograph, please?"

The label on the ribbon takes me back to Italy for an instant. I put the plant down on the piece of furniture and open the card. It conveys an affectionate, cheerful thought.

The voices of my grandchildren, who have just arrived from the United States for the holidays, fill the house with excitement and chaos. Tomorrow is Christmas Eve and we'll finally all be together. The truth is, though, that I'm not ready. How will I manage to feed so many people? How can I possibly fry all those *struffoli*?

The world whirls around me dizzily and I feel as if everything is slipping out of my control. I go back to the kitchen, in search of certainties that I can't find. I head into the dining room, hoping that things will go better there. The table! Yes, the dinner table for tomorrow. I want it colorful and beautiful. In a frenzy, I take out the glasses and arrange the plates and cutlery. I fold the napkins carefully. I have fun deciding who will sit where.

I'm a Virgo and, most days, I even manage to bore myself with my compulsive perfectionism, but not today. Today it looks like the messiness is getting the upper hand. I start over again on the table, trying to keep my emotions at bay. Let's see, two, four, eight, plus five, thirteen, and four makes seventeen guests for dinner tomorrow . . . No, not seventeen, that's an unlucky number! Let me count over again.

From the photograph of him on the chiffonier, Carlo is smiling that special smile of his on our wedding day. I'll never forget the first time I felt his eyes on me, many years before, in a restaurant with a view of the Colosseum. I was not much more than a young girl, and he was already a successful man. The waiter came over to me with a note from him saying that the producer had noticed me. Then the stroll in the garden, the roses, the scent of acacia, summer as it was coming to a close. That was the start of my adventure.

I stroke the green armchair where Carlo would doze off while reading the newspaper. I feel cold; I must remember to light the fire tomorrow. Luckily, Beatrice, the youngest of my grandchildren, comes along to take my mind off my recollections. "Nonna Sophia, Nonna Sophia!" She's very blond . . . and very determined. Behind her, the others peer in, like a delegation of little rascals. It's time to get ready to go to bed, but they have no intention of doing so. I look at them, they smile at me, we make a deal.

"Why don't we see a movie?"

Amid shouts of joy, a battle breaks out as they choose which cartoon movie to watch. In the end *Cars 2* wins, their favorite of the moment. We all sit down together in front of the TV.

"Nonna, can you imitate Mamma Topolino for us?"

"Now, *mangia*. Eat!" I recite my line from *Cars 2*, making funny faces as I do so.

"Again, again, Nonna, please. Do it again!"

Hearing my voice, the same that comes from the mouth of a little car, drives them wild. Who would have thought they would enjoy it so much when I accepted, rather reluctantly, the proposal to do that peculiar dubbing job?

Little by little, Vittorio and Lucia, Leo, and Beatrice are mesmerized by the movie and, before it's over, they're fast asleep. I cover them with a blanket, look at my watch, and think about tomorrow. Outside it's started to snow, but with all the hustle and bustle inside I hadn't even noticed.

Comings and goings are always very special moments. They set the merry-go-round of recollections in motion, opening doors to yesterday, today, and tomorrow.

When I think back on my life, sometimes I'm surprised that it's actually all true. I say to myself, *One morning, I'll wake up and find out that it's all just a dream.* Not that it was always easy. There were hard times. But it was definitely wonderful and worthwhile. Success, too, bears its burden that you have to learn how to cope with. No one can teach you. The answer is inside you, where all answers are.

I tiptoe back to my bedroom. It's comforting to spend some time alone. I know that if I stop for a moment of quiet, I can find the peaceful beating of my heart, and calm.

As soon as I'm in the bedroom I realize I'm still wearing my apron. I untie it, take off my shoes, and slump onto the bed; the magazine I'd been reading in the morning is still open to the same page. The excitement of embracing my family again has made it hard for me to sleep these past few nights, and I feel lost if I don't sleep. It's the engine that helps me to travel through my days.

"*Buon riposo!*" (Good night!), Ninni shouts out from the other room. "*Cerchi di dormire!*" (Try to get some rest!)

Ninni, Ninni . . . she's been with us for nearly fifty years. She was Carlo Jr. and Edoardo's Nanny, and when they grew up she stayed on to take care of me. Now, whenever my sons come to the city with their children, she takes care of those little rascals with the same enthusiasm as ever. Sometimes I wonder where she finds the patience to put up with us.

"*Sto già dormendo*" (I'm already half asleep), I tell her to reassure her. But instead of sleeping I just lie there, my eyes wide open as I stare at the ceiling.

As I try to calm down, thoughts race through my mind. Will my grandchildren like my *struffoli*? The ones that my Zia Rachelina would make for us in Pozzuoli, the small town where I grew up, were much better than mine. You know, the flavors of our childhood are always better than others.

I feel restless, the way you do when you slowly slip from reality to a different world, one of dreams or memories. I can't keep still, so I put on my bathrobe and go into the study at the end of the hall. To do what, I don't know. I look at the shelf, I move aside some books, bric-a-brac, pictures, paperweights. I fret, as if I'm looking for something. Then I see a dark wooden box at the back of the shelf. My heart skips a beat. It takes me by surprise, but I recognize it right away. In an instant, I pull it down and open it. Before my eyes are letters, telegrams, notes, photographs. That's what was pulling me here; this is the thread that guided my footsteps on this cold winter night.

The wooden box holds my treasure trove of memories. I'm tempted to leave it as it is. Too much time has passed, too many emotions. But then I muster the courage to pick it up, and I slowly carry it back to the bedroom.

Maybe this is my Christmas gift, and it's up to me to open it.

TOOTHPICK

A MOTHER FOR A GRANDMOTHER
AND A *MAMMINA* FOR A MOTHER

I open an envelope with the word "Nonna" on it, written in my childhood handwriting, and I see myself again as thin as a rail, my mouth too big under my yellowish eyes, and my expression one of surprise. I can't help smiling when I see my own handwriting, and in an instant I'm in Pozzuoli again, remembering the uphill struggle of my childhood. There are some things that, however hard you try, you just can't forget.

In that letter I thanked Nonna Sofia for the 300 lire her son, Riccardo Scicolone, my father, had sent to me on her behalf. My father did not live with my mother, my sister, and me. He even managed to be absent by mail. Nonna Sofia was a cold, distant woman, whom I had only seen once in my life. And yet, in my letter I told her how my first Holy Communion and Confirmation had been the most beautiful day of my life, and that my *comare* (my godmother), had given me a gold bracelet. I also told her that I'd been promoted "to fifth grade, with the highest marks." In other words, I told her things that any grandmother would like to hear, as if she were interested, as if she loved me. I even asked her to thank my father for his thoughtfulness.

I wonder now who had encouraged me to write to her. Perhaps it was Mamma Luisa, my mother's mother, who even in the hardest of times insisted on good manners. She had welcomed me into her home when I was just a few months old, and really did love me. Her love was simple, warmhearted, and unselfish. Or perhaps my mother had encouraged me, as she would find any excuse to make some contact with my father in the hope of getting him back. She resorted to every possible ploy. After all, she was just a young girl whose youth had been stolen when she got pregnant with me. If I think back, it was no accident that I called grandmother and grandfather Mamma and Papà, while my mother was simply Mammina, Little Mother.

As a young girl my mother, Romilda Villani, oozed allure. Fascinating and very talented, she didn't care too much for school, but she played the piano very well and, thanks to a scholarship, she had been able to enroll at the Conservatorio di Musica San Pietro a Majella, in Naples. For her final exam she had prepared Liszt's *The Bells*, graduating with praise and distinction. Despite their limited economic means, my grandparents had bought her a baby grand, which sat proudly in the small parlor at home. But my mother was a restless beauty and had even greater dreams.

A contest held by the American film studio MGM fueled those dreams—and also ended them. MGM was looking all over Italy for someone who resembled Greta Garbo, the absolute queen of all female movie stars at the time. Even though Romilda was just seventeen, she wasted no time. Without telling her parents, she went before the jury, certain she would win. She was right, and just like in some fairy tale she did win, and was awarded a ticket to Hollywood for a screen test. But her parents, Papà Domenico and Mamma Luisa, wouldn't hear of her leaving. She was simply not going to go and that was that. After all, America was on the other side of the world.

Our family legend has it that the people from MGM traveled all the way to my grandparents' home to try to convince them to let Romilda go, but left shaking their heads, incredulous and disappointed that they would not give their permission. So the prize went to the runner-up.

Romilda never forgave her parents, and as soon as she could she left them to pursue her dream: Rome and Cinecittà—Cinema City, the large studio complex that was the center of Italian filmmaking. She was going to get what was coming to her, at whatever cost.

But the young Garbo of Pozzuoli hadn't taken into account the unpredictability of love. Her fateful encounter with Riccardo Scicolone Murillo, who would become my father, happened in the street, in Via Cola di Rienzo, one evening in the fall of 1933. He was tall, handsome, elegant, and had a way with women. Immediately struck by that gorgeous girl in search of glory, he had to win over her heart, and what better way than to invent a story that he worked in the movies, which he really didn't, of course. By that time, Romilda had learned that there were long lines in Cinecittà for aspiring actresses looking to land the same bit parts she was trying for, so she could hardly believe she had found her prince and champion.

Riccardo was twenty, had some money, and came from a family of noble origins. Having had no success as an engineer, he had found a temporary job at the Ferrovie dello Stato, the state-run railroad, on the Rome-Viterbo line. Soon afterward, Romilda and Riccardo met again in a small hotel in the center of the city, where they would make love all night long. But then I came along to ruin everything. When Riccardo found out that Romilda was pregnant, he grew confused about what he wanted, and gradually turned cold toward her. I was just not a part of the plans he had made for his life, nor was my mother.

To defend her daughter, Mamma Luisa arrived unexpectedly in Rome, demanding that they get married. Riccardo was almost convinced to do the right thing, but he stopped short, manufacturing a weak excuse: he had never received Confirmation, and he claimed that making amends for that was more complicated than he had expected. So the marriage never took place. But whether or not he wanted to, my father did give me his last name as well as a drop of blue blood. It's amazing to think that even though I never had a real father, I can still call myself Viscountess of Pozzuoli, Lady of Caserta, a title given by the House of Hohenstaufen, Marchioness of Licata Scicolone Murillo.

A SUITCASE STUFFED WITH WISDOM AND POVERTY

I was born on September 20, 1934, frail and not particularly pretty, in the ward for unwed mothers at the Clinica Santa Margherita in Rome. As I always say, my layette was a suitcase stuffed with wisdom and poverty. Mammina insisted that they put a bracelet on my wrist, because she was terrified that I'd be switched with another baby. For a while, Riccardo, whose own future was uncertain and who was conflicted and wracked with doubts, hoped that his mother, Sofia, would take us in. Romilda had tried to ingratiate herself with Sofia by giving me her name. But once again Riccardo failed to deliver on his promises to my mother. Sofia would not open her house to us, so he rented a room for us in a boardinghouse, where for a few weeks we lived together as a family. Or almost as a family.

Unfortunately, there was no money, the room was not right, and everything else was wrong, too. Papà was too arrogant to accept just any old job, and he didn't have the credentials to be able to get the jobs to which he aspired. When my mother's milk ran out, she began worrying about my health. Her fears became real the day she left me in the hands of the landlady while she went in search of a job. When she came back, I was on the verge of dying: the woman, perhaps well meaning, had given me a teaspoonful of lentils, which had made me seriously ill. And Riccardo? He had disappeared, again.

Romilda did the only thing she possibly could. Somehow she managed to buy a train ticket for Pozzuoli and took me back home with her. Penniless and husbandless, with a dying infant in her arms and the "guilt" of having ruined her family's reputation, she was desperate. She had no idea how her family, the Villanis, would react when they saw us, and was afraid that they, too, would turn us away. But when Mamma Luisa came to the door, all it took was one glance at her daughter with a baby in her arms for her to throw open the door and embrace us as if she'd been expecting us. She took out the brandy, the fancy glasses, and, after an emotional toast, immediately got down to work taking care of me.

"A woman's milk is what's needed here," she declared. Wasting no more time, she summoned the wet-nurse Zaranella, famous throughout the region of Campania, to our home. To help me survive, all the Villanis made a vow to San Gennaro and gave up meat for months. Actually, they gave it all to Zaranella, who in turn gave it back in the form of rich, nourishing milk. No one ever complained about this sacrifice, neither Papà Domenico, affectionately called Mimì, nor Zio Guido, nor Zio Mario, nor Zia Dora. United we stand, divided we fall, is what the family always believed.

But Zaranella's mik wasn't enough to restore my health. I was tormented by a barking cough. "This child is sick," declared the doctor, holding a stethoscope to my chest. "Some fresh mountain air would do her good . . ."

And so Mamma Luisa made plans for the whole family to leave the small apartment on the Lungomare and move to a higher altitude, on Via Solfatara. It was the right choice. After they carried me out for one walk in the cool evening air, a grin appeared on my pale face. "She's saved!" said Mamma Luisa and, calm at last, went back to her other everyday concerns.

Papà Mimì, a small, stocky man, was department head of a munitions factory in Ansaldo, which in a few years, after World War II started, would make Pozzuoli the target of fierce air raids by the Allied forces. Papà Mimì worked very hard, too much so for his age, and in the evening he'd come home exhausted. All he wanted to do was read his newspaper and get some peace and quiet, but instead he would find a huge family that was always in turmoil. Mamma Luisa tried to manage us all as best she could, with her willpower and lots of imagination. Their two sons, my uncles, worked in a factory, but only occasionally, and Zia Dora was a typist. However, all their earnings together weren't enough to put bread on the table every day.

Perhaps more than bread and even more than love, the main ingredient in Mamma Luisa's cooking was imagination. I remember her *pasta e fagioli* (pasta and beans), simmering cheerfully in our small kitchen, releasing into the air the aroma of the sautéed vegetables with lard, when there was any to be had. That smell of home and family protected us before the war, and it also kept us safe during the war and its bombs, death, and violence. Even today, when I remember that homely, comforting aroma, I start to cry and that time all comes back.

Mamma Luisa also made *farinella*, similar to polenta, pasta with squash, *panzanella*, a salad made with stale bread and vegetables, and boiled dried chestnuts. It was very humble cooking, based on hardly anything at all. And yet, compared with the hunger that we would suffer during the war, we ate like royalty, especially at the end of the month, when half of Papà Mimì's salary would end up in Mamma Luisa's meat sauce. Impossible to forget, it was so delicious.

The building on Via Solfatara had a red marble entrance of a shade so beautiful that it had no reason to envy the Hollywood villas I was to see during my career. It was a warm, almost orangey tone, a typically Neapolitan hue. When I saw it many years later it was different, with sad purplish nuances. Perhaps because of time, or the wounds of war, or perhaps because my eyes had become clouded.

The apartment was small, but it seemed to expand like an accordion to fit us all in. Our family of seven had grown. My mother, to earn a penny or two, would play in the cafés and trattorie of Pozzuoli and Naples. Sometimes she'd go all the way up to Rome to meet Riccardo. And that's how one day she came back to her parents, shaking all over, to tell them she was pregnant again.

"Of course, because God rubs salt into the wounds," was Mimì's reaction, resigned before the lack of judgment of that hard-headed, untamable daughter. This time the young Sci-colone didn't let himself be persuaded to provide even a last name for his child. He wanted nothing to do with us and so my sister, Maria, was born a Villani, in 1938. She would bear that name for many years.

I saw my natural father, Riccardo, for the first time when I was about five. Mammina had sent him a telegram saying that I was very ill, in order to persuade him to come visit. Biding his time, of course, but eventually he arrived, and brought me a beautiful toy car with blue pedals, red wheels, and on the side, my nickname, Lella. I was so emotional and excited about seeing him that I was too nervous to look him in the face. To me, my father was Mimì, and no one else could take his place. Every now and again I wonder if my father's feelings were hurt when I couldn't meet his eyes. The fact is that the toy car he gave me still exists—I keep it somewhere in my heart.

Another time he brought me a pair of roller skates. I would race around on them in the entrance hall. Every day my sister would beg me to lend them to her. And I, being a sadistic older sister, would give them to her after they'd just been oiled. Poor little Maria took so many spills!

I lived my life as best I could, hidden behind a thin yet sturdy veil of shyness. Yes, I know it's hard to believe, but I was really shy, perhaps because of our situation: My father was absent, and my mother was too blond, too tall, too lively, and, above all, un-married. Her eccentric, excessive beauty embarrassed me. She was a *ragazza madre*, a girl-mother, as the saying goes. I dreamed of a normal, reassuring mother, with black hair, a creased apron, her hands rough, and her eyes tired—like Mamma Luisa, whom

I would find once again a few decades later in *A Special Day*, a movie in which I play a character named Antonietta, a devoted housewife and mother of six.

I prayed to God that Mammina wouldn't pick me up from school because it made me ashamed in front of my schoolmates. The religious institute that I attended was run by nuns, and, afraid of being teased, I would enter the classroom first or last, after the other students were already in class. I was neat and diligent, and did my duty like a little soldier. But I wasn't at ease with the other children. Little girls, everyone knows, can be really mean. Because I was very dark and also really skinny, everyone called me Toothpick.

I did have a real friend, Adele, who stayed my friend throughout my life. She's no longer with us, and when she passed away she took with her my childhood and all its flavors, the good and the bad. She lived on the same landing as mine. As soon as we got up in the morning, we'd meet on the staircase and stay together until evening. After elementary school we were separated—she went to vocational school and I went to teaching school—but there was really nothing that could keep us apart.

Her family was slightly better off than mine, or maybe it was just smaller than ours, with fewer mouths to feed. Whenever it was Adele's birthday she'd be given a doll that she shared with me. In contrast, my grandmother would give me charcoal for the Epiphany, saying that I'd been naughty. But as she said it she'd look at me with tenderness in her eyes, so I would understand that it wasn't true, and that the problem, as always, was money.

When the war came we were even hungrier than before. Sometimes I just couldn't resist the smell of food that came from Adele's kitchen, and I'd approach it with hope that they'd include me. Sometimes, but not often, Adele's mother would invite me over to have lunch with them.

Many years later, when I went back to Pozzuoli to film a special for television, I made sure Adele was invited. From that moment on we never were out of touch with each other again, until the day I called and she didn't answer the phone. It was my birthday, one of the saddest I can remember. Adele had had a stroke and she was wheelchair-bound, unable to speak. She would weep silently when her daughters talked to her about me, about us, about our lives as children.

At school I was fascinated by the orphans, whom the nuns always sat in the last rows, so that they wouldn't forget their misfortune. I'd sit right in front of them, as if I fell somewhere in between their misfortune and an ordinariness that didn't belong to me. I would have liked to visit the orphanage adjoining the convent, but in between the buildings there was a long flight of stairs that was absolutely out of bounds to us.

The nuns were strict and I was afraid of them, even though they took special care of me. When they had to punish us, they'd tell us to put out our hands so that they could smack them. But they never even touched mine.

I was shy, really, but I did like to go against the grain. When I solemnly wrote to Nonna Sofia about my first Holy Communion, the truth is that I had already taken Communion a while back, in great secret. I had gone to church, stood in line, knelt before the priest and, lowering my eyes, I had answered: "Amen." When I got home I told Mamma Luisa about my adventure, convinced that she would be happy to have such a saintly granddaughter. "What have you done!" she shouted, in despair at my more or less innocent transgression. That transgression was simply my instinctive way of meeting with God. I searched for him, and sometimes found him, in the most unexpected places.

THOSE NIGHTS SPENT IN THE TRAIN TUNNEL

When war came to Italy, I was six. By the time it ended, I was eleven. It filled my eyes with images that I would never be able to erase. When I think of my first memories, I can hear the bombs falling and exploding and the antiaircraft siren wailing. I can feel the hunger pangs and see the cold darkness of those dreadful nights of war. Suddenly, all my fears come back. It might seem hard to believe, but I still sleep with the light on today.

The Germans were the first troops to arrive in our small town. They were Italy's allies at the time. In the morning they would march outside the house, tall, blond, blue-eyed, and I would watch them, entranced, from the window, torn between fear and excitement. To my little girl's eyes they seemed neither mean nor dangerous. But then I'd unintentionally overhear my grandparents talking about deportations and Jews, torture and pulled-out fingernails, retaliation and betrayal, and I'd know that something else was going on. I'd race to the kitchen and ask them questions, but they'd deny discussing such topics. "*Non avimm' detto niente*" (We didn't say anything), they'd reply impassibly. So I could tell that the soldiers were not as harmless as they looked to me.

At first, we were all in the eye of the storm, but soon our lives would be hit hard by the winds of war—and by the air raids. Little by little everything came to a standstill—school, the Sacchini cinema and theater, the band playing in the town square. Everything stopped except for the bombs.

For the Allies, Naples was a key target: it was one of the most important ports in the Mediterranean, at the center of the supply route to North Africa, which the Axis powers controlled. Along with Taranto and La Spezia, Naples was an important Italian naval base. Important industries were also located all around the city, which made the region even more strategic: Baia Domizia, Castellammare di Stabia, Torre Annunziata, Pomigliano, Poggioreale, Bagnoli, and not least our own Pozzuoli. At the outbreak of the war, the Allied attacks were aimed at military targets, but after a certain point, the bombs started to rain down on the town and the coastline. It took me a while to understand that the streaks the bombs left in the sky had nothing to do with the fireworks for the Feast of the Madonna of Pompeii. Houses and schools, churches and hospitals, hotels and markets were struck repeatedly.

I remember everything as though it were yesterday. As soon as the siren sounded, we'd race off to take refuge in the railway tunnel, on the Pozzuoli–Naples line. The railway was a main target for the Allies, like all routes of communication, but for us the tunnel was a place of shelter. We would arrive there with our mattresses and lay them down on the gravel, next to the tracks. We'd all huddle together in the middle—it was dangerous to stay close to the exit—and prepare to spend the night. Sometimes it was humid and cold, other times it was muggy without the slightest breeze. But it was always infested with mice and cockroaches. And it was filled with the roar of the airplanes and by our anguish and our fear that we would not make it out of there alive.

In the tunnel we'd share the little we had and we'd encourage each other. We'd cry and we'd try to sleep. We'd argue and sometimes women would even give birth. All together, one on top of the other, ranting and consoling one another, we hoped the nightmare would end. Then, at dawn or around four thirty, we'd rush out to avoid being run over by the early train.

Often the bombs would start falling unexpectedly—the siren didn't always work—and I'd be so frightened that instead of getting dressed I'd start undressing. It happened over and over again that the first airplanes surprised me naked, still at home.

Together with my mother I'd run breathlessly toward the shelter. But one evening shrapnel from a bomb hit me on the chin and I got to the tunnel scared to death and bleeding. It was nothing serious but it left a scar. A few months later, that scar would unexpectedly bring us a gift of food.

Hunger was the major theme of my childhood.

Sometimes, when we'd leave the shelter, my mother would walk us into the country, into the hills just outside Pozzuoli, where the shepherds' grottoes were. A friend of my uncle would give her a glass of fresh milk for Maria and me. They called it *'a rennetura*, which meant that it had been milked right after the calf had eaten. It was thick and as yellow as butter, and it made up for days and days of no food. Yes, because the longer the war continued and the bombing grew more intense, the greater the shortage of water and food. Rationing wasn't enough, all transportation was blocked, and the bombs had destroyed the water main. The people were on their knees.

Mamma Luisa would send me to do the shopping at Signora Sticchione's, where we had a sort of open account, which she jotted down on a scrap of the same brown paper she used to wrap the bread in. On the third of the month there was no money left and she'd give us credit, mumbling bitterly to herself: "*Ci risiamo 'n'ata vota* (Here we go again) . . ."

The truth is we were all more or less in the same boat. I'd purchase eight coffee beans in a teaspoon, a *cuppetiello*, which my grandmother would grind and use to "disguise" the barley she had to brew. We were also due a loaf of bread with the addition of a small bun, called *'a jonta*, which never made it home because I couldn't stand the hunger and I'd eat the little roll before getting there. My grandmother would ask me: "*Ma addò sta?*" (Well, where is it, then?), but she never rubbed it in. She loved me deeply and to see me in pain made her suffer so much.

As time passed there was no more buying food, no money,

no supplies. On some days, we wouldn't even have a crumb to eat. There's a vivid scene in Nanni Loy's *The Four Days of Naples*, a movie made after the war about the uprising of the Neapolitans against the occupying Germans, in which one of the young characters sinks his teeth into a loaf of bread so voraciously, so desperately, I can still identify with him. In those four famous days in late September, when Naples rose up against the Germans—even before the Allies arrived, it was the climax of a terrible period of deprivation and marked the beginning of the end of the war in Italy.

But before the end of the war, when the bombs that were falling on Pozzuoli had become unbearable, we were ordered to evacuate. Having no alternative, we took refuge in Naples with the Mattia family, Mamma Luisa's relatives. My uncles, Guido and Mario, who had gone into hiding to avoid the German conscription, had come with us on the train, but they had taken a terrible risk. At one station, the Germans had boarded the train to look for able-bodied men, and my uncles were almost caught. Two nuns who shared the compartment with us quickly hid them under their habits, saving them. This would later become a sort of legend, as well as a family joke. But at the time it was no laughing matter. We felt deep gratitude for these two women who risked their lives for perfect strangers.

The Mattias would not be as kind. They weren't brave enough to throw us out, but they took us in, reluctantly. I was all skin and bones, and Maria contracted typhus, which had spread throughout the city.

My mother went begging for food for us, but she didn't always manage to get any. She'd bring us a potato, a fistful of rice, or some of that black bread that was so hard on the outside, but stuck to the knife when cut because it was moist inside. Maria and I would always stay home to hold on to our place in the apartment, in case the Mattias refused to let us come inside again. We'd shape puppets with bread dough, and then place them to dry on the window ledge. The next morning we'd be so hungry we'd eat them all in one bite.

One evening, looking out the window, Romilda saw a woman pushing a baby carriage and carrying a loaf of bread. Counting on maternal solidarity, she threw herself at the woman, begging for a piece of bread as she pointed to our malnourished faces in the window. That mother was so moved that she shared her loaf of bread with us.

Then came September 8, 1943, when the Germans suddenly turned into oppressors as well as occupiers, and they gripped Naples in an iron vise, setting strict curfews and further conscription of our men. The Italian government had surrendered to the Allied forces, who had invaded the South, and the Germans could smell the scent of defeat. They took all their frustration out on us in a cruel and indiscriminate way. Exhausted by hunger, disease, and bombs, the Neapolitans reacted against them. I remember the day a young Italian sailor was arrested, his only fault being to have celebrated the news of the armistice, the hope that peace was on its way. He was shot on the steps of the university, right before the eyes of the other townspeople who, in spite of their shock and revulsion, were forced by the German soldiers to applaud.

Soon after, the city rose up spontaneously, from quarter to quarter, from house to house. People of all ages, of all social classes fought together. Still trying to keep control, the Germans called up men between the ages of eighteen to thirty-five for compulsory labor, but only 150 out of 30,000 showed up. By September 27, it was an all-out war between the Neapolitans and the Germans. A group of brave street urchins took part, as well, and became the heroes of the revolt. The Neapolitan uprising kept the Germans from organizing against the Allies and, after the four days of our revolt, they made a deal with the insurgents and withdrew. On October 1, 1943, General Clark entered the city leading the Allied troops.

The first Allied soldier I saw was wearing a kilt. He belonged to the Scottish troops that paraded through the streets of the city amid the laughter and the teasing of the young boys. The Americans gave out candy, biscuits, chewing gum. One soldier tossed me a piece of chocolate, but I had no idea what it was and didn't dare taste it. I took a can of instant coffee home and gave it to Mamma Luisa. It took her a while to understand that all she had to do was add some hot water to turn it into a beverage whose taste she had long forgotten.

"*LONE PINE . . .*"

After the war, it was time to start over again. We left Naples and walked back to our house in Pozzuoli. Maria, who was still sick, rode on Zio Mario's shoulders. The building had been bombed but it was still standing. We put cardboard and newspapers in the windows and stood in the long lines at the black market. Along with our hunger and thirst we now had to deal with lice, which tormented us for months and months until they were eradicated by that great American invention DDT. When the lice finally disappeared, it was a sign to me that the war had truly come to an end.

The Allies handed out real food—even white bread, which was a real luxury for us—and the farmers, little by little, began to cultivate the land again. But when winter came, the cold took our breath away. We were nine of us now at Mamma Luisa's, with the arrival of a cousin. We'd all stay close together in the kitchen, the warmest room in the house. But outside, the world was still a daunting place.

A division of Moroccan soldiers led by a French officer occupied the entrance to our building. Totally disrespectful, they acted as though it were their own home, loafing there from dawn till dusk. They made us feel unsafe and every now and then they'd come and bang on the door, rousing us from our sleep. More than fifteen years later, on the set for *Two Women* my memory of them would help me to make a dramatic part of the movie, when my character is attacked by Moroccan troops, even more realistic.

In the morning, when I'd go down the stairs to go to school, there would be condoms strewn all around the entrance. Naturally, I had no idea what they were and one day picked one up, thinking it was a balloon. Just as I had done after taking Communion, I went to Mamma Luisa joyfully, holding that small trophy in my hands. And again I quickly realized I had made a mistake. My grandmother wouldn't let me walk down there anymore—"No more balloons for you." She also spoke to the French officer, who from that day on kept a closer eye on his men.

My mother had started playing the piano again, in a trattoria with blue walls opposite from where we lived. My sister, who had recovered from her illness, would often join her to sing: "*Pino solitario ascolta questo addio che il vento porterà . . .*" (Lone pine, heed this farewell the wind brings with it). Maria was just a child, but she looked like a mature artist. I watched her and Mammina admiringly but, as usual, filled with shame, while the American soldiers felt right at home and raved about my mother and my sister's talent. Because of their appreciation, someone had the idea to welcome the soldiers into our good parlor on Sunday afternoons, to make a penny or two by opening a sort of domestic café. Mamma Luisa served homemade brandy, blending the alcohol she'd buy at the black market with cherry-flavored Strega, and Mammina would play while the soldiers hummed and sang songs by Frank Sinatra and Ella Fitzgerald. My job was to carry the bottles to be watered down back and forth and to learn how to dance the boogie-woogie.

One of those soldiers saw the scar on my chin and took me with Mammina to the troops' camp doctor, who, as if by magic, made it disappear. Not content to have helped me in this way, he sent us back home with a jeep filled with food supplies. There were even some *stortarielli*, short pasta made with white flour. We thought we had to be dreaming to see this much food.

At the time, Mammina tried to teach me to play the piano, which I loved, but every time I made a mistake she'd get angry and slap my head so hard I'd get a headache. I had to give it up, because of those headaches. I consoled myself by going to the movies at the Sacchini theater, which had reopened at the end of the war. That's when American movies invaded the theaters. I saw *Blood and Sand* over and over again, falling hopelessly in love with Tyrone Power and Rita Hayworth's ginger hair. Then came *Duel in the Sun*, which enthralled me in almost the same way. Lonely as I was, I would get lost in the dreamy gazes of Jennifer Jones and Gregory Peck, and I would dream of becoming just like them. It wasn't the fact that they lived the lives of stars that fascinated me, but their ability to express what they felt inside.

School had reopened, too, and I liked studying, even though as time went by my interest waned. The last year my report card was filled with low marks. To do my homework I'd wait for Zia Dora, the brains of the family, to come home from work. But she was so tired she'd often fall asleep between a Latin translation and a verb exercise. "*Zia, scetate!*" (wake up!), I'd whisper, feeling rather guilty.

My chemistry teacher loved me, as did my French teacher. I've always been good at languages, something that helped me a lot with my career. But at the time I had no idea what I might become; for all I knew I was going to be teacher, which is what my father wanted for me. Or at least this is what I seem to remember.

Many years later, upon returning to our home in Pozzuoli, I was amazed to find a notebook from when I was a little girl. Inside it, I read the words: "Sofia Scicolone is going to be an actress one day." I must already have had some idea about what my future would be. And yet, when Maria and I would organize little shows in the kitchen, and Mamma Luisa, who had started out as a seamstress, helped us to sew our paper costumes, it was my sister who performed in front of everyone, members of the family, and neighbors. I would stand in the corner to watch, and even that made me feel shy and embarrassed.

But things were starting to change. I was growing up, the ugly duckling was turning into a swan. Above all, the desire, the almost physical need to express my emotions, to translate into gestures and words the feelings I had built up inside and that I still could not interpret was growing inside me. I wanted to dive into a wider sea. Little did it matter that I couldn't swim.

II

THE FAIRY-TALE FACTORY

PRINCESSES IN CARRIAGES

My transformation from ugly duckling to swan is clearly portrayed on a cover of *Sogno*, an Italian photo-romance magazine that I pull out of my treasure chest of memories. Now yellowed, the cover shows my face in a close-up that peers out at me, across another time and age to reawaken my memories. The year is 1951, and on it is a name that stretches way back into the past and has almost been forgotten: Sofia Lazzaro.

The war had ended, Italy had gone back to living, people to dreaming their dreams. It's hard even for me to recognize the Toothpick I had been until just before then behind the languid gaze of a heroine of *fotoromanzi* (photo-romances). In only a few years, my figure, face, and name had all changed. Even my city had changed.

My adolescence was a full-fledged revolution, as unpredictable as revolutions always are. Time can speed up suddenly, old fears can make way for new challenges, and everything can take on a different appearance, while we head down unknown and unimagined roads.

I had blossomed very late compared with my girlfriends, and by the time I finally did, I wasn't expecting it anymore. As I was about to turn fifteen, I suddenly found myself living inside a curvy, glowing body, filled with life and promise. Whenever I walked down the streets of Pozzuoli, the boys would turn around and whistle after me.

The first person to notice my maturity was my physical education teacher. He was a handsome, well-built young man, accustomed to thinking of the world as a basic floor exercise. One spring day he showed up at our doorstep, with a grave expression on his face, hat in hand, to ask my mother for my hand in marriage.

"Donna Romilda, I have true feelings for your daughter. I

have a house, and I even have a steady job. If you were to agree, we could marry in September."

"Dear Teacher, I'm truly sorry but it's out of the question. Sofia is too young to marry."

My mother dispatched him kindly, but without a moment's hesitation. She felt sorry for that mild-mannered young man, but she had other plans for me. I watched the scene from a distance, as if it had nothing to do with me, but I felt very relieved. I was still trying to figure out who I was, let alone think of getting married.

Another boy had drawn my attention for a short time. His name was Manlio and he lived in La Pietra, a few train stops from Pozzuoli. We'd seen each other on the street, had felt attracted to each other, and one afternoon I found the courage to move beyond the borders of my small world and go look for him. All I can remember now are his red eyes and an enthusiasm I wasn't prepared for. Maybe he'd had something to drink, or maybe it was just the ardor of youth, but he scared me. I wasn't ready, and I ran off without looking back.

While I may have looked like a woman on the outside, inside I was still a bashful, introverted girl. I knew I had to throw myself into what I wanted to do, but I didn't know how or where. And maybe not even why.

It was a beauty pageant in Naples that finally offered me a springboard. I would never have gotten that far if Mammina hadn't taken me there, in spite of my shyness and our poverty. She was like a fairy godmother who, against all odds, gets Cinderella to the ball. No doubt about it, those years of my life have the feel of a fairy tale that comes true.

One day in the fall of 1949, a neighbor came to see us, holding a newspaper clipping that said that the *Corriere di Napoli*, the city's afternoon newspaper, was organizing a beauty pageant to elect the Queen of the Sea and her Twelve Princesses.

The winners were to ride through the city streets in a carriage, transforming, as if by magic, the ruins left by the war into an enchanted kingdom.

Romilda's eyes sparkled and she shot me a knowing look. The moment she had been waiting for for a long time, our moment, had come at last. We still barely had enough money to eat, so no way was mother going to let this opportunity slip away. Her own chance had been denied her by her parents, and she'd never forgotten it. She would have done anything to get even somehow. I answered her submissively, which I usually did: "If you really insist . . ." I wasn't quite old enough to enter the pageant, but she twisted my hair up to make me look more mature, and threw herself wholeheartedly into the job of preparing me for the big event.

Not even Mamma Luisa dared disapprove this time, and, although reluctantly, she contributed in her own way. A proper ball requires a dress and slippers, so Luisa took down the pink taffeta curtains from the windows and in no time at all turned them into an evening dress, perhaps not exactly elegant, but at least dignified. As for slippers, I only had one pair of shoes, and they were dark and worn: all that could be done was to paint them white to make them look brand-new again. "Holy Mary, I beseech you, don't let it rain," my fairy godmothers whispered in quivering voices.

So Mammina and I took the train, in a third-class carriage, headed for Naples. It was cold, and I'd put on my everyday coat—the only one I had—over my dress. Everybody kept staring at me, I looked like I was dressed up for the Mardi Gras. All it would take was a gust of wind, a drop of rain, a minute's delay, to turn my carriage into a pumpkin and shatter the dream.

The pageant was to start at Cinerama, the movie theater on Via Chiaia, and end at the Circolo della Stampa, inside the municipal authority building, a beautiful villa that is now abandoned. At the time, however, it was the pride of Naples, and the city was making every effort to rebuild everything the war had destroyed. I followed my fate like a lamb to the slaughter, but as soon as I'd gone in I realized I'd been noticed. Maybe the judges were struck by my diffidence, so different from the attitude of the other girls, more than a hundred of them. They might prove luckier than I was, but they were acting like a gaggle of geese, flocking together. I took a deep breath and jumped into the audition: As I paraded in front of the members of the jury, against the glistening backdrop of the Gulf of Naples, my inherent shyness made way for an animated cheerfulness and confidence.

This always happens to me, even today: before going out on stage I'm overrun by my fears, but as soon as the spotlights come on I let myself go, and I manage, who knows how, to show my best side.

After what seemed like forever, the jury announced the names of the winners. I still remember how thrilled I was to hear my name among those of the newly elected princesses. It was really only half a victory, not having been chosen as queen, but that didn't matter. I didn't completely fulfill the canons of classical beauty, which undoubtedly had complicated matters. And yet the fact that I was different would be one of the secrets of my success. For now, I needed to believe in myself.

I was overwhelmed but also energized by the applause, photos, interviews, and a lovely bouquet. My debut in the world had been a success. The pageant winners paraded down the city streets accompanied by a band, while the people showered us with flowers. The queen sat by herself at the front of a golden carriage, we princesses in the back. Via Caraccioli, Via Partenope, Piazza Municipio, Via Agostino Depretis, Corso Umberto, and from Piazza Nicola Amore, up Via Duomo, Piazza Cavour, then down Via Roma (now Via Toledo) and again toward the sea.

When I think back on the scene, it was almost like being in a Vittorio De Sica movie! I was in seventh heaven. Who cared that it was raining—the rain made everything seem more romantic, more unreal. And my shoes stayed white. The record books say that Tina Pica, the noted actress, Sergio Bruni, the popular singer and "Voice of Naples," and even Claudio Villa, the great singer and star of musicals, were there to celebrate the most beautiful girls of Naples.

At the time, of course, I didn't realize just how much that day would change the course of my life. Like any young girl, I focused on the prizes, which seemed too beautiful to be true: several rolls of wallpaper with a large green-leaf pattern, which made Mamma Luisa happy, a tablecloth with twelve matching napkins, and no less than 23,000 lire, about 36 US dollars at the time, a sum I had never in my entire life seen all in one place. But, most importantly, the prize included a train ticket to Rome, which, at the time, didn't particularly impress me but made Mammina tremble with excitement. We were holding our passport to Cinecittà, the center of Italian filmmaking, Hollywood on the Tiber.

But first Mammina did sign me up to attend an acting school in Naples, which she paid for with the money she earned from the piano lessons she had started giving again. To be honest, it wasn't so much a school as an example of what they call *arrangiarsi*—the art of making do—by a genuine Neapolitan. That actors' studio in the shade of Mount Vesuvius is where I took my first steps. The school taught a method of acting based on the years of experience of a single master, Pino Serpe, who bragged about carving actors and actresses from stone. How? By teaching us to make faces. All our facial muscles were trained to express the vast range of human emotions: horror, joy, desperation, sadness, surprise, arrogance, hope. Our eyebrows were absolute protagonists. It might sound silly, but this simple game of imitation forced me to come out and show others what I was capable of doing. And it would be of great help when it came time for me to enter the world of photo-romance magazines, which was just around the corner.

A few years later, when I had arrived in Hollywood, I received a letter that read: "My name is D'Amore, we used to take lessons from Serpe, *t'arricuorde?*" (do you remember?). I was touched that my acting school friend remembered me. I pictured him clearly: he came from the countryside, and unlike many of us at the time, he seemed to have a chance in the world—his family had food. He'd pay our teacher with bread, salami, and eggs.

Maestro Serpe arranged a few auditions for me. He got me a bit part in Giorgio Bianchi's *Hearts at Sea*, and in Mario Bonnard's *The Vow*. Most importantly, he informed me that in Rome MGM was looking for extras for an epic film to be set in ancient Rome. Once again, when Mammina heard that about MGM, she knew exactly what she wanted and, against my grandparents' will, she decided we were going to relocate. Maria, who was still a little girl and whose health was poor, stayed with my grandparents in Pozzuli, while Mammina and I, filled with eagerness and fear, headed off toward our dream.

QUO VADIS

Rome welcomed us with open arms, or so it seemed. I can't say the same for my father, whom Romilda called as soon as we came out of the station. She was so naive that she didn't even know how to use a token-operated public phone, and had to go into a café and ask to use their phone to make her call. Evasive as always, Riccardo reluctantly agreed to meet us at his mother's, but he was clearly disturbed by our unexpected arrival.

Nonna Sofia offered me a glass of milk and then, without

even asking us how we were or patting me on the head, left us to wait for him in the living room. When Papà came in, he glanced at me absentmindedly, his eyes filled with resentment. He didn't seem at all surprised to see how I had grown and used every last ounce of energy to discourage us from going ahead with our plans. If it had been for him, we would have headed right back to Pozzuoli, leaving him with his new family. Because in the meantime he'd married another woman, and they had had two children, Giuliano and Giuseppe.

I'll always remember the day he'd come to Pozzuoli, several years before, to inform my mother of his imminent marriage. Until that moment I hadn't really understood the great suffering between them, because all he ever did was spurn us. When little Maria walked into the room, he asked scornfully: "And who's this?" even though he knew perfectly well who she was.

In Nonna Sofia's sitting room, Mammina had no intention of being demoralized by the coldness of her first and only true love. Not for a moment did she even consider backing down. When we left my grandmother's house, she turned to some distant cousins of ours to ask them if they would put us up. They, too, tried to send us back home, but they eventually had to give in, and lend us a sofa to sleep on. They certainly didn't make us feel comfortable, but nothing could stop us from pursuing our destiny.

The morning of our second day in Rome we set off on foot for the "fairy-tale factory" on Via Tuscolana, dressed in black so that we'd look more elegant.

History with a capital H hadn't spared Cinecittà, either. The war had reduced its almost 100 acres to a pile of rubble, just like much of the rest of the country. In November 1943, most of the cameras and other equipment had been plundered by the Nazis and shipped north by train, although some were saved and hidden in storehouses around Rome. The large buildings had been used as German military storage spaces, but seven of the most important studios had been destroyed by the Allied air raids. When Rome was liberated, the area was transformed into a refugee camp. The Pisorno studio, halfway between Pisa and Livorno in Tirrenia, which predated Cinecittà's founding—it was the first city in which an entire film could be produced, beginning to end—was used as a US military logistic command base. After the armistice, the workers, stagehands, directors, and actors who hadn't supported Mussolini's Social Republic of Salò, the last Axis stronghold established in Northern Italy after the invasion of Southern Italy by the Allies, had taken out the few machines they'd managed to hide and started working again, waiting for the rest of Italy to be liberated. Filming of *Rome, Open City* began in 1945, and the movie was released in September, less than a month after the end of the war.

With very few resources and tons of ideas, everyone had to start from scratch. People's lives were starting up again and there were lots of beautiful and powerful things to describe. For Italian directors the time had come to get back to work. It was the dawning of neorealism, which was to change the history of cinema forever. Roberto Rossellini, Vittorio De Sica, and Luchino Visconti went into the streets to document the reality of working people and the poor. They focused their cameras on people's—and especially children's—gestures and faces, and on everyday objects. Meanwhile, American troops were flooding Italy with Hollywood films that made viewers dream a different kind of dream, one that brimmed with freedom and hope.

A new kind of war began between Italian filmmakers and producers and the major American film companies. As a young state undersecretary in charge of entertainment, Giulio Andreotti, who would later become Italy's forty-first prime minister, did everything in his power to ensure Cinecittà's rebirth. Andreotti managed to get a law passed that froze all the earnings from American films in Italy, thereby bringing money and work to Rome. When MGM arrived in the city to produce *Quo Vadis*, it was instantly Hollywood on the Tiber. And this is where my story as an actress really begins.

One morning in May 1950, Mammina and I hopped onto the blue streetcar that was leaving from Termini Station, and got off at the last stop. To my eyes, it looked as though the entire Roman army had camped outside the entrance to Cinecittà in search of a job, willing to work for anyone that had something to be done. As we made our way through the crowded field, we saw a multitude of people standing in line. Each was seeking to be hired as an extra or to get a bit part. We took our place in that line, putting all our hopes in it.

As soon as he arrived, Mervyn LeRoy, director of *Quo Vadis*, had all us would-be actors parade by so that he could choose the most promising faces. My mother had told me to always answer "Yes" in English, whatever the question asked might be. Too bad LeRoy spoke English and I didn't.

I got ready as best I could for the scene.

When he called my name I stepped forward and put on my nicest smile.

"Do you speak English?"

"Yes."

"Is this your first time in Cinecittà?"

"Yes."

"Have you read *Quo Vadis*?"

"Yes."

"What's your name?"

"Yes."

"How old are you?"

"Yes!"

LeRoy burst out laughing and, perhaps touched by my inexperience, gave me a small part all the same, one that had no lines in it. My role was that of a simple handmaiden, who tossed flowers at a triumphant Vinicius, played by a very handsome Robert Taylor. Mammina spent the whole day with a huge bronze basket on her head, and in the evening she couldn't move her neck at all. We later discovered that the other extras, who were much savvier than she was, had refused to take that part at the last minute, leaving this newcomer with the heavy task.

I still remember the din, the lights, the cries, the stifling heat, hundreds and hundreds of people standing for hours, and being moved from one set to another like post office packages. The extras were on the lowest rung of the ladder, and they weren't always treated kindly, especially whenever they accidentally spoiled a scene so that it had to be shot over again. Each time I ended up in the front row, with the cameras in front of me, I deceived myself into thinking they'd get me in the shot, too. They did, but the truth is I was out of focus, just a tiny detail, really, in a majestic picture. Most times I felt very small, but I knew I was in the right place, and I knew in my heart that, with plenty of patience and perseverance, I would eventually succeed.

One of the extras, although we had no way of knowing it, was a young Carlo Pedersoli, the future Bud Spencer, at the time an Italian swimming champion. Thanks to his athletic build he had been assigned the prestigious role of a legionary. A very young but already famous Elizabeth Taylor had also been given a small part. She was just a few years older than I was, but she'd become a world-class star thanks to *Lassie Come Home*.

I was stunned to see in person Robert Taylor and Deborah Kerr, whom I had admired so many times at the Sacchini movie theatre. I couldn't take my eyes off them. It was a dream just to be able to breathe the same air as they did.

But every rose has its thorn, and the sharpest was yet to jab us. Once we'd passed the director's test, the names of the extras who'd been chosen were called over the intercom so that we could be registered on the payroll. After "Villani" came "Scicolone," but two Scicolones showed up. One of them was me. The other one was my father's wife.

I don't remember exactly what happened, but I'll never forget how deeply mortified I felt at that precise moment. My father's wife went on a rampage. Mammina did her best to defend me, heaping on the woman her own frustrations. The real guilty party, as always, was nowhere to be seen. Finally, the production clerk came to my rescue: "Scicolone . . . Sofia."

It was clearly an unnerving situation for both of us, or, I should say, for the three of us, and luckily it never happened again. I wasn't much more than a girl, and I had no interest in the affairs of adults. Besides, what good was that name without the love of the man who bore it? I had grown up without a father and would never really have one.

In any case, the work would earn us 50,000 lire (about 80 US dollars), which we used to buy food for two whole weeks. And then what happened?

And then we used up all the money and, along with our money, Romilda's hopes dwindled as well. One day, looking me straight in the eye, she said: "Sofi, maybe the time has come to go home . . ." Although I was still a girl, I wouldn't let myself be influenced by her fears, however justified they might have been. "What are you saying, Mammina? We have to stay here and keep at it. Sooner or later . . ."

Maybe the light in my eyes convinced her that I was right. One thing was for sure, it was proof that the dream, *her* dream, was now mine, too.

In the meantime, however, we received news that Maria had fallen sick again, so Mammina had to rush back to Pozzuoli, leaving me alone for a few days at our cousins' house. I was scared to death, and tried to be even more invisible than before. Brought up by Mamma Luisa, I knew not to be a nuisance. I'd go to bed after everyone else did, and get up at dawn, making sure all my belongings were tidy so they wouldn't get in anyone's way.

Before she left, my mother had lectured me at length about all the hazards of the city, with which she had become familiar. But I had always been sensible. I had a good head on my shoulders and a mission to accomplish, and I didn't run the risk of falling into easy traps. To spur me on there was some good news, too: I had been noticed by the director of *Sogno*, and this meant my entrance into the magical world of photo-romances.

I CANNOT LOVE YOU

"What's wrong, why aren't you saying anything?"

"His father killed my father. I cannot, I must not fall in love with him."

"Today my revenge begins, and it will be frightful. Can you see my heart, Mother, can you see how it bleeds, how it aches . . ."

"No, Greg, no . . ."

Rereading the lines from the comic books of those days, I feel as though I've been catapulted to another planet. Maybe even then the dialogs had brought a smile to my face. And yet, the genre of the photo-romance was the real postwar publishing boom, and it embodied the desire of Italians, especially women, to laugh and cry freely once more, to flee from a reality that was still harsh, to suffer because of someone else's love pangs, and not because of the bombs or the food shortages. Obstructed relationships, terrible torments, unspeakable sins, switched identities, betrayals, and jealousies sparked the emotions of the readers, both men and women. The stories made no particular demands on its readers; the magazines had no ambitions to do anything but entertain.

The Communists, a strong party in postwar Italy, called the photo-romances the opium of the people, the Catholics called them an instrument of perdition, the intellectuals—many of whom actually wrote and invented them—called them third-rate literature. But at least at the beginning, the photo-romance encompassed an element of transgression, youth, and modernity. They could be disconcerting. The power of the photography, the conciseness of those speech balloons and captions, those young, handsome bodies and often bold plots contributed to changing the rules of the game and expressing the urgent need of women, who'd come out of the war stronger than ever, to find a place for themselves in the sun. Whichever way one looks at it, the photo-romance taught many Italians to read and write, and it contributed to unifying the country, North and South, the country and the city. In time, the Communist Party became aware of this, too, and used it for its electoral campaigns, as did the Church, which employed it to entice the faithful with the stories of the saints, the absolute shining star being Saint Rita of Cascia, the patroness of impossible causes, who had made peace between warring families in the Middle Ages.

The first to have the idea of combining the romantic novel and comics were the Del Duca brothers. They owned the Universo publishing house in Milan, which published *Intrepido*, a history magazine for kids, and delivered romantic novels in installments from door to door. The fruit of their imagination was *Grand Hôtel*, the top photo-romance that offered tormented passions and impossible adventures in a series of comic strips illustrated by two great artists, Walter Molino and Giulio Bertoletti. It was the first step toward the genre of the photo-romance. In 1957, Molino drew me as the main character in a comic book novel, *La peccatrice* (*The Sinner*), in which he managed to capture both my facial features and my expressions. *Grand Hôtel* first appeared on the newsstands in 1946, with its "chained souls" and "golden teardrops." I really liked the drawings, and I remember that in Pozzuoli one copy would be bought for a whole building, where it would then be passed on from one hand to another. There must have been lots of buildings considering that the first issue was reprinted fourteen times in the space of just a week.

The following year Rome answered with the magazines *Bolero* and *Il mio sogno* (*My Dream*), which was soon shortened to *Sogno*, both focusing on photography, which had a more immediate effect and was quicker to produce. That's how the photo-romance as we know it took shape, and *Grand Hôtel* soon followed suit. The first cover of *Il mio sogno* showed Gina Lollobrigida's face, and many of the ones that came later would show mine.

For those of us who aspired to the world of cinema, appearing in a photo-romance was almost a forced passage. It served to make you known, and it also taught you how to act in front of the camera lens, how to respond to the director's orders, and to overcome your inhibitions at emoting. As the insightful journalist, Vincenzo Mollica, so rightly put it, you learned to come to terms with your own expressiveness. That's how it was for me, as I finally had the chance to put to good use the faces I'd been taught so patiently by Maestro Serpe. In the evening, I would spend hours practicing in front of the mirror: I'd go from desperation to sadness, from furious hatred to the most foolish love, from scorn to concern, from rage to passion by simply raising an eyebrow, widening my eyes, pouting my lips.

There was no real set—we were still at the dawning of what was soon to become an industry—but just a makeshift room in which all the photography was done with some lighting and a couple of pieces of furniture as props. We'd read the script and, much like a human jukebox, produce the corresponding facial expression. It was hard work and I took it very seriously.

Different shots per pose, just under twenty images per episode, three or four days a week, less pay than the movies, but much more gratifying than the lack of a real job. Sometimes I was the "prisoner of a dream," at other times an "adorable intruder," or maybe a "princess in exile," or else, like the great Alberto Sordi in *White Sheik*, I'd wander about "in the garden of Allah," with lots of sand everywhere, wearing huge earrings and funny head-dresses.

The photo-romance allowed me to stay in Rome and earn a living, to familiarize myself with two different businesses, to meet the right people, and to get some training. It also allowed me to have fun. And God knows I needed it after all those years of hardship in Pozzuoli and Naples. I became a queen of the genre, along with Vera Palumbo and Anna Vita, and it helped me to understand that I might even make it some day.

Naturally, the photo-romance was fueled by the plots and intrigues of Hollywood cinema, but it also drew upon the *feuilleton*, the light literature or entertaining stories in news-papers or magazines, and the adventure novel, in the tradition of Liala, Italy's most popular romance author, and Carolina Invernizio, a popular serial novelist. *Grand Hôtel* had a more jet-set style, while *Bolero* preferred the exotic. *Sogno*, by constrast, was for all seasons. We who worked for the photo-romances were small, homespun stars. As I leaf through those magazines today, I find, to my surprise, letters that our readers sent us and our flirtatious replies. I wonder who really did write those let-ters, the ones that came in as well as the ones that were sent out.

To Benito, Caserta: "Next time, for the second stage of your platonic love, you may use the 'tu' form to address me. See how bold I was to be the first of us to use it?" Signed Sofia Lazzaro. Yes, I was now "Lazzaro," because Stefano Reda, the head of *Sogno*, had changed my name, his opinion being that my beauty was so stunning it could even raise the dead.

While I played the parts of unyielding princesses and seductive Romanian exiles, proud maids, and gypsy heroines, I
continued to attend the movie productions: I managed to get
myself bit parts in lots of movies, some of which were even
made by important directors. For instance, I appeared in *Variety
Lights*, directed by a young Federico Fellini and Alberto Lattuada. I had a very small part in a theater production, as did
Carla Del Poggio, Alberto's wife. During the breaks, while the
stagehands changed the lights and the sets, Mammina, who had
come back to Rome with Maria, and who would always accompany me to work, played the piano on stage, to Federico's
delight. I'd go from the set for *Bluebeard's Six Wives* to that of
Tototarzan, from *The Return of Pancho Villa* to *White Leprosy*,
forever trying to watch, to understand, to learn the trade.

Little by little I began to get myself noticed. The production
companies starting calling me to offer me small parts, my photographs began to appear in the press, and the following year,
1953, I was given my first lead roles in *Aida*, the film version of
the great tragic opera by Giuseppe Verdi, and *Two Nights with
Cleopatra*. Thanks to my photo-romance comic strips, I was becoming a real actress.

The photo-romances taught me a lot, and gave me a chance
to measure just how much the public appreciated me. But like
everything, that stage of my life had to come to an end.

On the cover of the April 5, 1953, issue of *Sogno* I gaze toward the horizon with an inspired and vaguely nostalgic look.
Underneath the picture, a discreet but heartfelt caption:

*SOFIA LAZZARO, the unforgettable interpreter of so
many of our photo-romances, has been whisked away to the
movies: but Sofia hasn't forgotten the readers of* Sogno, *and
to them she fondly bids farewell and promises to remember
them forever.*

III

THE IDEAL MAN

THE ROSE GARDEN

Whatever it is I look at—my children's eyes, the photographs scattered about in my home, the thousands of sketches accumulated over the course of our life together—it's Carlo I see before me, smiling and self-confident. Even now that he's no longer here, he inhabits my thoughts and inspires my plans. My story—personal, professional and, above all, familial—centers on my encounter with Carlo Ponti. From the moment we met, it was all one long, very long beginning, which we experienced together, without ever once leaving each other.

It was an evening in September 1951, and the umpteenth beauty pageant was being held in a lovely outdoor restaurant overlooking the Colosseum, on the Oppian Hill. It was Miss Lazio or Miss Rome, I can't remember now. A westerly breeze was blowing, the air was sweet and still smelled of summer. I had by then become a habituée of that sort of event, with what seemed like a habit for always coming in second. But that particular evening my thoughts were elsewhere. I was there to have fun, to take my mind off things, to dance, something I was very good at. I was with a girlfriend from Naples—she was a few years older than me, and, just like me, had come to Rome to seek her fortune. Two young men had accompanied us, because in those days good girls didn't go out alone.

The last pageant I'd entered, a year before, was Miss Italia. I'd made it all the way to that one after entering Miss Cervia (Cervia was and still is a resort town on the Adriatic coast). Although I hadn't won Miss Italia, I had been selected for the big national event. Armed with patience, Mammina and I had headed north, in search of the victory that fate seemed to want to deny me. It was important to be seen, to meet the right people, to draw the attention of the photographers, hard work that there was no way of getting out of if you wanted to be successful. And I was there to win my battle, to set things straight for myself and my family, to offer Romilda the dream she hadn't been able to live herself.

What I most remember about that evening so long ago in Salsomaggiore is the swimming pool, around which we were supposed to parade in our bathing suits. My heart was racing, half the country was following us, not like the Queen of the Sea contest, which was still a local event. Only a year had gone by since I'd become a princess in that pageant, but to me it felt like a lifetime.

Our "godmothers" were Gina Lollobrigida and Gianna Maria Canale, finalists in 1947 right behind Lucia Bosè, who would be my role model for a long, long time. I'd had my hair cut to look like Bosè's, and in fact it did, to some extent. Her story had aspects of a fairy tale: she had started out as a salesgirl in a famous pastry shop called Galli in Milan, and had ended up working with the greatest filmmakers of the time. All the girls of my generation wanted to believe in her fairy tale, which promised rebirth, glory, and happiness.

The high point would be the gala evening. That was when we were supposed to file past the audience that had paid to get in. As usual, my problem was, "*E mo' cosa mi metto?*" (Whatever am I going to wear?) The patron of the event, Dino Villani, came to my aid, maybe touched by my lack of experience and lack of means. That afternoon, he sent me to see a friend of his who owned a beautiful boutique, a delightful lady, accustomed to dealing with socialites, but also with young Cinderellas, not all of whom were going to make it as far as the ball.

"*Cara*, try this one on, it should look good on you . . ." she said to me in her lovely Emilian accent, as she held out a long white dress with fringe that she'd picked out without a moment's hesitation from among the rest. My eyes sparkled as I looked at it, I didn't even dare touch it.

She helped me put it on, almost forcefully.

"Signora, but I . . ." I tried to explain my reluctance.

"Don't worry, dear child, it fits you like a glove. Now all you need to do is think about this evening. Tomorrow, when it's over, you can bring it back to me."

I thanked her with all my heart and went back to the hotel feeling reassured.

Her small gesture, so generous and selfless, meant so much to me at the time. That's exactly how it is: what we do or don't do for others can be far more important than we might imagine.

The dress looked good on me, but unfortunately it wasn't enough. As was always the case, the jury, chaired by the great journalist Orio Vergani, didn't know quite what to make of my peculiar beauty. They couldn't completely trust all my sharp corners—"too tall, too thin, ungainly"—but they couldn't pretend they didn't see me either. And so they gave first prize to Anna Maria Bugliari, and made up a special category for me, as if to say a critics' prize or a special award: I got up on the podium wearing a lovely sash that read, "*Miss Eleganza*" (Miss Elegance). Ironic, really, if I think about the randomness of my choice of outfit.

Nineteen fifty was the first year the winners were announced over the radio. My pictures, taken by Federico Patellani and Fedele Toscani, father of the famous photographer Oliviero Toscani, and one of the first newspaper photographers for the *Corriere della Sera* (*The Evening Courier*), an Italian daily newspaper, made the rounds with the movie and photo-romance producers all the same, and maybe that unusual mention aroused some curiosity about my name.

So exactly twelve months later I was sitting at a table with my friends on the Oppian Hill, right below the stage where the jury was seated, when suddenly, a waiter came up holding a note for me. It read: "Why don't you join the pageant, too? It would please me if you did."

"What does this guy want?" I thought to myself. "And who is he anyway? Nothing doing, I'm not in the mood this evening."

But my friends insisted: "These are movie people, this might be your big chance!"

When I received the invitation a second time, signed Carlo Ponti, I gave in. As I had in other pageants, I came in second, but this time there was a small, but essential difference: I had attracted the gaze of the great producer.

Carlo was thirty-nine, twenty-two years older than I was. He had already made a name for himself, and he was at the height of his brilliant career. He made sure he told me when he came over to introduce himself, at the end of the contest, that he had scouted some of the greatest stars, names like Gina Lollobrigida, Sylva Koscina, and my very favorite one of all, Lucia Bosè.

"Shall we take a stroll through the park? It's a charming place. They call it 'the rose garden,' you won't believe the scent . . ." As he spoke he helped me up, and placed my light organza shawl over my shoulders.

Here we go again, I thought to myself, preparing to have to rebuke him if he made the moves men usually tried. The truth of the matter is that Carlo was very businesslike, and instantly won my trust. He told me about the movies he was making, he asked me about myself, about my plans for the future.

"Where are you from, Signorina? Ah, Pozzuoli. If I'm not mistaken, it has a beautiful Roman amphitheater . . . I was there a few years ago."

"It's right behind my house; we can see it from the windows," I answered, grateful he'd found something we had in common.

Right from the start he conveyed a wonderful feeling of assurance and familiarity, as if we had always known each other. I had the strange impression that he'd understood me, that behind my impetuous beauty he had read the traces of a reserved personality, my difficult past, my great longing to be successful, seriously, and with passion. It wasn't just a game for me, it was much more than that.

He understood and came right to the point.

"Have you ever had a screen test?" he asked me right off the bat, as our stroll was coming to an end.

"Well, to be honest . . ."

"You have a very interesting face," he continued, with an authority that was hard to say no to. "Come see me in my office and we can run a test, see how you look on the screen."

He gave me his address and said good-bye, so kindly it sounded almost formal. He was used to beautiful women, but I think he was especially struck by me because I was so different from the others. I had aspirations, but held within me the sound principles of my Pozzuoli provincial and religious education. I was not open to compromising myself.

Carlo was born in Magenta, a town near Milan, where his grandfather had been mayor. He would have liked to have studied architecture, but in the end he'd chosen law, even though he'd always loved art and literature. He'd started working in the cinema almost by accident, dealing with contracts. In 1940, when he was still very young, he'd founded the ATA, the Artisti Tecnici Associati film production house, in Milan, challenging the monopoly in Rome. He made his first movie in 1941, *Old-Fashioned World*, a historical drama that was the first colossal Italian film success, directed by Mario Soldati. It starred Baroness von Altenburger, stage name Alida Valli, and launched her career, but because the movie was about the Italian struggle against the Austrians in the nineteenth century, Carlo was suspected of being anti-Fascist and so was jailed briefly.

After the war Carlo married the lawyer Giuliana Fiastri, the daughter of a general, and they had two children, Guendalina and Alex. Carlo then moved to Rome to work with Riccardo Gualino, founder of the legendary production house Lux. Carlo respected and admired Gualino, but he was too resourceful to stay behind the scenes, and in 1949, together with Dino De Laurentiis, who had also been raised in Lux's shadow, he'd created his own production company, which boasted great directors such as Vittorio De Sica and Alberto Lattuada, Luigi Zampa and Roberto Rossellini, Alessandro Blasetti, Mario Camerini, Luchino Visconti. It's hard to say if I realized all this at the time.

I do know that my gut feeling told me to accept the invitation I'd received in the romantic rose garden. I don't remember whether I went there the next morning, or whether I let a day or two go by, but I was eager to find out whether his interest in me as an actress was sincere and well founded, as it had seemed to be. My mother got ready to come with me, but that time I stopped her.

"Mammina, it's better if I go alone."

The look she gave me was a blend of concern and offense, and she tried to insist. But I had made my decision, and she could not make me change my mind.

I showed up, all out of breath, at the address Ponti had given me and found myself standing in front of a police station. I was exasperated, and my instinctive mistrust, which my mother had no doubt instilled in me, made me think that it had to be some kind of ugly prank. *There, he was kidding me all the time. He's a producer just like I'm a ballet dancer*, I thought. I felt my anger rising, mixed with a feeling of bitter humiliation. *How could I have believed him! I was stupid, so stupid!* I thought of my father, and the tricks with which he'd drawn Romilda into his web.

Thank heavens, though, not all stories are the same, and mine had yet to be written. A young policeman who noticed my confusion reassured me: "If you're looking for the Ponti–De

Laurentiis production company, it's the next door down from here." I felt silly and childish, thanked him with a big smile, and got ready to enter the heart of Italian cinema. In a few days I was going to be seventeen.

THE FAVORITE

After about half an hour Carlo was ready to see me. I'd never been in such an impressive, luxurious office. I still remember how in awe I was when I saw all those telephones in a row on the desk. "They're for all the different intercontinental lines," he answered, with his irresistible smile, before I could even ask. I didn't say much because I wasn't sure what to say, but strangely enough I felt comfortable, as if I'd always been there. His experience and my freshness met somewhere in the middle, and we were starting to get to know each other.

Behind the desk Carlo had a trunk, which he'd inherited from a film he'd just produced with Gina Lollobrigida—maybe *The White Line* or *A Dog's Life*. He opened it and pulled out a beautiful dark pink dress. "You might be able to use it for some of the photos," he said courteously.

"Maybe, but I'm not sure . . ." I answered shyly. In the end I accepted it, although without trying it on. Even if I had wanted to, I wouldn't have known where, and just the thought of it made me blush.

Taking advantage of a set that was already mounted, Ponti led me to a theater located next to his office, and wasted no time in having me do a screen test. It was neither easy nor fun. And the results were terrible.

"Here, you, put this on," the technician said to me, holding out a bathing suit. His rudeness made me gasp. And to think that I was there with the producer. *Who knows the kind of treatment I'd get if I were alone*, I thought, horrified. I got changed behind the folding screen and then came out to where they were. I felt naked and my bashfulness stung like an open wound. Totally indifferent, the cameramen handed me a cigarette, ordering me to light it and then to walk back and forth while looking into the camera. I'd never smoked before, nor had I ever been alone in front of a movie camera. I felt totally incompetent, and the camera operator seemed to agree with me.

"Doc, she's impossible to photograph. Her face is too short, her mouth is too big, and her nose is too long." As usual I was "too much" of something. But that's the way I was, what fault was it of mine?

This first attempt was followed by others, equally disastrous. I was trying not to get discouraged, but my hopes were fading and the cameramen weren't in the least concerned about being kind to me. They didn't seem to realize that I was just a kid, that their words could crush me. At last, a somewhat more sensitive, or maybe just slightly older makeup artist came to my aid. Perhaps I reminded him of his daughter, or a younger sister, sparking his compassion.

"Signori, what they're saying is just nonsense. All they need to do is change the lighting so that the shadow cast by your nose will be shorter!"

His spontaneous, genuine words helped me to keep going. When, sometime later, Carlo tried to suggest the idea that a touch-up might be helpful, I wouldn't even let him finish what he was saying.

"Sofia, have you ever thought about . . .you know, softening your . . . your . . . dominant profile . . ."

"Carlo, if you're suggesting that to be able to make movies I'm going to have to slice off a piece of my nose, well then I'm going back to Pozzuoli because I have no intention of getting a nose job."

"No, Sofia, that's not what I meant . . ."

"Don't think I can't see what you were getting at. I'm not stupid. It's out of the question, and that's that. When you change a person's nose you change everything, and I don't want to change."

I didn't want a small, turned-up nose. I knew perfectly well that my beauty was the result of a lot of irregularities all blended together in one face, my face. Whether I won or lost, it was going to be in the original version.

I was so young, and before me was a powerful man, much older and more experienced than me, who held my fate in his hands . . . I don't know how I found the courage to stick to my guns. Maybe it was the boldness of youth, or maybe a tiny voice inside me was telling me to keep at it and not to give up anything I thought was important. I think Carlo was also taken aback by my determination and self-confidence, despite the hint of shyness and vulnerability I still conveyed. He would always say that he'd seen the artist in me, even before the actress—that something sparkled inside me. I'm not really sure what he meant by that, but it sounded like a compliment, and as such I've always treasured it.

During that period I wasted no time. I was always running from one set to another, from one photo-romance to another. I was trying to find the right path, even though it was hard to navigate those different worlds. In the first half of the year I'd had a bit part—which was much better than playing an extra—in *Milan Billionaire* and in *It Was Him . . .Yes! Yes!*, in which I'd been forced to act bare-breasted for the French market. In the former I played a girl who worked in a café, in the latter I had two roles: I played a bridal gown model and a concubine. Both were directed by Vittorio Metz and Marcello Marchesi and, although there wasn't anything special about these movies, they'd allowed me to see how professional actors like Isa Barzizza, a great actress of the stage and films, Tino Scotti, and

Walter Chiari, worked. "It's all good experience!" I'd tell myself, in my youthful wisdom, driven by ambition.

In *Anna*, a 1951 hit about a night-club singer turned nun, directed by Alberto Lattuada, starring the actress Silvana Mangano and leading man Vittorio Gassman, I was even given the chance to say a few lines. Lattuada, whom I'd met a year earlier on the set for *Variety Lights*, in which I'd had a very small part, had encouraged me from the start, reassuring me that I'd rise through the ranks. That might not seem like much, but for a young beginner like me encouragement like his was enough to keep me going for months.

In *Anna* and after that, in *The Piano Tuner Has Arrived*, I was credited for the first time as Sofia Lazzaro. I was earning 50,000 lire a day, the equivalent of about 80 US dollars at the time, a real fortune compared to what my family was accustomed to.

I made one of my first bit appearances the following year, in the spring of 1952, in *Girls Marked Danger*. It was a thriller directed by Luigi Comencini, also starring Silvana Pampanini, who had gotten her start as Miss Italia, and Eleonora Rossi Drago, and American actor Marc Lawrence as the male lead. Just a few hours' work outdoors, near Genoa, allowed me to appear on the movie's presentation cover for the United States, which read: "Hands Off! They're TNT! 'Girls Marked for Danger!'" We were three young Italian beauties ready to conquer the world.

But my real debut in a leading role took place in the spring of 1952 in *The Favorite*, the movie version of Donizetti's opera, directed by Cesare Barlacchi. I have always loved music—as a child I had virtually breathed it in my home—and I felt very much at ease in such a melodramatic production. I worked hard to learn the part, and I was paid many compliments. I dare say I was almost taken seriously, although the movie didn't make a cent. For the arias, I was dubbed by Palmira Vitali Marini. It was excellent training, maybe even a passport to my role for *Aida*, in which I was soon to be paired with none other than the renowned lyric soprano Renata Tebaldi and her amazing voice. Later, I was to have the honor of meeting this great singer a few times, even though she was always busy traveling around the world. She was a marvelous person. That I had merged my acting with her singing as one person was a source of immense pride for me.

WHITE SHANTUNG

My time of subsistence living seemed to be over at last. With my first earnings, which we stuck under the mattress, the three of us—Mammina, Maria, and I—moved to a small furnished room, at first on Via Cosenza, and later on Via Giovanni Severano, near Piazza Bologna. It was a tight fit, but we were happy to be together.

Maria, who had arrived with Mammina from Pozzuoli, was going through a difficult period, and the big city was no help. She'd been very sick as a child and was still fragile. She'd suffered when Mammina and I left home, even though she was surrounded by the generous, loving arms of Mamma Luisa. The real problem was that she didn't have a last name because our father had never recognized her. She was only eleven and was ashamed to go to school, where she was forced to make her illegitimate status known. So while Mammina and I were out all day long, working or looking for new jobs, Maria would stay at home by herself. Even today I can't bear to think about how distressing it must have been for her, how much she must have felt abandoned, invisible. Unfortunately, at the time we had no choice, although I knew deep inside that we were going to have to find a solution, and I kept telling myself that I would do so as soon as possible. Our father, on the other hand, rather than helping us, created more problems for us, and not just by never being around.

Early one morning we were surprised by someone knocking at the door. When we opened it, we found the police standing there.

"Villani Romilda? Scicolone Sofia? Come with us."

"Why? What have we done? What's the meaning of this? How dare you?"

They didn't even give us time to get dressed nor did they bother to answer our questions. Mammina and I were whisked off to the police station, and asked to explain how we supported ourselves. Someone had filed a formal complaint, questioning the legality of our presence in Rome, and suggesting that we'd turned our apartment into some sort of house of ill repute—that we were immoral as well as breaking the law.

"Someone filed a complaint against *us*? A house of ill repute?" Mammina asked. "*Us*? Who was it? Who, who can possibly hate us so much they'd want to soil our name?"

At that point, even the police officers were embarrassed, because they realized they'd been dragged into a family dispute that had nothing to do with the law. Our accuser was none other than Riccardo Scicolone, my father. I still cannot fully express the storm of emotions we felt, the surprise, hurt, disheartenment, fury, and shame that raged inside us. When we recovered our sangfroid, we managed to demonstrate the source of our earnings quite easily, and then headed right back home. But the wound my father had caused us was a deep one, and, for me, it would never heal.

In that room on Via Severano, Mammina often cooked in the bathroom, on a portable hot plate, even though our landlady had told us not to. We'd wait for her to finish eating and take a nap so that we could prepare a quick sauce in the hope that the aroma wouldn't reach her nose.

It's a habit I've always kept, even when, as a successful actress, my destiny has taken me abroad, whether to small or large hotel rooms. Even today, when I'm away and I start missing my home, or I'm too tired to go out, I turn to my hot plate. After all, it takes so little to make a plate of pasta.

We eventually moved from the furnished room to a small apartment, which was also on Via Severano, and started to live like a real family. I had taken the reins of my—our—life. My mother continued to accompany me to auditions and many other places, although her enthusiasm always had a veiled hint of pessimism. Maria hadn't spread her wings yet, but her time was soon to come. In any event, although I played the part of the head of the family, I was still subject to the rules of the Villani home. Whenever I got home late, I'd have to tiptoe in to avoid being scolded by my mother: she was going to do everything in her power to keep me from making the same mistakes she'd made.

"Do you realize how late it is? Who were you with? Does this seem like the right thing to be doing? You and him alone? Just who do you think you are? Sofia, Sofia, have you learned nothing from our situation?"

By that time, however, whenever I went out it was with Carlo. True, he was married and we had to be careful, although there was still nothing between us. Only later would our fondness turn into love. At that point it would be too late to go back, but for the time being, I was content to be lucky enough to finally have someone beside me who knew how to speak to me, who could give me advice, who supported me in the parts I chose, which is crucial when an actor is just starting out. I was trying to get ahead but without taking any false steps, and knowing that Carlo was on my side was a huge help. There was something fatherly about his presence, too, and I'd never had a real father. He gave me a rootedness and stability that kept me grounded, while the world around me seemed to swirl dizzyingly, excitingly.

Carlo had a lot to teach me, and I wanted nothing more than to learn. Little by little he was becoming an essential part of my life, without my realizing it. Or maybe I did realize it, but had a hard time owning up to it.

In 1950, I had tried, in vain, to join the Experimental Film Center, but they'd told me I wasn't suited to it. I liked the environment; there were beautiful gardens and a huge glass windowpane that I remember clearly. It was a very professional school, maybe too much so for me. By that time my place was on the movie set more than in a classroom. It was there that, ever since I'd worked as an extra, I'd observe everything, try to absorb as much as possible, and discard anything I couldn't use. I would spend day after day there, accumulating experiences. But it was Carlo who helped me shed my Neapolitan accent and hone my elocution. Carlo also suggested I read some very good books out loud, recording myself as I did so that I could hear the mistakes I made. He taught me how to answer questions during interviews and even how to dress well and find my own sense of style.

One day, I don't remember what the occasion was, Carlo came to see me with a huge package, an elegant one with the label of one of the finest boutiques in Rome. I opened it trembling, pleased by his attentions. Inside the box was a beautiful white shantung woman's suit.

"Thank you . . ." I said softly. I was very moved.

"You should always wear suits," he replied, ". . . and always white ones." I pretended to agree with him, but I knew it wasn't true. In those days, I could wear anything I wanted to, everything looked good on me.

One of the first evenings we spent together we went out to dinner. I wasn't used to eating at a restaurant, and I thought it would be best if I ordered something soft, so I wouldn't have to struggle with the different utensils and be embarrassed. I ordered an omelet. But just as I was about to use my knife to cut the first slice, Carlo looked at me sharply and whispered, "No, not the knife, you don't need it." From that day on I never ordered an omelet again, that's how ashamed I felt . . .

Every situation I found myself in seemed to be a test. And every situation presented constant challenges. My life was like a minefield through which I slowly made my way. I went from launch to launch, movie to movie, and dinner to dinner. Facing each challenge allowed me to get closer to what I dreamed of becoming.

LIKE A FISH

It may have been Carlo who called Goffredo Lombardo, or maybe it was Goffredo who noticed me. The truth is that when the Neapolitan producer summoned me in 1952 to offer me the leading role in *Africa under the Seas*, directed by Giovanni Roccardi, I was again ready to say "Yes," just as I had done with Mervyn LeRoy. This time, however, the stakes were higher and the risks were a lot greater.

The movie tells the story of a rich industrialist who hosts a group of scientists on board his yacht in the Red Sea. He takes advantage of the trip to bring his daughter with him, too, a bored, spoiled, and rebellious young woman, who ends up loving underwater diving, as well as the captain . . . Most of the story takes place in the water, if not actually underwater.

"Signorina, you come from near Naples. You know how to swim, don't you?" Lombardo asked me.

"Of course, Doc," I lied, without realizing the trouble I was getting myself into. "Like a fish!"

I wasn't the first or the last Neapolitan who didn't know how to swim, but I'm sure I was the first to sign a contract to act on the high seas. Besides blessing me with this role, Lombardo was also the person responsible for my artistic christening. He didn't like my acting name Lazzaro, and liked Scicolone even less. He wanted to give me a short name that was easy to pronounce, a name with a certain allure. So, while staring at a poster hanging behind him which showed the beautiful Swedish actress Märta Torén, he recited the alphabet: Toren, Soren, Roren, back to the *L*, Loren. Yes, that's it! Sofia Loren! And while we were at it, he decided to also replace the *f* with a *ph* and voilà, it was the right name for an international star. People in Pozzuoli somehow became convinced I'd changed my name to Sopìa, with a *p*, although they didn't understand why.

The drama of *Africa under the Seas* took place off the coast of the island of Ponza. There I was standing on the deck of the large motorboat, the movie cameras ready to start filming, the director shouting into his megaphone: "Jump!"

I didn't wait to feel scared, I just pretended I knew how to swim and jumped in.

Almost as soon as I hit the water I was grabbed by the strong arms of the stagehand who was responsible for all the underwater shooting. In just a few days he would teach me all there was to know about swimming. At that moment, however, my savior was furious at the director, who had me jump in just a few yards away from the churning propellers. They'd made me take a huge risk and had endangered my life. Thanks to the stagehand, however, I had survived, and I went on to learn how to handle scuba tanks and snorkels, fins, wetsuits, and fish. At the end of the movie I really had become a fish, and I had overcome one of my many phobias, as well.

HEAVENLY AIDA

My first big opportunity—although every opportunity is a big opportunity, especially when you're starting out—came on the wings of the heavenly music of Verdi. While we were working on a movie together (I think it was *The Vow*), the excellent actress Doris Duranti told me that at Scalera, one of the most famous movie studios in Rome, the film director Clemente Fracassi was starting to shoot *Aida.* "Go find out," she suggested. After all, I had already acted in *The Favorite*, where I had proven to be quite skilled at playing the opera stand-in. The producers had had a black actress come over from America, but they weren't convinced she was the right choice. That's how I got the part, maybe thanks also to the intervention of Renzo Rossellini, Roberto's brother, who was the movie's musical consultant.

I didn't have much time to learn the lines before my first shoot, and I was supposed to synchronize them perfectly with the singer's. So to be able to concentrate and learn my part quickly and thoroughly, I would lock myself inside the small office of the production studio, in the freezing cold of winter. Neither the office nor the set had any heating, and it was so cold that I could see my breath. So before each take, they'd make me chew ice to lessen the puff of cloud that emerged whenever I'd say my lines. And they had one of the stagehands follow me around with a hair dryer out of range of the camera's frame!

Each and every day, I'd spend four hours, which seemed endless, in makeup. My entire body, from head to toe, was made up to transform me into Aida. Darker makeup was used at the hairline and on my forehead to hide the tulle of the wig. But I have to admit it was worth it. Providing Renata Tebaldi's voice with a body was a special emotion for me, and one that would be hard to repeat. In the end, we were like one person. I was the only member of the cast who had to act, and not just sing, and this made my job even harder. The audience wasn't supposed to know there was a record guiding the way my lips moved. Even Carlo was amazed. I think that was when he really started believing in me.

I started to believe in myself, too, and with the money I earned—a million lire, about 1,500 American dollars at the time—Mammina, Maria, and I were able to move to a larger apartment on Via Balzani and I was finally able to set right my sister's honor. My father, as little as he'd ever been in our lives, had pretty much abandoned us. I no longer tried to love him. So when he'd heard I'd made some money and contacted us to ask for it, I had no difficulty giving him all the money I'd earned for *Aida* in exchange for his name for my sister. That name, which for me had been merely a hollow shell, for my sister was salvation. Maria Villani became Maria Scicolone and she could finally go to school and start living without shame.

There's no need to go into more about that heartbreaking exchange. The important thing was that with my own means, and as well as I knew how, I had gone back over our family history, to try to understand things that had been too big for me to deal with when I was a child. And I had drawn my own conclusions. Not all men were like Riccardo Scicolone; I knew that not every story was the same. In the future, I wanted a different kind of person by my side, someone who could really make me happy. I still wasn't completely sure who that could be, but life would soon show me that I had already met my ideal man.

IV

WHO'S THAT *PICCERELLA*?

THE BENCH

"Sofia, Sofi, when you were fifteen you said 'yes' to me," reads the signature on a photograph of Vittorio De Sica, the great director, which I pull next from my treasure trove of memories. Well, did I really have a choice? Without De Sica I would never have become what I am, I would never have found my true voice. His talent and his trust are two of the greatest gifts that life could ever have given me, and I will keep them alive forever in my heart.

That day at Cinecittà—I was actually nineteen, not fifteen—I was wandering from set to set. Who knows what I was looking for, but I do know that I loved the hustle and bustle of the scenes, the noisy crowd of extras, the papier-mâché backdrops that each time would open up to a whole new world. I liked spending my days there. There was work to be found. On every corner you might come across an idea or have an important encounter. And every encounter could turn into a unique opportunity, to be seized at once.

Cinecittà was a wonderland, a landscape of dreams in the making, all shuffled up like a house of cards. Ancient Romans sipped coffee with young soubrettes, great *condottieri* chatted with chorus girls, working-class women had a sandwich with men in tails. Throughout the lots, small time wheeler-dealers did business, while the most impassioned film directors were also busy talking to technicians and stagehands. And everyone was checking out the extras.

It was a universe of the imagination, and I raced through it at full gallop, pursuing my destiny. I raced and dreamed, and yet I wasn't just a dreamer. My feet were firmly rooted to the ground, I was ready to make the big leap forward. I was down-to-earth and always on time. I really wanted to work, and I was willing to risk everything I had on my own certainty.

That day, while I was walking along the lanes, I could tell that two men sitting on a bench smoking were watching me. One of them was Peppino Annunziata, who would eventually become my never-to-be-forgotten makeup artist, as well as a kind of bodyguard, chosen by Carlo to stay beside me at all times. The other man was Vittorio De Sica himself, the greatest creator of neorealist films that Italian cinema has ever known. I could hear them conferring in a Neapolitan accent and realized that I was the subject of their discussion. The musicality of their conversation made me think of home. Glancing in their direction, I broke into a smile.

"Sophia, Sophia, come here, I want you to meet . . ." Peppino called me over.

De Sica turned to me with his beautiful, melodious, kind voice, flattering me, giving me the usual compliments that men in those days would always give pretty girls. He also gave me some fatherly advice:

"It's a jungle out there. You have to keep your eyes wide open . . ." he said. "But if you have passion, and it looks to me like you have lots of it, trust yourself and everything will work out fine!"

I could hardly believe it. That was the renowned Vittorio De Sica sitting there talking to me.

Vittorio De Sica began his great adventure in cinema as an actor—and had been called the Italian Cary Grant. He went into directing during the war and made *The Children Are Watching Us* in 1944, a deeply affecting film about a neglected little boy. He succeeded in capturing the spirit of the moment, the struggles of real working people, the call of the street, the poverty of postwar towns. De Sica threw himself into filmmaking heart and soul, searching in the faces of ordinary people for traces of the new world that was rising up from the heaps of rubble. He restored the voice of the elderly and of children, shoe-shiners and the homeless, prostitutes and the unemployed. He denounced the injustices he saw, and his emotions were stirred in the same way as the emotions of his characters—and of his audience.

Vittorio's experience as an actor and his filmmaker's eye made him a well-rounded maestro. He understood the person in the actor standing before him with infallible instinct, so that he could get what he wanted out of them, sometimes even without having to say a single word. He would, if necessary, even go so far as to make children cry deliberately for the sake of a scene, as if he were stealing their emotions! Whether they were the marvelous kids in *Shoeshine*, or the destitute in *Miracle in Milan*, great actors, would-be ones, or nonprofessionals from the towns where he filmed, all of them responded to his guidance and encouragement, and did what he wanted them to as well as they could.

A short time after that first encounter on the streets of the studio, I saw him again in the offices of Ponti–De Laurentiis. He was then working on *The Gold of Naples*, a tribute to Naples written in six episodes. Perhaps Carlo had mentioned me to him, thinking I might be suited for the part of the *Pizzaiola* (the Pizza Girl). Vittorio had no recollection of me from the Cinecitta lot, but I had not forgotten his encouragement from the bench where I'd seen him for the first time. We talked about this and that, he asked me a few questions, where I came from, what I was working on. I told him about Pozzuoli and my debut in *Sogno*, about *The Favorite* and *Africa under the Seas*, and I confessed that screen tests terrified me.

"Interesting," he said. He was only pretending to listen to what I was saying as he observed me with his third eye, which was trained to discover the actor behind the appearances, the talent that lay behind the insignificance of a resumé diligently rattled off. I did my utmost to make a good impression, but he was noncommittal, and motionless as he watched me. I was honored by his interest, but convinced by his demeanor that nothing would come of it. "*Torna cu' 'e piedi pe' terra, Sofi', 'e suonn' nun servono a niente*" (Put your feet back on the ground, Sofi, dreaming is useless), I thought.

Just as I had resigned myself to not getting the part, De Sica shifted suddenly to the informal "tu" form of address and said, "You leave for Naples tomorrow. I'm going to make a movie in episodes, taken from a collection of stories by Giuseppe Marotta, the Neapolitan writer. The cast is first-rate."

I was floored and looked at him in awe. "One of the episodes is all about a young woman named Sofia," he continued with his mysterious serenity. "She's exactly like you, no need to do a screen test to find that out. I'll have someone get you your train ticket."

Of course I said yes. The cards had been dealt and I'd come up trumps. I should have known that good things come of having the courage to dream.

GOLD FEVER

So I set out, my eyes closed, toward the fairy tale of my life.

My mother, who was always mistrustful, tried to make me stay: "*Ma si' asciut' pazz? Ma addò vaje ca manc' 'e cunusc' a chisti ccà? Chi te dice ca teneno bbuoni penziere?*" (Are you crazy? Where on earth are you going with someone you don't even know? How do we know he has clean thoughts?)

But I, by that time, knew exactly what I was doing: "*Ma no, nun ce pensà*" (Please, don't worry about it), I tried to reassure her. "Everything will be fine."

She was happy they'd chosen me, of course, but she couldn't help being anxious, making mountains out of molehills, asking silly questions like: "What will you wear?"

She didn't even know what part I'd been given. And for this

part, I didn't need anything special. *Pizzaiole*, the women who make pizza in Naples, wear ordinary clothes.

I behaved with Mammina as though I were a grown-up daughter, showing off a self-confidence that I didn't at all have. Inside, I was both terrified and excited.

Am I up to this? I wondered. *What if De Sica is wrong? What if he thinks I'm a real actress? Maronna mia, ch'aggia fa'?* (Holy Mary, what should I do?)

I remember my first day on the job as if it were yesterday. In February 1954, it was freezing cold, and I had barely slept from anxiety. Standing before the maestro, I felt like a child, my legs shaking, my voice a mere whisper. I hadn't been back to Naples since the Queen of the Sea pageant, where I'd been a pawn in a spectacle that had already been written, a little statue chauffeured around in a carriage. Now I had the leading part in something that had to happen right there, right before our eyes, and that in one way or another depended on me. Naples' *bassi*, the city's poorest quarters, were counting on me.

Vittorio knew what he wanted, and he showed me the way: "Sofi, you have everything you need inside already. Let it all come out, let yourself go! Fish out the emotions in what you've seen, in what you've experienced, go back to Via Solfatara, that's where it all starts."

Vittorio had recognized that, underneath my reserve and my sometimes animated persona, lay a pool of strong memories. Within my youthfulness, he saw a sensitivity, born out of a difficult childhood, that was seeking a way to express itself, to be transformed into art.

"Act with your whole body, down to your toes and the tips of your fingers, they're just as important as your voice, your eyes, your face," he would never tire of telling me. Of course, he was exaggerating to some extent, but those words held an important truth. When you act, you do it completely, with your feelings and with your head, your skin and your guts, your memories and your heart. In our business, this is the only secret that really counts.

That first morning I was feeling so nervous that to overcome the cold and build up some courage I even took two sips of cognac. And then suddenly it was evening! The day had gone by in a flash, so fast I hadn't even noticed. After twelve hours' hard work, when we all met for dinner, I was a different person. It had been like playing, Vittorio acting along with me from behind the movie camera, I in front of it. We had acted, but most importantly we'd had fun. With his special touch, he'd released me from all my worries. Both of us had gone back to being two crazy Neapolitans, who improvised with sheer joy. Vittorio was fond of saying that "Neapolitans, like children, always look good on camera."

The shooting went on for twenty days, and they were twenty days of celebration. The movie was based on well-known short stories about the people of Naples, written by Giuseppe Marotta. So the film was a big event for the people of the Materdei quarter of the city, where the shop in which my character, the Pizza Girl, worked—Pizzeria Starita. People flocked to the streets just to see us act, wanting to get swept up in the magic of their city lit up by the spotlights of the set. So great was the confusion caused by the crowd of street urchins and people with nothing else to do that even the fire department had to be called in. But ours was a fire of cheerfulness and vigor, the kind of fire that was good for everyone.

As the filming continued, my confidence grew. I started walking just like the Pizza Girl: head held high, chest out, my whole life ahead of me. I can still see Vittorio behind the camera, showing me how to respond and move, so that I embodied the very soul of my character—and everything he expected of me.

"You're good, keep at it!" he'd shout into the megaphone,

satisfied. I'd look at him, finding it hard to believe that all this was really happening to me. He pushed me beyond my limits. He helped me climb over the wall that hemmed in my deepest feelings. A few years later he would do even more, and lead me into an even greater performance in the land of tragedy.

Although comedy was no less difficult for me at the time, I realized that in that lighthearted world, everything revolves around the rhythm, and it would take very little to fall into coarseness or parody.

The Sofia of "*Pizze a credito*" (Pizzas on Credit), my episode in the film, runs a small frying shop with her husband, Rosario—played by Giacomo Furia, with whom I became good friends, and who would always be like a brother to me. Everyone stops at the couple's shop, more because of Sofia's attractiveness and flirtatiousness than because of the quality of the pizza—night watchmen and lawyers, drivers and priests, clerks and young kids are all charmed by her. Even the brother of famous Neapolitan singer Giacomo Rondinella, Luciano, flirts with Sofia, serenading her from his cart, to the joy of the onlookers both inside and outside the movie.

"EAT NOW AND PAY IN EIGHT DAYS!" says the sign, as well as the words that the husband and wife shout out to attract customers.

"*Venite, venite a fa' marenna! Donna Sofia ha preparato 'e briosce!*" (Come on in! Come in and have a snack, Donna Sofia's made brioches for everyone!)

The turning point in my episode, "*Pizze a credito,*" happens one Sunday morning, while everyone else is in church and Sofia meets her lover in his apartment and leaves behind the emerald ring her husband had given her, "the most beautiful ring in the Stella quarter of Naples." Rosario had used up all his savings to buy the ring—for love, but also to put on airs. Their bad luck in losing the ring instantly becomes everybody else's, and on a wintry, rainy day in Naples, the people in the streets don't hesitate to say what's on their minds, as they follow the main characters around in their search for what they've lost.

I will never forget the great actor Paolo Stoppa, who plays Don Peppino, an inconsolable widower who has lost everything and has decided to end it all. But instead of jumping off the balcony, he finds consolation in a plate of spaghetti. A disciplined professional, he watched my first lighthearted footsteps with affectionate detachment. We would work together in other films in the future.

And we took many footsteps, running from one house to another, from one story to another, surrounded by a world in motion, a world made up of wit and commonplaces, superstitions and gossip, humanity and backbiting. It was a real, everyday world, that sought a way, a wholly Neapolitan one, to overcome obstacles and free itself of the yoke of power, to exorcise death—which was always lying in wait right around the corner or on the slopes of Mount Vesuvius—while enjoying a *jurnata 'e sole* (a sunny day).

In each episode of the movie, the characters—all of them excellent actors, Totò, Mangano, De Sica, De Filippo—have something that's bothering them: Totò's problem is a thug who's been living in his house for the past ten years; Silvana Mangano used to be a prostitute, a past she hopes to free herself of through marriage; De Sica, who in this film became an actor among actors again, has a gambling addiction, something that, alas, plagued him in real life, too; the great Eduardo De Filippo is an arrogant old duke who, when driving past, expects everyone to clear the way ahead for him. The people use their most disrespectful, insolent form of expression to get back at the duke, what's known in Naples as *'o pernacchio*. But although *'o pernacchio* broadly equates with "giving a Bronx cheer" or blowing raspberries, in this case it really has nothing to do with that. That's more banal, anyone could do it, and it lacks resonance. *'O pernacchio*, as the Neapolitans use it, lets you say to a person of power that he or she is "*'na schifezza, 'na schifezza, 'na schifezza*"—in other words, simply foul, disgusting, the pits. The person who is the receiving end of *'o pernacchio* suffers tragic humiliation. The person who learns how to execute it fully savors catharsis.

Everyone knows that Naples is a city where the high and the low are jumbled up together, where poverty and nobility live side by side. Intellectuals like Eduardo and Peppino, Vittorio and Totò, who was known as the Prince of Laughter, and was one of the most popular actors in the history of Italian films, spent much of their time with the common people, surrounded by them, so they could describe them just as they really were. And the people knew this and loved them for it.

At the end of my episode, I make a triumphant stroll along the streets, wearing my ring once more. My generous neckline and impudent smile actually revealed me to myself, before revealing me to others. More importantly, that walk delivered me into Vittorio's hands. From that moment onward he became one of the strongest influences of my life. He and I would work together for the next twenty years, and another thirteen movies, and he would teach me everything I know, supporting me, helping me to get my bearings. Often with the help of the great screenwriter Cesare Zavattini, he found me the characters that were most suited to my personality, pushing me toward the gale winds of drama or the light breeze of comedy, where the risk of overdoing things is high, and where sometimes the chance of getting through it all safely is slim. We really loved each other, like father and daughter. I admired him unrestrainedly, and he always helped me to do my best. And the two of us were soon to be joined by Marcello Mastroianni, thus completing our perfect triangle.

The Catholic Cinema Center, also known as the CCC, didn't like the "Pizze a credito" segment. Too much adultery, too happy, too sensuous. But everyone else did, except for my mother, who peppered everything with her usual dose of pessimism. She'd come with me to see the premiere of the movie—she was always right there beside me at every important event—and as soon as they turned the lights back on, she exclaimed resentfully: "That Ponti guy has ruined you . . . the episode with Silvana Mangano was much more beautiful than yours!"

"Mammina, what are you saying," I replied, trying to calm her down. "They're very different, extremely different. One's a comedy, the other's a tragedy . . ."

She always wanted the best for me, and she could never stop believing that the world wasn't out to get us, to take away what was ours, all the things we'd earned with so much hard work. She had been so deeply affected by the disappointments in her own life, early on. I, instead, was completely forward-looking. And nothing could stop me now.

My triumphant walk in the wet dress in the movie became famous, giving me a tad of glory and a passport to my future, but the rain that showered me from artificial rain-making machines, also made me sick from pneumonia, which I had a hard time recovering from. During the last few days of shooting, I'd gone to work with a fever, and on one of the last evenings in Naples, while we were all out celebrating the end of the movie, I collapsed and had to be taken back to the hotel. Maybe I'd overdone it, but of course, what I got back from the experience was priceless: "A love of life, endless patience, constant hope," as Marotta wrote. In other words, the gold of Naples, which was soon to carry me all the way to America.

THE *PICCERELLA* GROWS UP

Totò, Prince Antonio Griffo Focas Flavio Angelo Ducas Comneno Porfirogenito Gagliardio De Curtis di Bisanzio, was the undisputed king of this golden side of Naples. I had followed him around on the set so many times since my arrival in Cinecittà in 1950, watching him, timidly and adoringly, as I performed my bit parts, as one of the extras in *Bluebeard's Six Wives* and as a young girl in *Tototarzan*. Even before I'd moved to Rome, I'd gone to Scalera, one of the production companies where the prince was working. I was still not much more than a girl, out of work and without a penny to my name, and I'd entered the room on tiptoe. One of the members of the production staff, maybe touched by my youth, had let me sit down to watch. Totò, eyeing me, had asked one of his assistants: "Who's that *piccerella* (that little girl)?

Hesitantly, I'd approached him to introduce myself: "Scicolone Sofia, I'm very honored . . ."

He was very sweet, he smiled at me, and offered me some of his precious time. "What's a young kid like you doing here? Where are you from?"

"I'm from Pozzuoli, I'm here to work in the movies . . ."

"Ah, the movies," he'd sighed, making one of his famous faces just for me.

For an instant his ironic and irresistible wistfulness was all for me. I drank it down like a glass of fresh water, and it made me feel stronger. If the great Totò was offering me a minute of his attention, then anything was possible. It was a sure sign of all the good things that were going to happen.

But the prince didn't just take time out to chat with me that day. Before I left, he put a 100,000-lire banknote in my hand, perfectly aware of the poverty I'd been trying to hide. I think he'd seen the hunger in my eyes: for food, work, or maybe simply for the movies. Mammina and I were able to eat for a long time with that money, it was as if we'd hit the jackpot.

His daughter, Liliana, describes how one afternoon, seeing me show up in his dressing room on the set for *Bluebeard*, Totò nearly fainted.

"It's dangerous to contemplate certain panoramas at two in the afternoon; all these promontories and valleys are giving me double vision," he said.

Having had the honor of meeting him, I can safely say that the king of comedians was always acting, even when he wasn't on the set, and that he would give anything for a good line.

I ran into Totò again in 1953 on the set of a movie, *Poverty and Nobility*, based on a comedy written by Eduardo Scarpetta. Totò played Felice Sciosciamocca, a penniless scribe whose name means "with mouth agape." His character was hired, along with his family, by a young marquis to act the part of the love-stricken man's aristocratic relatives for his bride-to-be, Gemma (yours truly).

"Talk about Carthage and all the Carthaginians," exclaimed Totò when he saw me wearing the future bride's costume. "We'll welcome you into the bosom of our family, if you welcome us into yours . . ."

The prince was absolutely irresistible. Spending time with him dispelled every fear, dissipated any embarrassment. Also because he'd invent half the script on the spur of the moment, and no one could stop him. In *Poverty and Nobility*, Toto has a famous scene that has gone down in the history of cinema, where he stuffs his pockets with spaghetti. It speaks volumes about the hunger of our people, of the ravenousness of Pulcinella, the character in our commedia dell'arte who represents the Neapolitan essence, and of the starvation I saw with my very own eyes in Pozzuoli during the war. Hunger that you can only fend off with a smile, with the lightness of spirit that we Neapolitans are filled to overflowing with.

Naples will always be Italy's most beautiful city, inhabited by its most beautiful people. It's a city that has witnessed so much indecency, so many ugly things there that today it needs to be able to imagine a better tomorrow. That might explain why, in 2013, when my son Edoardo approached me about doing a short film, *Human Voice*, based on a play by Jean Cocteau, right there in Naples, I accepted with immense joy. It's my small contribution of hope to the land I adore.

Life has taken me far away from my roots, but my heart will always be right there, in the light, the language, the Parthenopean cuisine. The more time goes by, the more speaking Neapolitan dialect comes naturally to me. Maybe it's because I express myself better in Neapolitan, I can say things that I can't say in Italian, let alone in English or in French. I put so much love into this language that even my children understand me when I speak it, and now even my grandchildren do.

The same goes for Naples' traditional dishes, which take me back home, to the kitchen on Via Solfatara, where I'd spend my days, amid the scents and aromas of poverty. It was in that kitchen that Mamma Luisa's singing and the warmth of the stove kept me company, and that, when there was enough money, the meat sauce bubbled in the pot.

Nowadays I don't cook that much, and I eat very little. My mind is filled with a million thoughts. But when my children come to visit me from the United States and they ask me to make something special for them, I isolate myself in my kingdom and I'm in Pozzuoli again. The recipe that gives me the greatest satisfaction is "la Genovese," those ten pounds of onions sautéed until they're soft, to which I add the rolls of stuffed meat, and let everything simmer for four hours. In today's world, where everything is so fast, four hours seem endless, but in that amount of time I can savor my childhood from so long ago.

But to go back to Totò, I was to run into him again in *The Anatomy of Love*, directed by none other than Alessandro Blasetti. Another great master of Italian cinema, Sandro believed in me even when I was still a nobody. *The Anatomy of Love* was another movie in episodes, a medley that gathered together all the leading names of the times, from De Sica to Mastroianni, from Yves Montand to Alberto Sordi, from Eduardo De Filippo to the magical Quartetto Cetra. Assigned to the typewriter were Alberto Moravia and Vasco Pratolini, Giuseppe Marotta and Giorgio Bassani, Achille Campanile, Sandro Continenza, and Suso Cecchi D'Amico. I was working with Totò, in an episode where he, a professional photographer, has his camera stolen while trying to pick up a beautiful girl, played by me.

They say that Blasetti was quite taken by my ability to accompany the great ham. I who always loved to learn the script by heart, sometimes even before I had to, had understood that it would be pointless here to do so with the prince. Totò loved to improvise, he filled the screenplay with little gestures, inventions, dreams. Better to go along with him, try to keep up.

On that occasion, the fact that I'd grown up in Pozzuoli helped. Our Neapolitan spirits—which consisted of intuition, scent, wit—came together and made sparks.

Although I would never work with Totò again, I would soon afterward meet Blasetti in another movie that since then I've always kept close to my heart.

A SCOUNDREL IN A TAXI CAB

The first person who believed I'd be perfect for *Too Bad She's Bad* was Suso Cecchi D'Amico, the only woman in the field of the great scriptwriters back then. "The oak tree whose branches produced so much Italian cinema," as Lina Wertmüller describes her. While reading Alberto Moravia's *Roman Tales*, Suso had run into a lovely episode that takes place right at the beginning of the short story "Il fanatico" ("The Fanatic").

One day Suso and I met on a train. After catching sight of me at the station, she came to the car I was traveling in and sat down next to me. Her familiar manner put me at ease.

Looking me straight in the eyes she simply said: "I have the perfect story for you."

"Why not!" I replied, enthusiastically. Suso had worked on the story with the screenwriter Ennio Flaiano, Moravia himself, and Sandro Continenza; they'd taken it to Blasetti, who was looking for a story for a movie. The producers' first choice had been Gina Lollobrigida, who was considered to be number one at the time. But Suso had seen me at Cinecittà while I was working with Bolognini on *We'll Meet in the Gallery*, and she'd been impressed by my cheerfulness. In the movie, I had danced the mambo, which I would dance again in *Woman of the River* and in the *Bread, Love, and . . .* series, wearing a gorgeous red dress.

After our brief encounter on the train, Suso, backed by Flaiano and Blasetti himself, insisted that the producers give me the part.

Sandro was happy to have me on the set again, and he was offering me my first opportunity to play the leading role. Until that time I'd always played bit parts, and in *The Gold of Naples*, although I'd had an important part, it had only been for one of the episodes. Now I was going to have to hold the stage for the whole movie, aided by two of the very finest partners, Vittorio De Sica and Marcello Mastroianni. It was the start of a long, successful, blissful journey.

On that occasion I also met Mara, Blasetti's daughter, who worked in production. Her eyes had seen the stuff of the actress in me, even though I was still a novice, but for a long time she continued to talk to me as though I were a child. We still keep in touch, laugh together, and we like to remember the good old days, as if they were yesterday.

It wasn't until Gabriel García Márquez died that I found out that he had been hiding in the folds of the set for *Too Bad She's Bad*. One of the greatest contemporary authors, Gabo, like so many others, had come to Rome in pursuit of the dream of Cinecittà, and he'd entered the Experimental Film Center thanks to the Argentine filmmaker Fernando Birri. In a recent interview he described how, in *Too Bad She's Bad*, he was the third assistant director—in other words, the bouncer. That's why, during the shooting, he hadn't been able to approach me as he would have liked to: his job was to keep out the curious onlookers. What a shame! It might have been the start of a great friendship.

In *Too Bad She's Bad*, a splendid black-and-white movie, Marcello and I met for the first time. We immediately fell in love—silver-screen love, of course.

I still remember the first time I saw him. I was standing on the steps of the building where we were to make the movie. He, from a few floors up, was watching me.

"*Ciao*," he greeted me, as though he were somewhere up in the air.

"*Ciao*," I answered, shy and excited.

We got along instantly, and our relationship was intact through all the years of his life, without ever a wrinkle. On that first set we grew familiar with each other against the backdrop of postwar Rome, a carefree, brightly lit city. The people there had started traveling again, going to the beach, swimming, loving each other and having fun. We felt good together, Marcello and I. What a couple we were! Simple, beautiful, real.

In the movie Marcello plays the part of Paolo, a kind but not particularly intelligent young man who has lost his family in the air raids and is trying to make a new life for himself by driving a car for a taxi company. He can't resist uninhibited Lina who, while trying to rob him, hums "Bongo bongo bongo" with adorable arrogance. My character was new and unusual for the times: the descendant of a family of thieves. She accompanies her father, a scoundrel, played by a marvelous De Sica, as he commits perfect thefts. Again, Vittorio guided my steps, as well as those of young Mastroianni, who had worked only in the theater until then.

Ten years older than me and much more self-confident, Marcello came to the set delightfully unprepared. By contrast, I applied myself like a schoolgirl, for fear of making mistakes and looking bad. I also had some very long parts in some very long scenes, as if I were the only one speaking. I remember one of them in particular, which took place on the steps where we'd met for the first time. When I finished my long recitation, Marcello hugged me, laughing: "How do you manage to remember everything, how do you do it?"

"Because I study. You don't study. You could remember everything if you wanted to, it's just that you wait until the last minute to get down to work . . ."

What fun we had! We were young and irresponsible and the world was our oyster.

A lot of the credit goes to Blasetti, no doubt, who knew how to relate to us actors: he knew how to get the best out of us, he respected, appreciated, and loved us. He was a perfectionist, famous for doing the same scene over again. Even after the tenth try, he'd take Marcello, Vittorio, and me by the arm and say: "Beautiful, but . . . ," and we'd start over again from scratch. We might do two dozen takes.

Sandro expected from others the same dedication to hard work that he had and the same passion that he felt. With me, both were guaranteed. Maybe this explains why we always got along so well.

Vittorio, working as an actor, was humble and respectful and accepted everything that the director told him, without ever judging or disagreeing. Often, however, Sandro called him over to discuss a particular scene, changing it over and over again.

"What do you say, Vittò, is this how we should do it? Or do you prefer the close-up?"

Sandro had immense respect for his collaborators, and he knew that having De Sica as a colleague was invaluable. They were a great pair of gentlemen, of the kind you don't see around anymore.

Blasetti's moviemaking technique was unsurpassable and he had an outstanding eye for the stills. He would come to the set wearing thirties-style boots and knickerbockers, because there was mud everywhere, and his wife had gotten tired of having to constantly clean him up and clean off his shoes and trousers. Sometimes he'd wear what resembled a funny pilot's uniform.

Blasetti was also very interested in the technical side of film-making, and even asked a factory that made mining carts to adapt one of them for the movie camera, in order to create tracking shots. Known as the Mancini cart, named after the owner of the factory, it was used for years in Italian cinema. Blasetti would also spend hours talking to the stagehands. He adored cinema and everyone that was involved in it. Although he did know how to smile, he was very authoritative, and for all of us working with him it was a lot like being in school.

We were friends for the rest of our lives. He was always discovering something; if he'd been born a few centuries earlier, he might have been an explorer. Meanwhile, he'd discovered me, and I will always be deeply grateful to him.

Interlude

Images, notes, letters, poems. My treasure trove of memories, which I've set down on my bed, has the fragrance of life, and it makes me travel in time. It takes me back to the days of my youth, now so far away. Its luminous streak of memories and hopes also points the way to tomorrow's path of dreams that can still come true.

I sip the tea Ninni quietly left on the bedside table for me before she went to bed. Everything is ready for tomorrow, Christmas Eve, but I feel distant, lost in this sea of memories where my life ebbs and flows. Happiness and melancholy intermingle in mysterious forms—there cannot be the one without the other. Many people dear to me are no longer here, but they continue to speak inside me, through the achievements of my sons, through the imaginations of my grandchildren, who will bring great cheer to our table.

The thought of them brings me back to the here and now. I can already savor the preparations, all of us together in the kitchen making the meatballs that Livia the cook used to make, a family tradition at Christmas. I can already imagine the children's tiny hands covered in flour, the balls of meat of all different sizes dredged in breadcrumbs, the smell of fried food that compensates for the cold and lights up the winter with happiness. But the river of memories is calling me. And I trustingly abandon myself again to its flow.

V

MAMBO

THE GHOSTLY ORCHESTRA

As I thumb through the photographs, I stop to smile tenderly at one image I'd forgotten, a photograph of Carlo lightly stroking my head. It is worth a thousand words. That small gesture sums up all the depth of our feelings. I turn the picture over and read: Summer 1954. It was there, while making *Woman of the River*, that we finally understood we'd fallen in love. The girl who'd had to grow up too fast had become a woman, the extra had become an actress, and our intimacy had turned into love.

In the photo, we're on the set, during a break from the filming. Behind us is the Po Delta, with its gentle light, green fading into blue, water turning into sky. In that humid air swarming with mosquitoes, the actors and stagehands rode back and forth by bike or boat, just like the characters in the movie. The landscape melted into the canals, the small bridges, the grayness of the swamps encircled by reeds. And behind the dunes was the sea, which can sweep you off your feet and take you far away.

Carlo created *Woman of the River* especially for me. The production was completely his, without the contribution of his longtime partner, De Laurentiis. If I'd realized at the time how much he'd invested in it I would have been paralyzed. But even without knowing, I felt the great weight of responsibility upon my shoulders. After *The Gold of Naples* and the Roman summer spent with Vittorio and Marcello acting like scoundrels in *Too Bad She's Bad*, I was far from home, the lead female character starring in a dramatic role. Casting me was an act of faith on Carlo's part, faith in my talent that was beginning to blossom.

The idea of a dramatic role excited me because it gave me a chance to express my deepest feelings, something that I found hard to do in real life. Yet it also felt like a huge challenge, and I worried that it might be too much for me. *Will I manage?* I wondered, frightened. No one answered.

To make sure all went well, Carlo had, as always, thought big, bringing together all the most important names of film-making at the time. Rereading them now, one after another, I'm awed: for the scripts, he signed Alberto Moravia and Ennio Flaiano (who would also write the stories for *8½* and *La dolce vita*); Giorgio Bassani, Antonio Altoviti, and a young Pier Paolo Pasolini, who'd just arrived in Rome to teach in a high school somewhere in the outskirts, together with the director, Mario Soldati. Scriptwriter Florestano Vancini, who'd made a documentary on the delta in 1951, was there, too.

And, last but not least, we were also joined by writer-producer Basilio Franchina, who would prove to be one of the luckiest associations of my entire life. Sicilian-born, a reporter, author, and scriptwriter, a movie and art enthusiast, Basilio had been the neorealist filmmaker Giuseppe De Santis's assistant director in *Bitter Rice*, in 1949, one of Ponti–De Laurentiis's biggest hits, and worked often with De Santis. Set in the rice paddies of Vercelli, the film had crowned Silvana Mangano in the part of the *mondina*, a peasant rice worker, and turned her into an international star. Mangano worked alongside Vittorio Gassman, then a budding star, and a very handsome Raf Vallone, resolute, wise, and good-hearted. It's a richly layered story, filled with emotion and social critique, and the title, *Riso Amaro*, is a pun in Italian. *Riso* in Italian means both rice and laughter, *amaro* means bitter, so the title reflects the bittersweet story. Silvana dances an unforgettable boogie-woogie before surrendering to her tragic end.

To create a character that would fit me perfectly, a character with more than one mood, Carlo and Soldati had found inspiration in that damp clime, populated by beautiful women wearing bandannas and shorts, and by small-time crooks whose sole purpose in life seemed to be to make the women suffer. The movie was to contain a spectrum of moods, maybe a few too many, ranging from the sentimental to the dramatic until the final catastrophe takes place.

My character, Nives, is a worker in an eel-pickling factory in the delta, in a town called Comacchio. An independent young woman, she had won the town's beauty pageant and lives surrounded by friends and coworkers. For these working-class women, life is often harsh, but in their world, people stick together. They toil away with little time for distractions. Young and fresh-looking, Nives resists the attentions of handsome Gino, a smuggler who doesn't want to settle down, played by Rik Battaglia, who looked a lot like Burt Lancaster.

"*Que bel ritmo tiene el mambo, que sonriso tiene el mambo,*" Nives sings, sensuously. But as often happens to strong, passionate women, as soon as she falls in love she's done for. In a long race across the swamp on his motorbike, Gino overcomes her resistance and Nives gives in to this tall, dark, and handsome man, fooling herself into thinking that they can have a family together, a house with a cooking range. Nives embodies the big and small hopes of ordinary people. Gino, however, feels trapped. He lives his life on the run, escaping—from himself, from the police, and, when he finds out that Nives is pregnant, from her. Who better than I could understand all this? It was a story I'd heard before.

On the set we worked hard, nonstop. As the drama gradually built to its tragic ending, my anxiety grew and the pressure became unbearable. I didn't feel anxious during the day, when I was busy in front of the camera, but it would creep up on me in the evening, when everything was calm. I'd lie down to go to sleep and all the things that had happened during the day, the scenes, the details, Soldati's words—always a bit cold—Rik's pranks, a line that I hadn't said quite right, came back to me. I kept going over every detail, the lines I'd done wrong, the gestures I could have done better. As these thoughts went through my mind I'd start to feel very short of breath. Inside me I could hear the shrill sound of violins, playing for me all night long, keeping me awake.

"Doctor, what's wrong with me? I'm scared, a few months ago I caught pneumonia . . ." I asked. I was afraid that I was still feeling out of sorts and winded from getting sick when filming *The Gold of Naples* in that artificial rain. That pneumonia had crippled me at the end of the shooting.

But the doctor had no doubts:

"Don't worry, Sophia," he said. "It's just a question of anxiety. Your lungs are perfectly fine. Your asthma is clearly psychological in nature. You must try to stay calm, control your emotions."

Hearing his reassurances, I didn't know whether to be happy or even more concerned. Everyone knows how hard it is to tell your mind what to do. As soon as I would lay my head on the pillow, I'd start to wheeze, and during the worst nights I'd even run a slight fever. I was living a double life, during the day active and strong, during the night in a state of shock, assailed by that ghostly orchestra.

Carlo, whenever he was around, tried to reassure me, minimizing the problem: "It's nothing, change your sleeping position and I'm sure the Stradivariuses will vanish . . ." But I was suffering, and I was afraid I'd never make it to the end of the movie.

As the days went by, the situation got worse, but, as if to make up for it, I received a wonderful gift: Basilio Franchina. At first, Carlo had asked him to direct *Woman of the River*, but then he changed his mind and instead gave him the job of scriptwriter and executive producer, expressly asking him to deal with my dialogues. Basilio didn't take it badly; instead, he got down to work with his usual passion. While we were getting to know each other, he became aware of the problems I was having, and he made himself available so that I was never left on my own again. Our professional relationship turned into one of brother and sister, and this cheered me up, gave me strength, and helped me to find myself. I would never again be able to manage without him.

When each day came to an end, I'd go to sleep accompanied by his gentle warning:

"Sophia, don't start with those violins again!"

"I won't," I'd say to him, "as long as I know you're by my side."

Basilio knew just what to do and say to help me with my crisis, quietly becoming a part of my life. Like all real friends he offered me the greatest gift: he encouraged me to be myself.

SET ANOTHER PLACE AT THE TABLE

I've always had a sort of sixth sense about choosing the people with whom to share my most intimate, private side. And I'm hardly ever wrong. When I am mistaken about someone, I move away calmly, on tiptoe. I don't want to hurt anyone. I don't like to suffer, nor do I want to make anyone else suffer.

Generally, I'm somewhat of an introvert; I love peace and quiet and to be alone. Social life wears me out. I don't get too familiar with strangers, nor do I give much importance to acquaintances. I trust my instinct, I can quickly size up the person I have before me, how sincere they are, what their intentions are.

When I saw Basilio for the first time I knew instantly that we were always going to be friends.

He was an intelligent, cultured, extremely polite Palermitan, and very kind. Like many Sicilians he was reserved, discreet, and he never talked about himself, his loves, his ambitions. Basilio was a friend of the painter Renato Guttuso, and the directors Luchino Visconti and Roberto Rossellini.

Because Soldati had a sarcastic, detached manner, I didn't at all feel comfortable with him, and we didn't always agree on the set. He was all brains, too intellectual, he explained things the way he wanted to, and that was that. He showed no compassion for a young girl who'd just started working in cinema and was accustomed to trusting her instinct.

Working for Mario I felt suspended between my shyness and the growing awareness of how *I* wanted to act. Sometimes we'd be at loggerheads. I was still new to the business and art. I didn't have the right to speak my mind, nor would I have been capable of doing so. I was sure he wasn't the right director for that movie. He definitely wasn't able to help me.

Basilio, however, understood instantly what I needed to be able to do my very best. He was with me at all times, at makeup, before, during and after the shooting, besides trying to quell the ghosts that visited me during the night. He'd show me where the camera was, the marks on the ground, where to look in a scene. With endless patience, he taught me, offering me images that could inspire me for the more dramatic scenes. In the evening, in my trailer, we'd go over the script for the next day, analyzing the nuances, the two of us looking for the heartstrings to pull, the feelings to stir up inside me. He helped me to transform my insecurity into emotion, my weakness into passion.

Even though Basilio and I were working on the present, taking apart every word, every line of the script that I would be performing imminently, we were also anticipating the end of the movie, where the most difficult scene awaited me, one that would demand everything I had to give.

A clever psychologist, besides being someone who knew how to make a movie, Basilio first talked to me about the climactic scene only vaguely, only alluding to it. Then, as we gradually approached the fateful moment, when Nives loses her son in the delta, he started to get to the point. He waited for the right time to say something, when his suggestions would be the most effective: "Imagine a small, young, defenseless child. Your son. And you, Nives, are his mother. Outside there's water, water everywhere. And suddenly, you can't find him anywhere . . ."

Then he'd pile it on: "You look for him, you start to feel faint, you feel like you're losing your mind, everyone wants to help you, but you just don't know what to do . . ."

I would hang on his every word. I was there to believe in the reality of my character and the situation she was in. And I really did have to believe in it. Little by little, I let myself be influenced so that I could find the character that was waiting for me within. Thinking back to what De Sica had taught me, I traveled inside myself, pursuing what Nives's most authentic reaction to the tragedy might be. With patience and devotion I made every effort to find the smallest answers even in the most unexplored corners of my mind. We worked so hard that, when the time came to shoot that dramatic scene, I took a deep breath and did it right on the first take.

I had pulled through another challenge. Once more, I discovered that fear and vulnerability can help you if you pair them with hard work and discipline. And if you experience them with a true friend beside you.

Only once did Basilio get distracted, and did he pay for it! My antagonist in the movie was Tosca, played by a French actress named Lise Bourdin. When, after an intense courtship, Basilio managed at last to take her to the beach to make love in a corner concealed by the shrubs, all their clothing disappeared, both his and hers. I'll never know how the two absentminded lovers ever made it back to the hotel. Maybe they stole a sheet hanging somewhere, or they just ran as fast as they could . . . Of course, the whole crew found out and laughed about it for ages.

Basilio was a shining light for our family: for Carlo, for me, for both of us. He was always close to me during the difficult time years later when I was trying so hard to become a mother, and when Carlo Jr. was born in Geneva, Basilio got so drunk in celebration that, as he was walking down the hospital steps, he couldn't figure out where he was. He adored Carlo's and my children, and whenever he came to visit us he'd spend whole days playing with them. Still today, even though they're in their forties, Carlo and Edoardo remember him wistfully. "Wouldn't it be great if Basilio were here now, if he could see our children."

Our beloved friend passed away ten years ago, in 2003, in Rome. He died alone, in his home, leaving a sense of emptiness that I try to fill each and every day with my memories of our long life together, and with the deep affection we exchanged on every occasion. He loved all of us equally, and reserved for each one of us a special fondness. He wasn't just a friend of the family, he was one of us.

I have *Woman of the River* to thank for another important encounter. There I met Maestro Armando Trovajoli, who was to write the music for my most important movies, including *Two Women*; *Yesterday, Today and Tomorrow*; and *A Special Day*. A trusted collaborator of the Ponti–De Laurentiis company, he was one of the most appreciated composers on the Italian scene. He was the soul of Rome, the soundtrack of our lives. A great pianist and lover of jazz, he played with the biggest names, from Louis Armstrong to Miles Davis, from Duke Ellington to Chet Baker to Django Reinhardt. When I first met him, he was the director of a pop music orchestra for the Italian radio station RAI and, along with Piero Piccioni, he conducted *Eclipse*, an important weekly radio program. Dino and Carlo had hired him for *Bitter Rice* and later for *Anna*, in which I had a small part and Silvana Mangano had danced to the notes of "El Negro Zumbon," which became an international hit. And of course he is known for his work on the Quentin Tarantino film, *Kill Bill, Vol. 1*.

Armando married the film and television actress Anna Maria Pierangeli (later called Pier Angeli), who made him suffer terribly. After their divorce, he married Maria Paola Sapienza, a delightful woman who was absolutely crazy about him. They thrived on music, in their lovely home in Olgiata. In the 1960s and 1970s, he, together with the songwriters Pietro Garinei and Sandro Giovannini, were the makers of Italian musical comedy. Armando wrote the unforgettable "*Roma nun fa' la stupida sta-sera*" ("Rome, Don't Fool Me Tonight"), written for the 1962 musical comedy, *Rugantino*.

Each year, when the holidays came around, the first phone call I'd receive would always be Armando's. Or the first call I'd make would be to him. That's the way it always was, until the end.

"Hello, Sophia? Set another place at the table . . ." he'd sing-song, poking fun at himself and the comedy he'd written the successful music for.

". . . what difference does another friend make," I'd sing-song back, happy to hear his voice.

We were like children playing. Since Armando left us, Christmas isn't the same anymore.

I love to sing, like everyone did at home, Mamma Luisa, Mammina, Maria. Maybe I was the least talented of them, and above all the shyest. Singing in public always made me feel very embarrassed. And yet, I still like to sing.

Trovajoli was perfectly aware of the fact that my voice hadn't been trained, but he thought there was something brilliant and sensuous about it. So he preferred not to work on it too much in order to preserve its naturalness. De Sica had taken the same approach to my acting. He offered a few technical secrets, a touch of reassurance, and a lot of cheerfulness. And then he gave me the gift of a song.

In 1958, to the lyrics by Dino Verde, he wrote "*Che m'e 'mparato a fa'*" (The Things You Taught Me) just for me, and it was a huge success. He wrote it to fit me, adapting the notes to my voice. I could never have imagined someone writing a song for me, even less so a maestro like him.

He died just last year at the age of ninety-five. To say good-bye to him, I softly sang these words to myself: "*Capre, Surriento e 'sta luna, se ne so' iute cu' tté*" (Capri, Sorrento, and this moon have gone away with you).

THE RING

The end of *Woman of the River* marked the start of a new chapter in my life. My asthma vanished just as quickly as it had appeared, proof that it had been psychosomatic. I now had two new friends, and a dramatic role behind me that would make the neophyte Pizza Girl of *The Gold of Naples* into a well-rounded actress. But most important of all, I had a ring.

Yes, because the very last day of shooting, Carlo came to the set with a small leather case. During a break, he took me aside and handed it to me, without saying a word. I opened it to find a diamond ring.

It was a silent, luminous, timeless moment.

We never talked about our relationship, not even then, when he gave me the ring.

I rushed off and, as soon as I turned the corner, burst into tears of joy. Ines Bruscia—the script supervisor, who was soon to become my trusty confidante and go everywhere with me, in life and at work—chased after me, concerned, wanting to know what was wrong. But when she saw with her own eyes the reason I was so emotional, she was brought to tears, too. That in itself was remarkable, because Ines was reserved. She was also affectionate, modest, and efficient, and for many years she accompanied Carlo and me in our lives. Without her I would have been another person, a different actress.

I went back to Rome with a feather in my cap, new fears overcome—and a ring on my finger. When I proudly showed it to my mother, wiggling my fingers in the air to make the diamond sparkle even more, I got the only reaction a mother could possibly give, especially a mother like mine, with her personality, and her past: "What are you up to? (*Nun 'o vide ch'è spusato, tene ddoje figl' 'e vint'ann' cchiù 'e te?*) Can't you see he's married, has two children and is twenty years older than you? What can you possibly expect from him? Back out while you still can and make a life for yourself. You're still so young . . ."

Each time she asked me, "Have you talked about the future?" I simply didn't know what to say. The only thing I did know was that I loved him, and that he was the man of my life.

From Via Balzani, Mammina, Maria and I moved to Via di Villa Ada, in the Salario quarter, close to the Catacombs of Priscilla. But I was spending more and more time with Carlo, in his large apartment above the studios in Palazzo Colonna overlooking Piazza d'Aracoeli. His marriage had been over for a long time, although he was not divorced. And he had two young children. I was in pain for them, for us, and yet there wasn't anything I could do about it. I would have liked things to have happened more quickly for us, to have been clearer, out in the open. But the times would not allow that. I trusted our love, and I was ready to live that love.

Nineteen fifty-four had been filled with irreversible changes, major surprises, and personal developments. I'd met De Sica and Marcello, I was directed by Blasetti and by Soldati, and I'd sung and acted with some of the biggest names. I'd gone from comedy to tragedy without losing my identity. And my relationship with Carlo had grown stronger. I was turning into a star, and the whole world was starting to talk about me. In the spring I'd been to Cannes for the first time to present *Neapolitan Carousel*, film director Ettore Giannini's great movie, considered to be the only Italian musical capable of competing with the American ones. I'd played a small part in it where I sang, dubbed by a real singer, "*O surdato 'nnammurato*" (Oh Soldier in Love).

In June I'd also been to Berlin, where a famous photograph shows me sitting next to Gina Lollobrigida, with Yvonne De Carlo right behind us. In October, when I got back from filming *Woman of the River*, in Comacchio, I was off to London, where I was invited to Italian Movie Week.

The Gold of Naples and *Woman of the River* were both released in December, and I visited Milan for the first time ever, dressed as the Pizza Girl, handing out hundreds of pizzas to my fans thronging Piazza San Babila. When I got to the station I was welcomed by a festive crowd, and I was even greeted by the mayor. Suddenly, I was a star, with a press office dedicated to disseminating my image and getting me as much coverage as possible. Deep inside, however, I was still a child with wide-open eyes who wanted to be an actress, a woman who wanted to get married and have children, just like every other woman. I had my ups and downs just like everyone else, and I worked with passion and discipline, as I always had. I was growing inside my life, my great little story, putting it together day by day, line by line, page by page.

THE LUCK OF BEING SOPHIA

Just as 1954 had been a watershed, the year 1955 also started out well. At the Grand Gala del Cinema, held on January 15, the magazine *Guild* awarded me a prize that placed me in the company of Italy's other three greatest actresses, Anna Magnani, Gina Lollobrigida, and Silvana Mangano, who'd received the same prize in previous years. It was an important acknowledgment, confirming my growing success.

The world was changing, the war was a fading memory, and we were starting to see the first signs of the economic boom. Italian cinema was shedding its more overtly political nature and looking to make box-office hits. Italian comedic movies boasted such experienced actors, screenwriters, and directors, that they made money even as they produced some real masterpieces, capable of describing the whole spectrum of a country on the move.

For a few weeks I'd been working on the set of *The Sign of Venus*, a comedy with an all-star cast: De Sica and Peppino De Filippo, Raf Vallone and Tina Pica, Sordi and, most importantly, Franca Valeri, an amazing woman, who had also contributed to writing the story and screenplay. Franca has given me so much. We've always loved each other, and we always will. The characters' physical, geographical, and linguistic differences, played out with intelligence and wit, were the comic heart of the movie, which made us laugh even before the audience did. Dino Risi, whom I had never met before, was the director, and we would work with each other again immediately afterward.

I play Agnese, Franca plays Cesira Colombo, Agnese's cousin, who has left Rome for Milan to look for a job, and love. Franca describes her cousin as someone who walks "outward," not that she does it deliberately, of course, and that's why men ogle her. She, instead, has no one looking at her, so she stuffs herself with *patatesse* (potatoes), and lets herself be fooled by Signora Pina, the fortune-teller, into thinking that she's under the sign of Venus: a small window of opportunity that won't last more than a month or so, during which, if she keeps her eyes peeled, she can still hope to find her prince charming. The problem is that all the men she's surrounded by—photographers, poets, traffic officers, stolen-car salesmen—somehow fall in love with her cousin Agnese, when they're not thinking about their own affairs. The ending is bittersweet: poor Cesira ends up alone and disillusioned, her romantic dream vanished into thin air.

That summer, Risi had me on the screen again acting alongside De Sica in the third chapter of the *Bread, Love and . . .* series. The first two movies, *Bread, Love and Dreams* and *Bread, Love and Jealousy*, were directed by Luigi Comencini, one of the leaders of commedia all'italiana (the ironic, humorous treatment of serious themes), and had been huge box-office hits, thanks to Gina Lollobrigida, who had come to be known as La Bersagliera for her headstrong personality, and to the acting bravura of De Sica, who plays an older, still attractive commander of the carabinieri, transferred from his native town of Sorrento to Sagliena, in Abruzzo. "La Lollo," Gina's nickname, was the first Italian movie star and the prototype of the *maggiorata*, the "full-figured woman," as De Sica refers to her in the 1952 movie *Times Gone By*. This definition would also be used to describe me and some of the other actresses in my day, lumping us together in a single category, despite the fact that we were all quite different from each other, each of us on her own path.

When it came time for the third *Bread, Love and . . .* movie to be made, this one to be called *Scandal in Sorrento*, Gina Lollobrigida backed out. Maybe she didn't want to be trapped forever in the character of La Bersagliera, or maybe, since she loved to sing—she had a gorgeous voice—she was tempted by *Beautiful but Dangerous*, the fictional story of the life of the soprano Lina Cavalieri, which gave her a chance to sing on film.

So when they offered me Gina's part in *Scandal in Sorrento*, I didn't think twice about it. I had no reason to say no. The press had a field day, of course, concocting a rivalry between the two of us that had absolutely no reason to exist. We were two completely different women and actresses, and if one of us was successful it didn't mean the other one had failed. But that's life, and that was Italy, and during that period of affluence, the people enjoyed following certain epic rivalries: that between the Italian cyclists Fausto Coppi and Gino Bartali, the opera singers Renata Tebaldi and Maria Callas and, why not, Lollo-Loren. But both Gina and I were passionate about our work, and we had no time to waste in petty skirmishes.

My chance to star in *Scandal in Sorrento* was very alluring. Just the idea of working with De Sica again was enough for me to celebrate, since I'd had fun working with him and I'd learned so much. Thanks to his good spirits, his experience, his unfailing eye, I'd been able to take risks and improved without thinking, managing to show sides of my personality that I usually kept to myself. In other words, I learned my trade. On top of that satisfaction, we would be making the movie in our native land, directed by Dino Risi, who understood me and knew how to get the most out of me after just working with me on two movies that year.

So there we are in Sorrento, where Vittorio, as Maresciallo Carotenuto Cavalier Antonio, has just returned from Abruzzo and accepted a post as head of the metropolitan guard, or "metrotulip guards," as the great Tina Pica in the role of his trusted governess Caramella, mispronounces it, hoping to overcome his sadness at being close to retirement. But when he arrives it's me he finds, Donna Sofia la Smargiassa, the show-off, a fishmonger by trade, and the strong-willed tenant of his home.

The Fishmonger sold fish the same way the Pizza Girl fried pizzas: "*Frutti di mare, frutti dell'amore, frutti d''o core so' frutti ingannatori . . . Triglie rosse, triglie vive . . .*" (Seafood, the food of love, and the fruit of the heart can be deceitful. . . . Red mullets, live mullets . . .). The character of this Sofia gave me the chance to express myself to the fullest, especially because I knew Vittorio had my back. "Donna Sofi, you've vulcanized me," says this Casanova dressed in uniform. It was once again an explosion of happiness and vitality, which peaked with the unforgettable scene of our Italian mambo, I in my red dress, he looking at me puzzled and trying, in vain, to follow my dance steps.

Maybe the scene was successful because of the spontaneity of the improvisation, as well as because of Peppino Rotunno's flashy photography. The dance hadn't been written into the script. It had just come to us, as a perfect line might, like taking a stroll, like going out to buy ice cream in town.

"Officer, shall we dance this mambo?"

"What's a mambo?"

"It's a Brazilian dance."

Some critics said the movie marked the death of neorealism. But the Academy of Italian cinema crowned it with two David di Donatello awards, and the public swarmed to see it, sending it to the top of the box-office sales chart. The Pizza Girl in black and white had turned into the Fishmonger in Technicolor, maybe less authentically of the "street," but no doubt more modern, and even more popular.

In the meantime, my name was traveling around the world, and my photo would bask on the cover of *Life* and *Newsweek*.

While still filming *Woman of the River*, I had met another marvelous director. One day, while we were shooting the last scenes at the lighthouse on Punta Pila, I saw a boat approaching us, steered by a man who was rowing so naturally it looked as though that was all he'd ever done in his life. I thought he might be one of the local fishermen, curious about the set, but as he came closer, wearing a bathing suit and a T-shirt wrapped around his head to shield it from the sun, I recognized him as Alessandro Blasetti, the father of Italian cinema. I was speechless.

"I'd like to have you with me in my next movie," he said, without even saying hello first. I burst out laughing and gave him a big hug. He was talking about *Lucky to Be a Woman*, on which I'd work with Marcello.

So in the fall of 1955 I was on the set with Marcello, in *Lucky to Be a Woman*. The movie is the perfect description of that world of small stars, paparazzi, and society reporters that breathed life into the Rome of that period. For Marcello, it naturally paved the way to *La dolce vita*. For me, it was a watershed: from that moment on Sofia became Sophia, ready to head to the United States.

VI

CARY'S ROSES

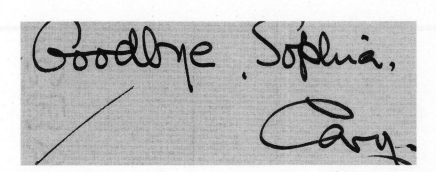

HAPPY THOUGHTS

My first personal encounter with American cinema was in the smile of Cary Grant—his elegance, his light footstep. How many other women had wished to be in my shoes? And instead it happened to me, to me with all my insecurities, my past, my yearning to improve myself. I had to show everyone that I was up to the great opportunity of working with this international star. To me, it felt like a responsibility, like a duty that had to be honored to the very end. No more, no less. So, when the time came, I put aside my fears, rolled up my sleeves, and got down to work.

Before I got the role to appear with Cary in *The Pride and the Passion*, Carlo had started to receive offers from other countries for me. He had gone to Los Angeles and sent me a telegram from there, as simple and to the point as a father might be.

"Sophia, if you want to conquer America, then you're going to have to learn English."

While he was dictating that to his secretary, he was already on the phone with the woman who was going to make this possible, the legendary language coach Sarah Spain.

"Miss Spain, this is Ponti. What are your plans for the next few months?" practically ambushing the poor thing, without giving her a chance to answer. "Miss Loren absolutely must learn English: she has to get to the point that she can think, eat, dream in English. Live in English, as if she'd been born in Dublin, or in New York. You will be her shadow, you will be beside her every second of the day, taking advantage of every opportunity."

"But I . . ."

"Please, don't say no. Whatever it is you were supposed to do instead, get out of it. We start bright and early tomorrow morning."

Sarah was Irish and spoke with a gentle lilt. A plump brunette, she seemed to roll, rather than walk. After a moment's bewilderment, she accepted the ambitious job and took up Ponti's request to the letter. This woman wasn't a teacher, she was a persecutor. She would arrive on the set—it was September 1955 and we were making *Lucky to Be a Woman*—two hours before makeup, she'd follow me around from one break to another, she'd eat with me, and in the evening she'd accompany me back home. Whenever I'd stop to chat with Marcello or with Blasetti, she'd drag me away without compassion. "*Sophia, come along. Take a look at this, what do you think of that? Would you like a coffee? What about your next film?*" Marcello would shrug, wink at me and grin. "If it has to be done, it has to be done. There's nothing you can really do about it."

Sarah started out teaching me grammar, continued with literature by T. S. Eliot and George Bernard Shaw, and included cartoons and songs, magazines, and newspapers. We read the *New York Times*, *Vogue*, Shakespeare, Mickey Mouse comic strips, Jane Austen, and *Little Women*. We listened to Frank Sinatra and Louis Armstrong, we learned George Gershwin's and Cole Porter's lyrics by heart, we discussed clothing, hairstyles, food, and current affairs. We painstakingly went over every single technical term on the set, from the lights to "Take One" to "Action." And we also watched every single movie I'd seen as a child so that I could become familiar with the different accents of the stars I'd loved so much. How odd to hear them speak with their real voices, after having grown up listening to the Italian dubbers. The tone of their voices could range so much, from kind to sarcastic, so different from the stiff tone of some of the Italian dubbers, who had done a superb job anyway. Although it did confuse me, I was tickled by it, too.

Sarah never left my side and I followed her around both tamely and stubbornly. I was lucky to have a good ear for languages. I did my homework diligently, improving day by day, and yet it wasn't enough. Because, meanwhile, something had happened that seemed like a miracle to me. And we all know that miracles don't have the patience to wait.

Carlo had found out that Stanley Kramer, the producer of *High Noon*, was in Spain where preparations were being made to shoot a costume drama on the Napoleonic Wars. Originally, Marlon Brando and Ava Gardner were supposed to star in it. But Marlon had backed out and was replaced by Sinatra. But Frank was on the outs with Ava . . . In other words, it was the usual Hollywood mess. The only sure thing was that Cary Grant would be in it, but by contract he had the right to approve his partners. And no way was he going to be content working with some unknown actress, let alone an Italian one.

As usual, Carlo wasn't discouraged by anything that got in the way of his plans. He called Kramer and invited him to Rome in order to show him *Woman of the River*. As soon as the viewing ended, the director made him an offer, taking him by surprise.

"How does two hundred thousand dollars sound for Miss Loren? I think she'd be perfect for the part."

Carlo let a few seconds go by, and then answered standoffishly: "Interesting, let me think about it, I have to look at her schedule, but in principle, I'd say yes, I think it can be done."

"It was the easiest decision of my life," he remarked that evening, as we waited for Stanley to join us for dinner. It was the amount of money you'd offer a star. Now it was just a question of my earning it.

After the contract was signed in late December, the United Artists machine got moving. It was early 1956, Cortina d'Ampezzo in the Dolomitic Alps was hosting the Winter Olympics and Montecarlo was preparing for Prince Rainier and Grace Kelly's wedding. Just a couple of months later Arthur Miller and Marilyn Monroe would marry. The Soviet Union was starting to crack with the unrest in its Eastern European satellites. In Italy the ground was being broken for the Autostrada del Sole, the major highway that would take eight years to build and eventually connect Milan with Naples via Bologna, Florence, and Rome. The world was changing quickly, and I was ready to face it.

In February I left to reconnoiter Spain and to meet my costars in *The Pride and the Passion*. What a surprise when I landed at Madrid's Barajas airport—I was greeted by five hundred fans shouting *"Guapa! Guapa!"* (Beautiful!) In Madrid I also met Lucia Bosè, the absolute legend of my youth when she was at the height of her fame in Italian neorealist films, and her charming husband Luis Miguel Dominguín, the great matador. To welcome me, they had organized a special visit to an arena, and what better company with whom to leap into the world of bullfighting? An outing among friends, a bit of time spent together, the chance to take some interesting pictures.

It was a clear winter afternoon when the Plaza de Toros de Las Ventas, bathed in sunlight, loomed up before me. They had given me a torera outfit to wear, and with the recklessness of a twenty-one-year-old, I had the crazy idea of going down into the arena by myself. I felt indomitable, as if my clothes were enough to protect me. At that point, Dominguín, maybe just to be funny, let the bull out of its pen. In the space of a few seconds, as that black cloud thundered in my direction ready to gore me, I was overcome by a mixture of excitement and fear I'll never forget. Dominguín, who may have been a joker, but who could also smell danger, jumped down into the *ruedo*, the arena, and dragged me away. Short of breath, covered in dust, I looked at him, laughing, totally unaware of the great risk I had run.

For the last part of the corrida, the *suerte suprema*, I took shelter in the *callejón*, where the bullfighters prepare for the fight, under the spectators' stand, and left the scene to him. As I watched the spectacle, I recalled all the times that, as a child, I'd seen *Blood and Sand*, and forced whoever had accompanied me to the Sacchini theater that day—Mammina or maybe Zia Dora—to stay there and watch that movie as many as two or three times. I'd fallen hopelessly in love with Tyrone Power, and at night I'd fall asleep thinking about Doña Sol des Muire, played by Rita Hayworth, and her beautiful face and hair.

My childhood always resurfaced to touch my heartstrings. Even now that I'd found my own way I remembered what I'd been like when, in between hunger and the war, without a father to guide me, all that was left for me to do was dream. Little "Sofia Stuzzicadenti" ("Toothpick"), with her problems and her daydreams, has always lived inside me, reminding me, yesterday and today, not to take anything for granted. This has been my greatest fortune, because it has enabled me to be happy each and every day for all the wonderful things I've been able to do, to measure the great distance I've come. A fairy tale loses its magic without real life, and the opposite is true, too. The most beautiful thing is to be able to walk in between, without ever having to forgo either the one or the other.

Although I had managed to survive a bull, the biggest challenge still lay ahead. In April, at the Castellana Hotel in Madrid, a huge American-style cocktail party was held to present the movie to the press and introduce me to Frank Sinatra and Cary Grant. I have to admit I'd never been so nervous in my life. I changed my dress eight times, tried out eleven different hairstyles, got in and out of heels of all different heights, finding no peace. As I put on my makeup I went over my lines with Sarah, who pretended she was Cary, then Frank, then the reporters ready to pounce on me and catch me off guard. She assailed me with questions, which I tried to answer appropriately: "*I'm so pleased to meet you, Mr. Grant . . . I'm looking forward to working with you, Frank . . . Sure, I love singing . . . No, it's my first time in Madrid. Yes, of course you're right, my English is still sort of shaky but it's getting better every day . . . I beg your pardon? Oh, yes, I definitely enjoy eating paella."* I focused on the English and thought about the two living legends I was about to meet. I would have been in awe of them even if they'd been from Naples. My legs were shaking and I desperately searched inside myself to find the right expression to wear with them. The good thing was they gave me all the time I needed to get ready. Cary showed up two hours late, Frank nearly four, by which time we thought he'd never show up at all.

The room was teeming with reporters and photographers, and only English was spoken—with all kinds of accents. I understood about a fourth of what I was asked, making up for it with an equally wide range of smiles, alternating my sweet smile with my sexy one, my mysterious one with the one that said I was confident. Photo-romances paled in comparison!

When I finally saw Cary's unmistakable profile standing out against the door, I thought I'd faint. Our moment had finally come. I tried to muster the courage I needed and approached him, feigning a nonchalance that I didn't at all have. His tuxedo with the shiny lapels, his slightly graying hair, his elegant ways took my breath away. He looked as though he'd just stepped down from the screen, a dream come true. *"E io che ce faccio ccà?"* (What on earth am I doing here?), I asked myself as our eyes met. *"Mo me ne fuje . . ."* (I need to get out of here now).

Too late. He held out his hand, looking at me with a pinch of mischief:

"Miss Lolloloren, I presume? Or is it Miss Lorenigida? You Italians have such strange last names I can't seem to get them straight."

It was a good line, of course, but those days everyone was talking about our rivalry, and I was very annoyed by it. It embar-

rassed me, and made the situation seem more difficult. "*Chist'*
nun se po' suppurta'" (I can't stand this guy), I thought to myself.

But suddenly, I was overcome by the urge to laugh, so I
laughed. All dressed up for the cocktail party, I chose the simplest road: to act the way I was, and not play the part of the
star. I liked looking Cary over, looking at him eye to eye, not
missing out on those genteel gestures, the way he bent his head
to one side while he eyed you with intelligent attention. I got
to know him, to appreciate his sense of humor, I knew how to
make him smile.

Who wouldn't have been bowled over by Cary Grant? It was
the start of a great friendship, a special partnership. Later, when
we were on the set for *The Pride and the Passion* for six very long
months, we'd have time to let fall our mannerisms as stars, and
show our more authentic sides.

In the movie, which takes place in Spain during the Napoleonic Era, the Spanish forces are British allies, and they have
had to abandon an enormous cannon. A British naval captain
(played by Cary) wants to recover it for Britain, but the leader
of the Spanish guerrillas (Frank) wants to transport it 600 miles
to fight the French at Ávila. So we, too, crossed the mountain-
ous area of Castilla y León, from Segovia to Salamanca, from
Burgos to Palencia, in pursuit of the cannon, the real star of
the movie. The crew numbered four hundred including technicians, stagehands, actors, and even military consultants. No
box-office success was ever going to repay the production for all
the money it was spending. Around the three main characters—
Grant, Sinatra, and me—was a whole sea of extras to stage the
great pitched battles of the drama. We and 3,685 soldiers—or
so the annals say—spent the last few weeks under the strong
walls of Ávila, as we waited to breach and capture it. These were
hardworking conditions. It was very hot and the set was chaotic,
bristling with confusion. It reminded me of the set of *Quo Vadis*

at Cinecittà, and also brought back memories of that emotion and impotence I'd felt as a debutante at her first test. I tried not to let my mind wander, to focus as much as possible on my part, and everyone was surprised at my resilience and good mood.

Sinatra was delightful, kindhearted, and fun-loving, even though he was still in pain over Ava Gardner, and so not exactly in the best of moods. On the outside he joked around, but inside he was suffering. He teased me in a mild-mannered way, and he pampered my sister, Maria, who'd joined me and was harboring the dream of becoming a singer. He'd try to trick me into making mistakes in English, which was still shaky, telling me that some obscene expression was instead an elegant phrase. He never sang while on the set, but in his dressing room he had a huge collection of classical music, ranging from Bach to Beethoven, from Verdi to Scarlatti. He introduced me to the music of Ella Fitzgerald, who he believed was the greatest singer of all time, and he opened wide the doors of jazz for me. He was irascible and generous, unpredictable and sincere, and he kept me company a lot of the time.

But it was the much more reserved Cary who really won me over, with his good manners and zest for life. The first time he invited me out to dinner I thought I hadn't understood correctly, so I asked: "*You and me?* Out for dinner? Are you sure?" What could he possibly have seen in me, a very young Italian woman who could hardly speak English and was less than half his age? And what were we going to talk about all evening? But he was unfazed. "*Yes, darling, you and me, out for dinner.*"

He'd bought a flaming red MG—his every desire on the set became an order—and we raced it around the gently rolling Spanish countryside. It was a magical evening, a timeless one, during which we chatted the way old friends do, inebriated by the fragrance of the late spring. He told me things about himself and about filmmaking, but lightheartedly.

"Hollywood is a simple fairy tale; if you understand that, you'll never get hurt." At dinner, he rattled off comments on the dishes we'd ordered.

I was charmed by his dry wit, his wisdom, affectionate manner, his experience. I would learn a great deal just by watching the way he approached life and his work.

We started spending more and more time together. I, just twenty-two years old, was often confused by a life that was going much too fast. He, at fifty-two, had lived a lot and suffered a lot, too, although it appeared as though he had everything. Cary told me his story, with both reserve and emotion. He was on his third marriage. He'd already had an outstanding career and would have many successes still to come. But he had had a difficult childhood. His older brother had died when he was still a child and his mother had never gotten over his death. She had slowly slipped into madness.

"One day, I must have been about ten, I got home and she wasn't there," Cary said. "Father told me she'd died, but the truth is he'd had her put away in an asylum. I only found out years later . . . and from that day on I went to visit her every chance I got."

His painful story touched me. I tried to imagine, behind his refined, mature appearance, that small boy faced with a tragedy that he couldn't possibly understand. When I begged him to continue, he searched for the words to go on.

"He sent me to an excellent boarding school, but I wasn't really interested in studying. What I wanted was a family."

He found one in a company of acrobats directed by a man named Bob Pender, who was both a teacher and a father to him. Grant ran away from school to travel around England with Pender, learning the art of the circus and vaudeville, finally ending up in New York City. By the time he got there he knew how to move, on stage and out in the world, with all the adroitness of a tightrope walker. After working on Broadway, and cleaning up his blue-collar Bristol accent—a lot like I had done with my Pozzuoli, Neapolitan accent—he went to Hollywood and was hired by Paramount. That's when he changed his name from Archie Leach to Cary Grant.

As our familiarity continued to grow, Cary showed me his vulnerable side, which so resembled my own. The George Cukor and Frank Capra comedies he'd starred in only let you get a glimpse of him behind the sophisticated wit. Maybe he'd found in me a person with whom he could express the deepest part of himself. "Tell me more," I'd say, as he would confide in me, but he'd often avoid going deeper and go back to his joking. He was, after all, Cary Grant, and he had a reputation to uphold. Maybe he felt too vulnerable to completely trust someone. Nonetheless, both of us realized that the feeling between us was beginning to be laced with love, and, for different reasons, we were scared.

I was very much involved with Carlo, who had become my home and my family, even though he already had a family, and it wasn't clear when we'd be able to get married and live together in broad daylight. And Cary was married to Betsy Drake, his third wife, who came and went from the set, although their relationship had been faltering for a long time.

When Betsy decided to return to America for the last time, she set sail from Genoa on the *Andrea Doria*. The ocean liner sank off the coast of Nantucket and forty-six passengers lost their lives. Betsy, luckily, lost only her jewelry, but Cary couldn't leave the set to join her, so he lavished all his attentions on me.

We worked hard and often went over the scenes for the next day together, but we also set aside some private time for us. We'd have dinner in some small family-run restaurants on the Ávila hills, sipping summer red wine and listening to the flamenco. I had a lot to learn, but something to teach, too.

One evening a gentleman approached our table.

"Mr. Grant, could I have your autograph?"

Cary rudely brushed him away from our table to defend our privacy. I scolded him gently.

"Why did you treat him like that? It's important to him, and it doesn't cost us anything."

Cary humbly said I was right and called the admirer back over. We both gave him our autographs along with a dedication.

Fortunately, we were staying in two different hotels, and this helped us to at least keep some distance between us. When we weren't working, I'd often sit out on the terrace of my room to get some sun. I tried not to overdo it, otherwise the following morning I'd show up too tanned.

Cary and I would talk about our dreams, which weren't about fame or wealth—which he already had, along with the respect and the love of the whole world—but about our more intimate dreams, which many took for granted: the miracle of a house, a person with whom to laugh and share one's life. "What kind of house would you like? Do you care for dogs? What names would you choose for your child?" I was charmed by his words, but I always stayed one step back. I didn't want to, and couldn't, raise his hopes.

In the meantime, we'd reached a turning point. The end of the movie was close at hand, and the situation between us showed no sign of being resolved. I was more and more muddled, torn between two men and two worlds. I woke up every morning wondering what was going to happen. I knew that my place was next to Carlo—he was my safe harbor, even though I was still waiting for him to make his decision; our furtive relationship couldn't go on much longer. I also knew for a fact that I didn't want to move permanently to the United States. I was afraid of having to give myself over completely to another culture, so different from my own. At the same time, it was hard to resist the magnetism of a man like Cary, who said he was willing to give up everything for me.

The last night, he invited me out, more solemn than usual. Inside I was afraid. I wasn't prepared for what he was about to say to me. Out of the blue, with a gorgeous sunset outside, he stopped, looked me in the eyes, and simply said: "Will you marry me?"

My words got caught in my throat. I felt like the character in a movie who has forgotten her lines. I had no answer to give him, I had never led him on, and had no intention of ever doing so. I couldn't show him a sign of certainty that I couldn't even find within myself.

"Cary, dear, I need time," I whispered breathlessly. I felt so small before this impossible decision.

He understood, and tried to soften the blow of my answer with a light touch of humor: "Why don't we get married first, and then think about it?"

The next morning I left for Greece, where I was going to make my second American movie, *Boy on a Dolphin*. When I arrived in Athens, I found a bunch of roses and a pale blue note in my hotel room.

"*Forgive me, dear girl—I press you too much. Pray—and so will I. Until next week. Goodbye Sophia, Cary.*"

We didn't see each other the following week, however—it was no more than a hope, promise, a dream. But I never forgot the words on the envelope—"*With only happy thoughts.*" His happy thoughts are still with me.

In fact, these shared dreams of family kept us united as friends long after the movie was finished. Cary showed me great joy when my sons, Carlo Jr. and Edoardo, were born. And I felt the same happiness for him, years later, at the birth of his daughter, Jennifer, whom he'd so longed for. And I was delighted when I met his splendid wife, Barbara, whom he loved to the very end.

MY TREASURE TROVE
OF MEMORIES

June 4, 1943. My letter to Nonna Sofia, in which I thank her for the check my father had given me on her behalf.

Corzudi 4 - 6 - 1943

Cara nonna

Ho ricevuto ieri la tua lettera con un assegno di £ 300. Ti ringrazio molto per l'interessamento che hai avuto per me; anzi siccome non posso scrivere personalmente a papà perché non ne so più il suo indirizzo, mi farai tu il piacere di ringraziarlo per i soldi che mi ha mandato. Ieri 3 giugno è stato il giorno più bello della mia vita ho ricevuto la prima comunione e la cresima ed a sono veramente felice.

Cara nonna appena dopo la comunione mammina mi ha portato a fare le fotografie che saranno pronte fra una settimana, appena le avrò la prima sarà spedita a te ed una a papà. La mia comare mi ha regalato

Tanti ringraziamenti e baci a tua Mamma e a zia Miranda

un bel braccialetto di oro con pietre azzurre, ti assicuro che è molto bello e mi è piaciuto tanto.

Giorni fa ho terminato i miei esami e sono molto contenta di dirti che sono stata promossa in quinta classe con maggiori voti.

Sei contenta? Tanti baci

Una aff.ma nipotina

Sofia Scicolone

Tanti ringraziamenti e saluti affettuosi.

Romilda

Mamma Luisa.

June 3, 1943. The day I received my first Holy Communion and Confirmation, which I wrote about in my letter to Nonna Sofia.

A picture of me when I was nicknamed Toothpick . . .

. . . and another taken when I started growing so fast that Mamma Luisa had to add several strips of material to the waist of my dress, made with fabric an aunt sent us from America.

My class during the last year of school. I'm the first one in the second row on the left.

My first picture in a bathing suit, when I was fourteen.

This was when I had a permanent pout on my lips because I thought it was an expression.

In the late 1940s I was still in Naples, attending Maestro Serpe's acting school.

In the early 1950s, after moving to Rome, I lived with Mammina and Maria. I got by entering beauty pageants and doing some advertising . . . some of which were shot on the balcony of our home on Via di Villa Ada.

Getting ready for a beauty pageant with some of the other contestants.

1950. In this picture I'm parading down the runway at the Miss Italia beauty pageant, wearing a white gown with fringe, kindly lent to me by a boutique owner who was a friend of Dino Villani, the patron of the event. On that occasion I won the title of Miss Elegance.

Sogno
SETTIMANALE DEL MARTEDI

N. 44
LIRE
30

Michelle attende selvaggiamente: ella ha tradito la sua migliore amica, è giunta al ricatto; di qualsiasi cosa sarebbe capace purchè il suo principe azzurro giunga a lei. Ora ogni fruscio del vento sulla sabbia, ogni rumore della notte le fa sobbalzare il piccolo cuore spaurito e tremante

SOFIA LAZZARO
in una inquadratura di "PRINCIPESSA IN ESILIO"
(Foto Latenza)

4 novembre 1951 ● Spediz. in abbonam. postale - Gruppo II

The cover of the November 4, 1951, issue of *Sogno,* when I worked under the name Sofia Lazzaro, with a dedication I wrote to Mammina. The issue contained this episode from "Princess in Exile," in which I played the part of Michelle Dumas, "a wild and moody type of girl" who tries to win over the handsome Prince Rojo.

A rare moment of relaxation with Mammina.

Yet I hardly ever had time to relax, as I mentioned in this note written years later, in which I regretted having somehow skipped my adolescence, busy as I was chasing my dream.

Rimpianti? non non Dire o meglio . Uno: non ho avuto adolescenza - già a 15 anni ero a Tu per Tu con il lavoro e con le ambizioni - non avevo più tempo per gl. obbandon. / per il fantasticare a vuoto / per giocare - non avevo più Tempo soprattutto per sbagliare -

1954. At last, the movies. Here I am with Totò, known as "the prince of laughter," in *The Anatomy of Love*, a comedy . . .

. . . and that same year with Carlo Mazzarella in *Neapolitan Carousel*, the first major Italian musical after WWII.

The words Vittorio De Sica wrote on this photograph many years after it was taken recall our first encounter at Cinecittà. I was nineteen, not fifteen, however, and he offered me my first important opportunity.

In those days, my beauty wasn't considered "orthodox," and the photographers and cameramen would say things like: "She's impossible to photograph. Her face is too short, her mouth is too big, and her nose is too long."

Many years later, I wrote these words in English in a notebook: "Don't ever try to disguise yourself in order to approach an ideal. Think of the irregularities of your face as *the Treasure*— which they really are."

Don't ever Try To Disguise yourself in order To approach an ideal. think of the impulsities of your face as the Treasure which they really are.

1954. On the set with Marcello Mastroianni. Here we are taking a break from shooting *Too Bad She's Bad*, a fast-paced comedy, in which we appeared together for the first time.

This picture was taken on the set of *Woman of the River*, also made in 1954, when Carlo and I realized we had fallen in love.

The poster for "Mambo Bacan," a song written for *Woman of the River*.

1955. A dinner party to celebrate *The Gold of Naples,* the film based on the eponymous book by Giuseppe Marotta (behind me). I'm sitting between Cesare Zavattini (left) and Vittorio De Sica. Behind us are the reporter Augusto Borselli and actor Paolo Stoppa.

An evening at Carlo's home, with all the friends who had worked on *Woman of the River.* From the left, Antonio Altoviti, Lise Bourdin, Carlo, Suso Cecchi D'Amico, me, Mario Soldati, Basilio Franchina, Gérard Oury, and his wife.

1956. With Cary Grant, in Spain.

1957. Cary and I, during two separate breaks on the set of *The Pride and the Passion*.

CARY GRANT

Forgive me, dear girl
I press you too much.
Pray — and so will I.
Until next week —
Goodbye, Sophia,
Cary.

SOPHIA, with
only HAPPY THOUGHTS.

When I got to my hotel in
Athens I found this note from
Cary. On his personalized
stationery he had written the
words: "Forgive me, dear girl.
I press you *too* much. Pray,
and so will I. Until next week.
Goodbye, Sophia, Cary." The
envelope reads: "Sophia, with
only happy thoughts."

On the set of *Legend of the Lost* with Carlo, shot in 1957 in the Libyan desert, also starring John Wayne.

HOTEL *Statler* WASHINGTON

Tonight, from New York — I'll be flying at the same time as you. You'll be in my prayers. If you think and pray with me, for the same thing and purpose, all <u>will</u> be right and life <u>will</u> be good.

C.

If this note means as much to you as yours do to me. I shall be glad I've written it.

Another letter from Cary, this one from New York. He wrote: "If you think and pray with me, for the same thing and purpose, all *will* be right and life *will* be good."

My career had become international. I was always flying somewhere . . .

During that hectic period in our lives, to get some rest Carlo and I would take refuge in Bürgenstock, Switzerland. In this picture, we're standing at the door to our home, saying good-bye to our neighbor, Audrey Hepburn.

27-1-958

Cara mammina, le lettere all'inizio
di un film sei tu sono sempre le
stesse. Piene di preoccupazioni. Tormento.
e specialmente in questo film.
Ho cominciato a lavorare subito e
tra prove e vestiti la settimana
è volata via. La seconda settimana
è volata via pur le prove.
Questo è un film particolarmente dif-
ficile - molto drammatico - ha bisogno
di molta concentrazione quindi,
non me ne volere se io non ti
scrivo spesso - Non posso dire
la stessa cosa di te perché io
ne 10 minuti al giorno puoi
anche dedicarmeli, se vuoi.

1958. A letter I wrote to my mother from America, in which I tell her about my work for a new movie, and I ask her to send me articles about me in the Italian press.

Sai che mi fa sempre enorme piacere
ricevere vostre notizie e specialmente
notizie dall'Italia.
Gradirei moltissimo avere i giornali
dove si parla di me come L'Espero
i servizi di Piediluco se sono usciti
insomma tutti i giornali che sono
usciti con le notizie sul mio conto
per la mia recente visita a Parigi.
Chiedi anche a Basilio il Paris-Match
col vero servizio. Ti chiedo queste cose
perché sono curiosa di sapere com'è la
stampa italiana in generale con me —
Vorrei anch Novella con la copertina
del film La Chiave e di a Marosa
di spedire il tutto via Aerea e
continuamente i giornali con le
mie notizie — Cerca di essere calma
per quello che riguarda le questioni
familiari e vattene per un po' di
giorni in qualche posto a riposarti.
Ah! come vorrei fare la stessa cosa!
Ricordati a sape un Marosa (che non mi scrive ma

(note a margine) fai
(note a margine) Ti abbraccio —
(note a margine) Ti mi

Early 1959. On the set of *Heller in Pink Tights*, adapted from a Louis L'Amour novel, in which I starred with Anthony Quinn.

With Zia Dora and a neighbor, when I went back to my hometown for *It Started in Naples* . . .

. . . which is where this picture with Clark Gable was taken, during a break.

1962. With Peter Sellers on the set of *The Millionairess*, a loose adaptation of the George Bernard Shaw play.

1960. On the set of *Two Women*, Vittorio plays a prank on me. Behind us Eleonora Brown smiles with amusement.

A scene from the movie.

On the set with Alberto Moravia, author of the novel on which *Two Women* was based.

A long interview with Moravia after the movie, which went all the way back to my difficult childhood, and was picked up by many magazines around the world.

Per Carlo Ponti
da parte di MORAVIA

Moravia

AM   Allora Sofia, lei è nata a Pozzuoli...

SL   No, sono nata a Roma.

AM   Ma ha abitato a Pozzuoli fino...

SL   Fino all'età di quattordici anni.

AM   Tutta l'infanzia dunque. Lei converrà che gli anni dell'infanzia per molti aspetti sono i più importanti della vita e che lei questi anni li ha passati a Pozzuoli.

SL   Ne convengo.

AM   Pozzuoli, una piccola città...

SL   Dica piuttosto un paese.

AM   Sono stato più volte a Pozzuoli per prendere il ferry boat per Ischia. Il porto è piccolo, con l'acqua oleosa, verde e sparsa di scorze gialle di limoni. Ci sono attraccate tante barche verdi, bianche e blu; sulla banchina deserta sonnecchiano al sole cani e gatti. La città è vecchia, rovine romane, con vecchie chiese, vecchie strade in ombra, ruine romane, il tempio di Serapide con le colonne immerse nell'acqua, i giardini pubblici...

SL   A Pozzuoli ci sono pure le industrie, la fabbrica di cannoni dell'Ansaldo in cui lavorava mio nonno. Adesso c'è l'Olivetti.

AM   E voi dove abitavate?

SL   Sulla collina, in una casa di appartamenti.

AM   Quante stanze avevate?

SL   Due camere da letto, il salotto, la sala da pranzo e la cucina.

AM   Come erano ammobiliate queste stanze?

SL   In sala da pranzo c'erano dei mobili di noce scolpito con dei

Vittorio, Carlo, and I celebrate after receiving, first thing in the morning, the news of my Oscar for *Two Women*.

I celebrate my statuette with Mammina and Maria.

This is true friendship, being happy together in the fullness of life's little and big miracles.

HOW DEEP IS THE SEA

After that dry hot summer in the heart of the Spanish Meseta, a period that was as exciting as it was laborious, it was almost a relief to be able to dive into the blue of Greece. I was tired, both physically and psychologically, and the sea, the wind, the sun of the beautiful island of Hydra made me feel right at home. I rediscovered the scents of my world, the light and the horizons reminiscent of where I'd grown up.

Boy on a Dolphin was an adventure film, a sort of archeological thriller where I acted alongside Alan Ladd. Alan was slightly shorter than me, so to shoot many of the scenes he had to stand on a stool. It wasn't anyone's fault, but it made him suffer, and he'd created a few too many complexes for himself. I, on my part, acted foolishly and wasn't very kind to him. I enjoyed poking fun at him and I played around all the time, as if life were nothing more than a comedy.

Back then, I was very different from the professional I was to become. I enjoyed working, I committed myself to it in full, but I was still a young woman and I needed to feel carefree. It made up for not having been carefree when I was a child. As a young girl at Cinecittà, I'd known I couldn't afford to make a single mistake—those hard times of the war were still so recent. Now that things were starting to look up, I could laugh and joke around. I didn't do it because I wanted to be mean—it was just a way to pass the time, to get the better of my nerves, the insecurity that never left me. And it was also a way to create my character, which in *Boy on a Dolphin* was in fact a lively, exuberant woman. As I'd never gone to acting school, I'd never done any theater, I had to find my inspiration elsewhere. And so sometimes I'd mix fact and fiction to better prepare for the part.

Even now, I draw from everything I possibly can to give my characters substance and physical presence: I draw from reality, memory, from other actors in other movies. Recently, I was struck by the last scene in *Blue Jasmine*, where Cate Blanchett has an expression on her face I'd never seen before. That expression crept inside me, and it lies there waiting to germinate a new plant, a new flower.

Jean Negulesco, the director of *Boy on a Dolphin*, was an American of Romanian origin. He was cheerful and bursting with life. We got along fine and in the evening he'd take us out fishing on *lampare* (boats used for night fishing). I loved spending the night out at sea. It took me back to when, while shooting *Africa under the Seas*, I'd sail out in the waters of Palmarola, near Ponza, with Antonio Cifariello.

Antonio was just a few years younger than I was, and, like me, came from Naples. Off the set, we were like two young kids, and it didn't take much for us to have fun. I was distraught when, a few years later, I learned of his death in Zambia. He had been making a documentary for RAI and his plane crashed. He was only thirty-eight and had a little boy. He had had his whole life in front of him.

Negulesco was enchanted by the landscape, by that sun-drenched, ancient nature that spoke to us about our origins. Whether he wanted to or not, he ended up putting the Mediterranean Sea at the heart of the movie. After all, he was an artist, too. Hidden where I couldn't see him, he sketched some wonderful portraits of me, which he exhibited in a show the following December, once we returned to Rome for the studio shoots. The profits from the show were dedicated to Hungary, which had just been invaded by Soviet tanks. Negulesco's wife was Hungarian and she loved her country dearly.

The Cold War was raging, but that Greek autumn for me was a period of calm and budding happiness. Carlo often came to see me, letting me know that he was working on a solution for us. And in spite of my mother's warnings I trusted him.

We celebrated Christmas of 1956 in John Wayne's hotel suite. He was just passing through Rome to do screen tests for *Legend of the Lost,* which we were to start shooting with the new year. To prepare for the Christmas party the whole crew went to Piazza Navona to buy gifts from the market stands: shepherds for the manger, handmade photo albums, special nougat candy from Benevento. The streets were filled with a festive din. Bagpipers were at every corner to serenade us, a tradition that goes back to ancient Rome, and the smell of roasted chestnuts was in the air. Our fellow actors who were American mixed in with the thousands of tourists, and they loved this typically Italian crowd and confusion, accustomed as they were to living on ranches and mansions with a view of the ocean. It was a brief time of normality before I had to leave again for the African desert. A few days later, on January 2, we'd be off to Ghadames, in Libya.

I had grown up on a little street, Via Solfatara, in a small town, Pozzuoli, but I was beginning to see the world now, and I could hardly believe it.

AFRICAN FEVER

Legend of the Lost was the last "American" movie I made before moving to the United States. The shooting was done in the harshest conditions, in the middle of the desert, close to the ancient Roman port of Leptis Magna, one of the jewels of the empire, and also to the town of Ghadames, which is known as the pearl of the desert. It was a surreal and fantastic place, brimming with magic, but with hazards, too. Cockroaches, scorpions, snakes, sandstorms, the heat, the thirst . . . And the

Tuaregs, "blue men," who both attracted and frightened me at the same time, with their mystery and their differentness. It's a good thing John Wayne was there to protect us!

I have never ceased to be amazed at the fact that the king of Westerns seen from up close was exactly as I expected him to be. Duke, which is what everyone called him, really was a cowboy, a big, solid, authoritative one, and very sure of himself. But he was always with his wife, a petite Mexican woman without whom he felt lost. To him I was just a little girl. He liked watching me play around, and whenever someone tried to put a damper on my exuberance, he'd say: "C'mon, leave her alone, she's young . . . Let her laugh." I remember it as though he were standing in front of me right now. I could have been his daughter, and when I was close to him I felt safe. I wasn't afraid of anything. He was our undisputed leader, but he never took advantage of his power over us—he didn't have any bad habits; he never threw any tantrums. He didn't need to. We all tried to anticipate his desires, to learn from what he had to say. He was a professional, who worked with the patience of a great person.

Only once did his legend run the risk of cracking. One day he fell off his horse—hard to imagine, isn't it?—and he broke his ankle. We expected him to swallow his pain with a shot of whisky. Instead, he started howling like a madman. We stood there looking at him our eyes popping out of our heads, astounded to discover the man behind the hero. But he soon got over it, and in no time at all he'd put his John Wayne costume back on, as if nothing had ever happened. I still have the stirrups from his horse hanging on the wall of my office. Accidents aside, he was a living legend, and he always will be.

The other main character in the movie, Rossano Brazzi, was quite the opposite of Duke. The embodiment of the Latin lover, Rossano was handsome and jovial, and so focused on himself and his good looks that he never even realized when I was joking. I'd say to him, *"Quanto sii bbello"* (You're so adorable), as though he were a child. Maybe he took me seriously. Rossano was always singing. During break after break, he chirped away as though he were still in *South Pacific*, which he'd filmed recently: *"Some enchanted evening, you may see a stranger, across a crowded room . . ."* with dreamy eyes and a fixed smile. He'd arrived from the set for *Summertime* with Katharine Hepburn in Venice, and it seemed from his look that he still was under the effect of her style and elegance. Rossano seemed sometimes to be in another world. However, when the time came, he was there to save my life. If it hadn't been for him I probably wouldn't even be here to tell this story today.

It was a very cold night, and my small hotel room was heated by a gas stove. There was room for a bed, a dressing table for me to put my makeup on, but not much more than that. I felt like a prisoner. I was always sealing the windows and doors because I was fearful, and it never even dawned on me that it might be dangerous. But that night I learned the hard way. I woke up during the night in the middle of a terrible nightmare. My head throbbing, I was in a state of confusion, and I felt like I might faint. I didn't know it, but I was asphyxiating from the gas stove's fumes. Somehow I managed to crawl on my knees to the door and open it, but then I collapsed. Rossano, who was just getting back to his room, found me unconscious and called out. "Help! Help! Sophia is dying!" They saved me in the nick of time; another second and it would have been too late.

The scare didn't stop me from continuing to work, even though that toxic headache lingered for a few days more. In the morning we'd arrive on the set wearing our fur coats, that's how cold it was. But then, as the hours passed and the sun became scorching, we took off layer after layer. The director, Henry Hathaway, was very ill at the time, but he stuck it out and saw the movie through. All of us worked together so well. We even came to the aid of the mayor of the nearby town of Ghadames, whose first wife became very ill one night and needed to be flown out to a hospital for treatment that wasn't available in Ghadames. Because the runway there had no lights, a plane couldn't land to take her to the clinic. We all decided to use the lights from the set and arrange them so that they would light up the runway and a small twin jet could land, get her on board and rush her to the hospital. It was a real triumph, and made all the effort it was taking to make the movie worth it.

When we left Africa we felt a sharp pang of regret. The desert was magical, a lost horizon. I now understood perfectly how it could bewitch and bind itself to the imagination of so many people. But my imagination was busy focusing on something else now, and not even the most beautiful desert in the world could stop me, for waiting for me at the end of the road was Hollywood.

HOLLYWOOD PARTIES

On April 6, 1957, I boarded an SAS flight to Los Angeles along with my sister, Maria. The tears ran down my face as I hugged my mother, who accompanied us as far as the stairs leading up to the plane.

"Mammina, you'll see, I'll be fine, and you will be, too. We'll write to each other, I'll call you every day, *statte accuorta* (take care of yourself)."

It was our first big separation. I was making a leap in the dark, into a celluloid world in another country, from which I didn't know what to expect. I was leaving the Pizza Girl, the Fishmonger, and a piece of my life behind. I was now an international actress, but one tiny part of me was still a girl venturing into the unknown.

In Los Angeles we were greeted in grand style by all the

American newspapers as well as a sea of people. At the foot of the plane was a little boy, John Minervini, who, with the shyness of a four-year-old, gave me a kiss on behalf of the whole Italian-American community. "*Welcome to America, Miss Loren,*" he mumbled, tripping over his words like at a Christmas pageant. I left a trace of lipstick on his cheek. He was the most photographed child that day.

Now and again Maria and I would look at each other and burst out laughing. We pinched each other's cheeks to make sure we weren't dreaming.

"Is this really happening to us? To Maria? To Sophia? Who could ever have imagined!"

And yet you can grow used to the role of the star. I soon learned that what was important was to see things for what they were, to not let all this emphasis, this impressive show, change my way of thinking. I knew exactly what I was looking for. I had wanted this success and it drove me to do even better. But inside me, I still yearned for a family, children, the normal life I'd never had.

Actually, America finally gave me the chance to live with Carlo. He traveled back and forth between Italy and LA, but when he was in Hollywood I had his undivided attention.

It had been a while since he'd finished with the Ponti–De Laurentiis company and created the Champion film company together with Marcello Girosi, a Neapolitan who spoke English very well. Girosi helped Carlo to expand his business across the ocean. They had signed an agreement with Paramount and I was entering the front door of one of the most important stables in the world.

My first Hollywood appointment was in fact a cocktail party organized by Paramount at Romanoff's, a famous Beverly Hills restaurant popular with the stars. In my honor they'd given everything a Mediterranean touch, with that slightly childish American way of transforming and reshaping reality. Everyone was there. I was the phenomenon of the moment, the person everyone wanted to meet, at the event not to be missed. I looked in one direction and there was Gary Cooper—so handsome he left one breathless—I looked in another direction and there was Barbara Stanwyck, smiling, and if I looked out the window I could see Fred Astaire chatting with Gene Kelly. *Mamma mia!*

At that moment, Jayne Mansfield arrived. The crowd of guests parted to let her through as she headed straight for my table. She moved forward, swaying on her heels, perhaps not completely sober, with something grand and imperious about each step she took. She knew that everyone had their eyes on her, and how could anyone not gape at her neckline, which was more than generous. It was as if she were saying: *"Here comes Jayne Mansfield. The Blond Bombshell!"* She sat next to me at the table and started talking—it was like a volcano erupting. As she got more and more worked up, suddenly I found one of her breasts in my plate. I looked up at her, terrified. She barely noticed, regained her composure, and left. One especially quick reporter took a picture of the scene, and the image went around the world. I refused to autograph it. Hidden behind Hollywood's enchanted kingdom were some coarse and grotesque sides, which I refused to have anything to do with.

That first party was followed by others, always the same and always different. For me it was one big adventure, a merry-go-round, a stellar whirlwind of faces, names, fashions. I was struck by the limousines and Cadillacs, the gaudy mansions, and also by the motels and drive-ins. I discovered supermarkets and shopping centers, drinks on the patio around the swimming pool, and cottage cheese with fruit salad. I met the legends of my youth, and felt like I was at the heart of the world. But all we ever talked about was cinema, and I missed my country, steeped in history, wit, humanity. Ordinary people just didn't seem to exist in Hollywood.

Maria and I settled into the suite of a lovely hotel, with a huge balcony. I appeared on *The Ed Sullivan Show*, then one of the most popular TV shows of the time. But as my celebrity status grew, so did my responsibilities and my fear of failure. Now everyone scrutinized me ready to judge and criticize me, to prove I was a fake. My English was improving fast, but my movie parts were becoming more and more important, more and more spoken, and they required my complete concentration.

Louella Parsons and Hedda Hopper, two of the gossip columnists with the sharpest tongues of all, simply terrified the stars. Luckily, they were always kind to me, because I was basically an outsider. After all, I was just an "Italian girl" who would be going back home sooner or later.

The first movie I made was *Desire under the Elms*, adapted from a play by Eugene O'Neill. I was expecting to play an intense, hard character, one filled with passion. At my side was Anthony Perkins, as handsome and neurotic as we all remember him in *Psycho*. A gentle, polite, somewhat sullen young man, he didn't know how to hide his restlessness. Between us there was a certain complicity. He helped me with my English, and I tried to make him laugh. His dressing room looked like a room a student might live in: a table, a few books. It had the austerity of a monk's cell.

The movie was entirely made in the studio—California didn't have the streets of our neorealism in Italy. This gave the film a very theatrical dimension, which was balanced by superb black-and-white photography. A few days ago, my grandson, while looking at the cover of the film, blurted out: "Nonna, were you Chinese before?" The makeup that was worn back then elongated the eyes in a striking way. I had been the first to use that effect with Goffredo Rocchetti, my makeup artist at the time. I set the trend, and everyone followed suit.

In California, I also finished shooting the last scenes of *The Pride and the Passion*, which we hadn't been able to finish in Spain because Sinatra had suddenly left the set. The rumor was that he had learned that Ava Gardner would not take him back, and she was the reason he'd accepted the part in the first place.

I started seeing Cary again, who hadn't given up on us. Heedless of the fact that Carlo was around, every day he'd send me a big bouquet of roses, call me, write to me. Maybe Carlo was hurt, but he never said anything. I was slightly embarrassed, but I was simply waiting for something final to happen. We couldn't possibly go on as we were.

At the start of the summer I went back to Italy for a short vacation. While I was in America, I wrote to my mother every day, but I also needed to see her, embrace her again. She, in my absence, had pursued her illusion of love. Riccardo had left his wife and gone to live with Mammina, only to abandon her for the umpteenth time. I'm glad I hadn't been there for that. I'd spent my whole life trying to protect Mammina from her impossible love for Riccardo, having long ago realized it was hopeless.

Maria had left LA before me and had actually been home for some time. Although Sinatra had encouraged her to pursue her dream of becoming a singer, she hadn't felt up to it. Maybe she also hadn't wanted to leave Mammina all alone. Such is the ebb and flow of history: Romilda, whose dreams had been shattered because of her parents, had given me my freedom, but not her younger daughter.

After a huge party in my honor at Casina Valadier, in the heart of Villa Borghese, Carlo and I moved to Bürgenstock, on the shores of Lake Lucerne, for some weeks together. Far from the limelight, we found the peace that had been missing from our everyday lives. It was an enchanted place, filled with woods and light, far removed from the excesses of the jet set. There we could read, take walks, spend time together without being afraid that someone might see us, accuse us, judge us. Our one heart rested in the silence and solitude of nature.

On August 8 we were back in America. Another set, another round. From Los Angeles I traveled to Washington, D.C., on the Super Chief, the train the stars rode in. Waiting for me there was Cary. We were going to make *Houseboat* together, one of those sophisticated comedies written just for him. But the magic of our period in Spain had ended. We were at a standstill.

In my treasure trove of memories there are letters and notes written in his elegant, joyful handwriting that still fill me with tenderness: they speak to me of a fondness that, although it changed over time, never waned.

> *If you can, and care to, have someone leave a note for me at the desk—a few words—any words. I need something from you today as all days—(perhaps it should be a punch in the nose, but a note bringing your love would please me more) . . . If you think and pray with me, for the same things and purpose, all will be right and life will be good. PS If this note means as much to you as yours do to me, I shall be glad I've written it.*

Two days before the shooting ended, Carlo and I were sitting on the hotel balcony having breakfast, a couple of croissants, and reading the newspaper. While leafing through it, we happened to see a piece by Louella Parsons announcing that our marriage by proxy had taken place in Mexico the day before.

I almost fell off my chair. Even Carlo, although it was he who had unleashed his legal office in search of a solution outside of Italy, was taken by surprise. His lawyers, evidently, had gone ahead with it without his knowing.

We were soon to discover that the marriage wasn't legal, and that it would cause us some huge problems back in Italy. But for the United States and the rest of the world, all our papers were in order. In the United States, in fact, living "in sin" was considered unbecoming. In America, unlike in Italy, it was not only possible to get a divorce, it was also quite easy. Which explains why Elizabeth Taylor got married eight times, as did many other stars.

It wasn't really the kind of marriage I'd dreamed of as a child, but at the time that seemed to be the best we could do. Despite the surprise, we dined by candlelight and started thinking about a short honeymoon.

On the set, Cary, who was slightly dazed and, at last, resigned, reacted in a truly gentlemanly way: "All the best, Sophia. I hope you'll be happy."

Then, Cary and I got married in front of the movie camera of *Houseboat*, he wearing a gardenia in his buttonhole, I in a gorgeous white lace wedding gown.

LIFE GOES ON

Carlo's and my troubles began a month later. The first jab came from the Catholic newspaper *L'Osservatore Romano*, the second one from a woman whom we'd never even heard of named Brambilla, who, on behalf of an association for the protection of the family brought charges against us for bigamy and concubinage, which would be considered a crime in Italy until 1969. In the meantime, having shelved the idea of a honeymoon, we'd left for London, where William Holden and Trevor Howard were awaiting me to make *The Key*.

On the plane, Carlo would have the final word about those last trying months. We boarded in the midst of a flock of reporters who bombarded us with questions about our marriage,

Hollywood, the movie we were on our way to shoot. An explosion of flashes, the kind of confusion that goes with stardom. I was hardly twenty-three, and of course I was dazed, but happy. I smiled at Carlo as I took my coat off and placed my bag in the overhead compartment. He looked like he was sulking, but I thought maybe he was just tired from all the hubbub, or something about work was on his mind. I got my breath back and started leafing through the in-flight magazine in search of my favorite perfume. I watched the passengers as they paraded by, trying to imagine what kind of jobs they had, their loves, their dreams. I was just starting to relax when I let an innocent comment slip. Or maybe it really wasn't that innocent.

"Cary sent me a bunch of yellow roses before I left. Yellow for jealousy? He's so adorable . . ."

Carlo turned toward me suddenly and slapped me in the face, in front of everyone. My face turned bright red with anger and shame, the white impression of his fingertips on my cheek stinging. I felt tears land one by one on my cheeks. I wanted to die, but inside I knew that I had somehow deserved it. And yet I still didn't regret what I'd said.

When you're twenty-three you're learning how to live, and Cary's love had given me so much. Maybe even the courage to fight for a normal life with Carlo. On the other hand, I may have been young, but I wasn't stupid. I knew that Carlo's slap, which may be hard to understand today, was the gesture of a man in love, who had seen his love threatened by another man, who had risked losing me and was only now getting over his scare, his hurt. I wept—but not for long because the plane was full. The flight attendant came over to me timidly, asking if I needed anything. I didn't know where to look, but in my heart of hearts I was content. This was the confirmation I had been seeking for a long time: Carlo loved me, I had made my choice, and it was the right one.

In London I fought my first battle on my own, and I won. As soon as I got there I discovered, to my chagrin, that Sir Carol Reed, the director, and Carl Foreman, the producer of *The Key*, had changed their minds about having me in the movie. According to them, I was too young to play the main character, and Ingrid Bergman was ready to take over from me. But I knew instantly that the script had nothing to do with it, and there had to be another reason. I'd read the script thoroughly, and there was nothing preventing me from playing the part of the sweet, mysterious Stella. The truth of the matter is they wanted a name, a big name at the time, and they thought that just mentioning Ingrid Bergman would be enough to make me step aside. Foreman visited me, taking advantage of the fact that Carlo wasn't around, convinced he'd already won by default. But he had no idea whom he was dealing with. I pulled out a toughness he wasn't ready for, and I defended my position.

"It's out of the question. I signed the contract, so the part is mine. I'm sorry, but I have no intention of giving it up. I feel as though that character belongs to me. And I know I can play the part well."

For me it was an important role, a dramatic one that would contribute to freeing me from the prison of the full-figured woman in which I risked being straitjacketed. I was never going to back down. He was speechless, but then started in again: "You know we're going to give you a load of money . . ."

"I don't care," I answered sure of myself, "I'm doing the movie, let me know when we start."

A contract was a contract, and he left with his tail between his legs.

Naturally, after having raised my voice, for the next few days I was scared to death. But by throwing myself heart and soul into the script I eventually won their respect. It was a beautiful story, set on the gray and stormy English coast. A story about

128

war, the sea, love, with a dramatic side that called for a certain presence. When we finished, Foreman congratulated me, telling me he was happy I'd put up a fight.

For the premiere of the movie, we were invited to the Royal Command Performance, where I made a small, innocent gaffe that went down in history. For the reception, to match my splendid gown by Emilio Schuberth, whose styles I had started wearing regularly, I had chosen a small jeweled headband, a diadem. Although I was growing up, I was still a young girl, who in her heart aspired to being a queen. Unfortunately, however, the person receiving us really was a queen, Elizabeth, and royal etiquette demanded that no crown could be worn before a member of the royal house. The queen didn't seem to be bothered by it, but the following day the newspapers had a field day publishing some of the most striking and imaginative titles.

During the same period, I crossed paths with Ingrid Bergman for a second time. I knew that Cary was in London to make *Indiscreet* with her, and one morning I went to see him on the set. But when Ingrid saw me, perhaps surprised by my unexpected visit, she missed her cue. These things happen even to the very best, and she was undoubtedly one of the greatest actresses ever, for whom I have absolute reverence. "Maybe it's best if I leave," I whispered to Cary, and I slipped out.

Carlo and I spent Christmas of 1957 in the snowcapped peace of Bürgenstock with Maria and Mammina. Our neighbors, who were as reserved and peaceful as we were, were Audrey Hepburn and Mel Ferrer, whom we would often meet during our walks in the woods. Our friendship was discreet, the company very pleasant; there was never any interference in each other's lives.

One day, while Mel was away for work, Audrey invited us to lunch. To get to their house, we had to walk along a trail surrounded on both sides by the peaceful, silent snow. It was like being in a fairy tale. The chalet was very beautiful, luminous, all decorated in white, set on a hill overlooking the lake. Audrey was all dressed in white, too, as was the table, on which she'd placed a few flowers and lots of candles. It was the height of elegance.

"This place is enchanting," I said. And she answered lightly: "I need solitude and beauty . . ."

We chatted amicably, talking about the movies, friends we had in common. We took a tour of the house. Then we sat down at the table. In came the appetizer, or so I thought upon seeing it. A leaf of lettuce, a curl of fresh cheese topped by a smidgen of raspberry compote. In the plate next to it, a crisp roll, bite size. The conversation was pleasant, the raspberry compote even more so, but when the help came back to take our plates away, Audrey got up from the table and with one of her airy, delicate, perfect smiles, she said: "I ate too much!" Our lunch was over. Diplomatically, I said: "It was so much, and all so delicious!" I was dying of hunger, and as soon as we got home I made myself a sandwich.

Audrey and Mel had been married nearly three years earlier in a delightful chapel just a stone's throw away from their home. A very tiny church, not much bigger than a room, it was as austere and solemn as a cathedral. Its greatness lay in the woods all around it and in its openness to all religions, from Catholicism to Buddhism, from Hinduism to Lutheranism. Each time I passed it I thought of how they'd been able to have their dream wedding. That dream was still very far away for me, just as Italy, too, was becoming ever more distant. The two of us had been banished as though we were criminals.

In January 1958, Carlo and I went back to Los Angeles, where we moved into King Vidor's mansion, which was unoccupied for a few months. We lived a very reserved life. When we weren't working we mostly stayed at home. In the evening, we watched television and went to bed early. It felt like we were in a quiet bubble in the eye of the storm.

My next challenge was called *The Black Orchid*, and I was to act alongside Anthony Quinn in the role of mafia widow who fights to make a new life for herself. It was another Italian, maternal role, paired with a great, solid, and experienced actor, who didn't do much to help me out, however. One morning, while we were sitting at a table preparing an outdoor scene, he scornfully asked me: *"Are you going to do it like that?!"*

"Dear Tony," I replied, "I do what I can." I was trying to control myself, but inside I was dying. However much I tried, it never seemed to be enough. "I'm going," I'd say, "I'm going back home." But then I'd start over again, as if nothing had happened.

Quinn had also had a complicated childhood, with a father who was an adventurer and a revolutionary, a friend of Pancho Villa. His mother was Mexican, of Aztec origins. After having done a thousand odd jobs, including stuffing mattresses in a factory, Tony had landed in the movies, and married Cecil De-Mille's daughter, which had paved the road for him. While he was grumpy and standoffish in front of the camera, away from the set he was very pleasant and really liked my spaghetti with tomato sauce.

The Black Orchid won me the first important prize of my career, the Coppa Volpi as best actress at the International Film Festival in Venice. When they told me I'd won—by then I was in Austria making *Olympia*, known as *A Breath of a Scandal* in the United States—my first instinct was to go there to receive my prize. But things weren't that simple.

"If we land in Italy together they'll arrest us," Carlo warned me while we were spending a week vacationing on the French Riviera. In the end, we decided I'd go by myself, after having received all the necessary assurances from Venice. He accompanied me to the train station in Saint-Tropez and, with some bitterness in his heart, watched me leave. In Venice I was welcomed by an incredible throng of people, they say as many as five thousand, who greeted me by shouting, "Welcome home, Sophia!" It was a welcome I wasn't expecting at all, and that made me feel right with the world once more, beloved by my public, acknowledged by my country. Before the members of the jury I was so moved I could hardly say a word. I kept my best smile for Tony Quinn. "See? I wasn't so bad, was I!"

The movie gave me another great satisfaction, which I will never forget. In Rome I watched the premiere while sitting next to the great actress Anna Magnani. When the lights went back on, Nannarella, who wasn't famous for being ceremonious, exclaimed, "*Brava*, Sophia, I really liked it!" Few compliments have ever made me happier.

After a short time in New York to make *That Kind of Woman*, a film that wasn't much of a success, despite the fact that a great artist like Sidney Lumet directed it, Carlo and I were again without a home. We traveled around the world like two exiles and in spite of our privileged life, we felt lost. In the fall we were in Paris, on rue de Rivoli. When we were about to leave, Yves Montand, Simone Signoret, Kirk Douglas, and Gérard Oury came to say good-bye. After our few months there, we had begun to feel like citizens of the world, with no home of our own but with friends in every harbor. In January—now it was 1959—we were again in Hollywood to honor our contract with Paramount.

This time I was appearing in a movie directed by George Cukor, *Heller in Pink Tights*, and once again Tony Quinn was my partner. Working with Cukor wasn't easy, and only in hindsight did I realize just how much he taught me. Unlike De Sica, who made suggestions but never forced you to do things a certain way, Cukor insisted I imitate him, making me feel like a puppet. He'd also spend a lot of time correcting my English. I was becoming more and more fluent, but was still far from being perfect. But in time he earned my gratitude, and this somewhat atypical musical Western found a place for itself among my favorite movies.

From the Wild West to Imperial Austria, all it took was a night on a plane. But even the set for *A Breath of Scandal*, a costume movie based on the life of Sissi, Princess Olympia of Austria, had its complications. Our director Michael Curtiz, who also directed the legendary *Casablanca*, had a heavy Hungarian accent, which was hard to understand, and which made shooting much harder than had been expected.

Before our collaboration with Paramount came to an end, we had one more film to make, *It Started in Naples*, with the great Clark Gable, which finally took us back to Italy. Gable was by that time a mature actor, oozing charm and bonhomie. Each time I saw him, his character Rhett Butler in *Gone with the Wind* came to mind—those wonderful kisses, those sunsets, his staggering good looks. I would gaze at him as we worked together with the eyes through which I'd first seen him, and it made me dream.

Gable was and wasn't there. He'd get to the set very early, right on time and very professional. He was always perfect. Perfect with his lines, perfect with his makeup, perfect with his schedule. So perfect that when five in the afternoon came around you'd hear the ringing of his wristwatch. Which meant that it was over, and that he could leave the scene midway through and just take off.

In August, Capri welcomed us with open arms, although we'd just received the news that the Italian court had charged Carlo with bigamy. The day of my birthday, the crew made me a cake with twenty-five candles, and Carlo, defying the authorities—and the whole world, it seemed—joined us.

Once again it all felt too impossible and too beautiful to be true. Another stage of my life had come to an end. Hollywood had given me everything it possibly could, and despite the trouble we had landed in, it was time to go home.

VII

A MOTHER WELL WORTH
AN OSCAR

Fino all'età di quattordici

Tutta l'infanzia dunque. Lei

zia per molti aspetti sono i

WHITE NIGHT

When I received an Oscar nomination in late February 1962, I could hardly believe it. "The Oscar?" "The Academy Award?" I kept rereading the names of the other candidates, Audrey Hepburn and Natalie Wood, Piper Laurie and Geraldine Page, saying to myself: "What is this, some kind of joke? Besides the fact that *La ciociara* (*Two Women*), is an Italian movie, spoken in Italian—when has anything like this ever happened before?"

And yet, of course I was flattered. It made me feel good, and I tried to fool myself into thinking that, having come this far—having become an international star with many good roles under my belt—it might even be enough. Deep down inside, though, I knew it wasn't true. Every step I took made me quietly dream of another victory. Maybe I was daring too much, but hope and ambition were a part of me. Still, I knew that disappointment was potentially always just around the corner, and that triumph was only for the few.

After much procrastination, I decided I would not go to the ceremony. If I lost, I'd faint. If I won, I'd faint anyway. I couldn't allow myself to do that in front of that audience, and before the eyes of the whole world. "I'm going to stay right here in Rome, on my couch," I said to myself, and that is indeed what I did.

That fateful evening, Carlo was nervous, too—although he feigned nonchalance. If I had to choose one word to describe him, that would be "presence": he had it in every situation, and projected it for others, for himself. He was a solid man, level-headed, highly focused on his work, on the goals he'd set himself. A movie enthusiast ever since he was a child, he'd dedicated all his life to cinema. A determined businessman, he always had an eye on the results, but he also knew how to put up a fight for a good movie. And if he didn't like the way it came out, he would personally get behind the moviola to edit it and put it back together the way he thought best. Cultured and sensitive, he was a man of few words, but he'd understood me right from the start, and he never once tried to force me to be different from what I was.

We'd worked so hard to reach that point. And we were perfectly aware that every small victory is made up of effort and sacrifice, and that any one achievement doesn't necessarily represent the final goal. We were a team, a solid pair, we complemented each other as in the best of families. Today the word to describe it would be "synergy," back then it went by the words "affection" and "mutual support." We'd traveled, and had been out in the open about our relationship, yet we'd come back home at our own risk, despite the charges against us.

That April 9, 1962, we were in our apartment in Piazza d'Aracoeli, where we had been living more or less officially for some time. Because of the time difference between Italy and California we were going to be up all night. Before us was a stretch of very long hours of sitting and waiting. Worldwide TV didn't exist yet. Too anxious to spend those hours chatting, we could neither rest nor read. On top of that, the phone kept on ringing, with voices submerging us in wishes that were sincere to a greater or lesser extent. The most brazen made predictions; sure of this and of that, they seemed to know everything. We looked at each other half smiling. However it turned out, it was going to be an unforgettable night, well worthy of an Oscar. Some music, a sip of wine, the umpteenth cigarette, a cup of chamomile, the window open to let in the springtime. And then what?

It was getting very late when I had a brilliant idea. Sauce, that's it, sauce, how silly of me, I should have thought of it before. In the kitchen I'd feel safer, I could distract myself from this whirl of anxiety that I couldn't stop. As I peeled the garlic, my thoughts flew back to Mamma Luisa, who'd died a few years before. Maybe she would have preferred for me to be a schoolteacher in Pozzuoli, with two rooms on the same landing, or maybe even on the floor above, Sunday dinners together, and maybe a few grandchildren underfoot. And yet, she would have been very proud of me tonight. After all, she'd been the one to teach me the value of discipline, the satisfaction that came with doing my duty, the pleasure of feeling right with the world. She would have been proud of my success that had been achieved with nothing more than willfulness.

My eyes were veiled with tears. Emotion can play such tricks on you. The phone rang one more time; it was Mammina again, for what must have been the twentieth time. She said she was calling to calm me down, but she was really trying to find a way to soothe her nerves. Carlo answered the phone with a slightly harsher tone than usual, even though they had great mutual esteem and respect, "Romilda, leave Sophia alone, we'll call you as soon as we get word." They were more or less the same age, and, in some ways, they were competing with each other, although Romilda had stepped aside somewhat when this authoritative gentleman had entered my life. She also still feared the "Scicolone effect": never trust a man, especially if he's married.

I sliced the onion to hide my tears and I felt better right away. Sometimes it takes very little to get your feet back down onto the ground, to regain the balance that surprises, whether good or bad, risk taking away from you.

At three in the morning I received a cablegram from Santiago, Chile, telling me that Doña Loren had won the Golden Laurel for best actress 1961. It was obviously a prank as Doris Day had won the prize that year. All the same, I wondered: Could it be an omen of victory or a trick of fate? Dawn was still a long way off and the thought of getting any sleep at all had vanished. Trying to think of ways to pass the time, I curled up on the sofa, waiting for the light of dawn, and soon Carlo joined me.

Luckily, time, even when it passes slowly, so slowly it seems to be going backward, never actually stops. The minutes became hours and the night turned to day. At six in the morning, according to our calculations, it was all over. But no call came through, no telegram, nothing. The silence all around us was almost physically painful. *At this point we may as well go to bed,* we thought. And yet we didn't dare get up. We just kept sitting there in the gray light of dawn, staring at the walls, the paintings, the photographs. And we finally dozed off like two kids.

But at 6:39 a.m., the phone rang. As heartless as an alarm clock, and just like a siren. Carlo literally pounced on the receiver.

"Who? Who? Cary? Cary Grant?" An abyss of silence, and then an explosion of joy, in his unlikely brand of English, sparked off like a firecracker at a country fair: "Sophia win, Sophia win, Sophia win!!!"

I snatched the receiver from his hand. On the other end was Cary's warm voice. "It's wonderful, Sophia, it's wonderful. You're always the best!"

I was smiling at Cary all the way across the ocean, I was smiling at myself, at us, at life. As soon as I hung up, I starting hopping all around the living room. Then, all of a sudden, I was overcome by a feeling of complete exhaustion. I didn't know how I was supposed to feel. I felt all empty inside. I ran into the kitchen to make sure the sauce hadn't burned.

Downstairs, outside the door, there was a throng of impatient reporters. Elbowing their way past them were Mammina and Maria, who promised them I would let them come in as soon as possible. My sister was holding a small basil plant: "This way you'll always remember where you're from."

Our embrace was one of the most intense moments in my whole life. My Oscar was theirs. Their happiness mine.

MOTHERS AND DAUGHTERS

To get to that night, I had embraced a role that I was given by Vittorio De Sica. He had been the first to catch sight of the promise of an actress within the extra, the actress within the full-figured woman, and now he could see the mother within the daughter. Yes, because this movie, *Two Women*, was entirely a question of mothers and daughters, which was anything but easy to unravel. And we had shot the film together over the last eight years between the lowly quarters of Naples and the piazzas of Trastevere, the alleyways of Sorrento, and the rugged, barren hills of Ciociaria.

Two Women is a novel by Alberto Moravia. One of Italy's finest twentieth-century writers, he would often get together with Carlo and share projects, readings, opinions. Carlo had immense esteem and respect for him, and I, too, loved him very much. Thanks to *Too Bad She's Bad*, which had been adapted from one of his short stories, I'd met Marcello, and Moravia and several other great writers had written *Woman of the River*.

Three years before the Academy Award, in Bürgenstock, Carlo was thinking about buying the rights to the novel, and he'd asked me for my opinion. I'd devoured it in two days, unable to put it down. *Two Women* had broken my heart. The story was about our land, about Italy, it was about me and my mother, about the war we'd lived through and the one we'd feared, about wounds that will never heal. In those pages I recognized the courage, hunger, and blind stupidity of bigotry and the ignorance that were part of the war, as well as the redemptive maternal instinct that thrives in every woman everywhere.

The main character, Cesira, was a *burina*, a country bumpkin working in Rome, trapped in a bad marriage when she was still very young. She finds herself widowed and alone with her daughter in Rome as the Allies bomb the city, trying to protect all that she has—her possessions, her shop, her daughter. The bombing is so terrifying that she decides to flee to her native village, Ciociaria, in central Italy. Everyone is saying that it's a matter of a few weeks until the war's end, that the Allies are at their doorstep.

Cesira's voice enchanted me: She is open-minded, with plenty of common sense and a fighting spirit, and she would do anything for her daughter, Rosetta. Her way of thinking, so honest, so real, but so fully aware of her limitations, clashes with the confusion of the war, with the banality of evil around her. In one scene, a train headed for Naples stops in the middle of the countryside, as if it were lost, even though it is on tracks.

The countryside is made of dust and rocks, of mule trails up steep hills, where the crops grow on graduated terraces. They clamber to get to the top, surrounded by mountains, in search of a safety that no longer exists. Huts and dilapidated houses, which are more like stables than the homes of God-fearing people, host farmers, and evacuees, all forced by the emergency to live together. Those long weeks that were to lead to the end of the war turn into months, and even seasons. People from the city and from the country, their lives, their ideas, so different, and yet so similar, are mixed together. But everyone is focused on him or herself, and on the little they have left. Ideals count less and less in the face of hunger, cold, fear. "English or German, it doesn't matter who wins . . . Let's just hope they get it over and done with soon!"

In real life Moravia had been evacuated to Ciociaria with his wife, Elsa Morante. He, too, had suffered from hunger and the cold, he'd experienced boredom and fear, he'd slept on mattresses made of corn husks that stab your back, in the midst of the bugs and the mice. He'd wolfed down carob bread and hard pecorino cheese, oranges and goat's entrails. Sixteen years later, he wrote his memories into Cesira and Rosetta who feel completely lost so far from home.

In a little town, mother and daughter begin to spend time with an idealistic character named Michele, who is very different from all the other townspeople—well read, he uses big words when he speaks, and no one seems to understand him. Yet he uses his ideas to try to reawaken the deadened feelings of people around him, to spark in them the longing to rebuild a better world. Little by little their friendship grows, as fresh as the sky, the cyclamens, and the maidenhair ferns that crop up along the edges of the balconies. But after the fall and winter have passed, and there are no provisions left, everyone is forced to eat chicory, sow thistle, and basil thyme. The English and German troops, at a standstill on the Garigliano front line, have squeezed Italy in their grip. After forty days of rain and mud, the north wind sweeps the clouds away and the skies clear up once again, but with that the bombing resumes, streaking through the sky and striking haphazardly. The Germans begin their retreat, but conscript more men as they go, and act even more ferociously than before, because it's clear that they've been defeated. The Americans arrive, kind yet detached, lazily climbing the Via Appia as they head for Rome, handing out candy and cigarettes.

In this war, everybody is up against everybody else, dominated by selfishness, fear. Everybody grabs what they can. Cesira's joy at the thought of their imminent freedom even makes her forget her friendship with Michele, who has been feeding her and her daughter all this time. But her joy doesn't last long. She and Rosetta are about to be violated in the most extreme way, in the very last moments of the war and at the hands of those who claim they are there to liberate them.

That summer of 1959, as Carlo and I strolled through the woods of Bürgenstock, *Two Women* was all we seemed to talk about, like an obsession. Carlo was hoping to find international backing and an international audience for this venture, but the Hollywood screenwriters, although they appreciated the book, couldn't see a movie being made out of it. "It takes too long for the tragedy to happen," they said. "It's too slow-paced, nothing happens until the end." But those of us who had seen the war up close, who had lived inside it, and who had learned to wait through it, saw the potential movie very clearly. It was a story we knew far too well.

In the book, Cesira is thirty-five, Rosetta is eighteen. At twenty-six I was somewhere in between. At first, Anna Magnani had been considered for the part of the mother, with me as her daughter. George Cukor was to be the director; he had recently directed me, and he loved Anna passionately. Excited about the idea, he flew all the way to Italy to see her, but she refused to budge.

"It's a great character, but I can't play Sophia's mother," she'd said without mincing words. "She's too tall, too overbearing. I appreciate her as an actress, but she wouldn't be right in the role of my daughter. I'd have to look up at her, what sense would that make?

Without Anna Magnani, Cukor backed out, and Carlo had to start over again from scratch.

At that point, De Sica came into play, along with Cesare Zavattini, the great screenwriter and early neorealist. A *ciociaro* by birth, De Sica, too, insisted on having Anna Magnani in the film, convinced that he'd triumph where his esteemed American colleague had failed. But Anna was a tough nut to crack, and she was much too sure of her position to give in. Vittorio tried several times, using all his charm and *savoir faire*. The last thing he tried was to get Paolo Stoppa to convince her by making a tentative phone call. "Nannarella, I'm having dinner with De Sica right in front of your apartment, can we come up a minute?" But it was all in vain. "The daughter has to be less of an imposing presence, you know, someone like Anna Maria Pierangeli . . . we'd be perfect together," she remarked.

The more Vittorio tried to convince her, the more adamant she became. Until, but maybe only to provoke him, she blurted out, "If you really want Sophia to be in it, why don't you get her to be the mother?"

No sooner said than done. Although he was unhappy about that "great refusal," the next morning De Sica called me in Paris to suggest I play Cesira.

"What are you saying? The character is much older than me. She's a mother! How can I do that?"

"Please, Sofi, think about it. She's a mother you're familiar with, you've seen so many like her, she's a lot like your own. We'll make Rosetta slightly younger and that will be that. Please, say yes."

Carlo was amused by the idea, and he encouraged me the way only he knew how to: "If Vittorio thinks you can do it, it means you can. Trust him."

The variety and depth of the feelings that a mother can express arouses all the heartstrings of any actress. Those facets, that complex and delicate psychology have always attracted me—maybe because, my own story being what it is—I have always strongly felt gut emotions. There's no getting around it: the woman-mother represents the most complete aspect of the female personality, and in this sense it challenges every actress to give it her all.

Vittorio guided me through this adventure: "Cesira is a well-rounded mother figure. She's humble, she's always worked, and she lives for her daughter. Her approach to things is simple and straightforward. You've already experienced all these things personally, Sofi. You know perfectly well what I'm talking about. You'll act with no makeup on, with no tricks. Be yourself, you become your own mother, and everything will turn out fine."

After all those years of Hollywood, *Two Women* was taking me back home, to the harsh reality of my childhood. The war, which had long been buried inside me, was now resurfacing to give a voice to this wounded woman in Moravia's story, to her suffering, to her courage. I thought about Mammina and how she'd fought to defend us, to get us food and water. I thought about how she must have felt those nights when the Moroccan soldiers camped out in the entrance hall came knocking on our door in a drunken state. About how she watched, without anyone noticing, as those young American marines came to our parlor to drink brandy. Because she knew there was danger everywhere, at all times, even in the places you felt safest.

When they introduced Eleonora Brown to me, the young girl who had been chosen for the part of Rosetta, I instantly felt responsible for her, for us. Her face was shy and intelligent and the work that awaited us was hard. How could I possibly become her mother? Suffer for her? How could I help her to place her trust in me? My instinct encouraged me to look at her with the same kindness I'd felt when I was looked upon as a child, with the same love I'd been protected and caressed with. And it worked.

Eleonora was born in Naples, the daughter of a Neapolitan woman and an American who had met during the war, and she was often accompanied to the set by her aunt. She was thirteen, little more than a child, with a child's eyes in the body of an adolescent.

De Sica was a master at getting nonprofessionals to act. He'd proven it in *Shoeshine*, in *Umberto D.*, in *Miracle in Milan*. But in *Two Women* he truly outdid himself. He always got what he wanted, whatever it took. While shooting one of the most dramatic scenes, the one where Rosetta has fallen in love with their friend Michele, played by Jean-Paul Belmondo, he even went so far as to tell Eleonora that her parents had had an accident.

"I'm sorry, dear, I'm so sorry . . ." he said in a dramatic voice filled with pity. "They're in the hospital now, their condition is serious, but there's no telling . . . Come on, come on, child . . ."

Eleonora started crying her eyes out, and we had to stop shooting. It was impossible to continue working. Vittorio had gone one step too far.

"Eleonora!" I said and immediately ran to her side. "It's not true! He's saying things that aren't true just to make you cry! Come on, get over it, smile . . ."

But the shock had been too much for her and we had to stop for a while.

Of course, it wasn't easy for a young girl to express such dramatic emotions spontaneously. When Vittorio failed to help her, or when he succeeded by overdoing it, I would step in, to mitigate, to inspire, to suggest. In a scene in which Rosetta is completely naked while I help her wash, it took everything I had to help her overcome her embarrassment and retain her sense of decency while she was so exposed.

In time we got to know each other very well and to love each other, like a mother and daughter, and her interpretation of Rosetta went down in cinematic history. The experience of that movie was so intense that we have stayed friends and often talk to each other even now.

We started shooting on August 10, 1960. The crew was staying on the hills around Gaeta. Carlo and I rented a large white house overlooking the gulf. From my window I could see Pozzuoli. "This is much more beautiful than Beverly Hills," said Vittorio. "You were born here, this is where you belong." The truth of the matter is I was completely at ease, with no makeup on, my ragged dress, white with dust under the summer sun. I liked being with the extras, in the grottoes, my feet bare while carrying a suitcase on my head.

Under the air raid sirens, I saw myself back in the railway

tunnel again, in the company of mice and cockroaches. I recognized the goat's milk and the grumpy grin of the shepherds, I gazed at those poor dishes with an appetite, at that dark bread we'd missed so much when food was so scarce.

De Sica kept me under control, he'd pull me back down if I flew too high, he'd lift me up if I was too dejected. But when we got to the anxiety, the despair, he freed my heart of all its restrictions, all impediments. He let the miracle come true, he let my Cesira come to light and find her own way.

It was the most difficult role I'd played in my entire career. Without Vittorio I would never have succeeded in wiping the slate clean so that I could start over in a new life, which at that very moment seemed to me to be the only one possible. As De Sica shot the scene, his eyes filled up with tears: "Use this. Take one is good!!" He knew how to apply pressure on my feelings with a skill that really turned me into a woman, so distant from the glamour of stardom.

Even now when I happen to watch *Two Women*, all I need is one scene, just one, to relive all the emotion just like the first time. A rock I throw at the Allies' jeep after their troops have violated Cesira and Rosetta and my cursing them—"Thieves, cuckolds, sons of bitches"—is an act of rebellion against all the hatred that had held the world hostage for so many years. The flame of that rebellion must always burn, even in times of peace, keeping us watchful and alive. So that nothing like this will ever happen again.

Two Women won twenty awards for me besides the Oscar, including a David di Donatello, a Silver Ribbon, and Best Actress in Cannes. It also led to a beautiful interview with Alberto Moravia, which traced back over my whole life. Reading it today now that fifty years have gone still brings tears to my eyes.

THE MYSTERY OF BEING NORMAL

As I read that interview and listen to the voice of the great writer, Alberto Moravia, in the questions he posed to me, I go back to Pozzuoli, to its small harbor, with its slimy, green water strewn with yellow lemon rinds. The Pozzuoli of old houses and shady old back alleys, of the Roman ruins and the Temple of Serapis, whose columns rise out of water since the earth around them subsided. But also the Pozzuoli of the construction sites, of the Ansaldo cannon factory, where Papà Mimì worked.

Led by Moravia, I return to our small apartment, with its carved walnut furniture and the kitchen, where I would do my homework while Mamma Luisa offered me cups of coffee and told me stories in dialect. In her palace, my grandmother would make bread topped with beans for lunch, the same dish that's known as *minestrina* (small soup) in Ciociaria. In the evening we'd eat pasta, because when the men got back from work they needed to have a filling meal. On the 27th of every month I'd go to Naples with Zia Dora, who'd buy me a chocolate drink with whipped cream and a *sfogliatella* (shell-shaped pastry), at Caflish's. That was where I saw Anna Magnani for the first time. There she was, exuding charm from a large poster above the theater where she was acting in a play.

In that Pozzuoli of my memories, I can feel my father's shadow, that of a stranger, who was drawn to our house by my mother's artful telegrams, but who couldn't wait to leave. *L'asino tra i suoni*, is how Neapolitans describe someone like him, like a fish out of water, not much more than an intruder. He was tall, distinguished-looking, with graying hair, a hook nose, large hands and feet, but slender ankles and wrists. A nice smile, a scornful expression. A real charmer.

As I recalled my father, Moravia started to dig mercilessly into my past. And he brought to light the wound from which

Sophia Loren was born. The differentness of my family—my absent father, my mother who was more beautiful than other mothers—had made me suffer tremendously. It had filled me with shame, and at the same time it was my fortune. It was the strength that forced me to work, to show others who I was, to choose a path for myself when I was still very young. In other words, "success is a surrogate for unattainable normality." I headed for Rome, fleeing a fatherless child to find myself in the body of the actress I wanted to become.

A few years later, Carlo would also have a dual role in my life. He was the producer who could help me to fulfill my dream of making movies, and he was also the man who could offer me the gift of the normal life I so longed for. But once again there was a differentness to our relationship. When we met, we faced obstacles that wouldn't allow us to be together, to be normal. These were difficulties that stymied me on the one hand, but, perhaps, spurred me on as well.

When I left Rome for Hollywood, just as I had left Pozzuoli for Rome, I was leaving behind a situation with no way out, to try to forge a normal path of my own. I couldn't find a normal life, however. It didn't exist for me. It was this impossibility that gave me the inner, psychological drive that enabled me to identify with my characters and bring them to life, to delve deeper into their reality and to learn more about myself and the world.

"You never suffer in vain," says Moravia, "at least when you have the willingness to know why you're suffering."

Signora Brambilla, the woman who took it upon herself to accuse Carlo of bigamy, stole the normal life I was seeking. And I responded with *Two Women*, which consecrated me in the eyes of the world. It was my destiny. Whereas in cinema I prefer passionate and tragic parts, strong and emotional characters, in life I want to be the exact opposite: objective, controlled, introverted. In short, normal. But a normal life escapes me, my joie de vivre, my liveliness, my temperament keep me from having one. So I try to find fulfillment through my art, playing characters toward whom I feel drawn precisely because they're so different from what I'd like to be in life. That's all. And yet it's so much.

THE DREAM

I had a dream that I'm on a beach, at sunset, and the sea is very calm, immense, smooth, like an endless stretch of blue satin. The setting sun is a fiery red. Suddenly, I start running along the beach and I run without ever stopping. I'm still running when I wake up.

Moravia read it this way, "in the manner of the oracles who would interpret ancient dreams": the sea represents the normality that I try in vain to reach. The sun is success. If I wanted to I could just stand here and watch the peacefulness of the sea; instead I want to chase after my sun. And, like all those who want to reach the sun, I have a long way to go, but I go on with my race because that sun, albeit very far away, comforts me and lights the way.

VIII

LA DOLCE VITA

MARCELLO

Marcello, Marcello . . . My race for the sun would never have been as vivid or as richly satisfying without Marcello Mastroianni. His gentle gaze, his kind smile have always accompanied me, offering me a sense of security, joy, and so many other emotions. Those twelve movies we made together have certainly left their mark. The first time, I was twenty and he was thirty. The last time, he was seventy and I was sixty. In between, we had our long friendship, filled with affection and tenderness that would light up with passion on the set.

We had chemistry between us, and it never let us down. The harmony that joined us—which could be sexy, happy, sad, ironic, always deeply human—was so spontaneous that many people wondered if there might be something more between us. And we always just smiled, shrugging our shoulders: "Nothing at all! These are simply the miracles of cinema, of life."

Marcello even confirmed this publicly, joking with Enzo Biagi, a famous Italian journalist and writer, who asked him about the two of us: "The woman I have had the longest relationship with is Sophia . . . We've been together since 1954 . . ." And then he added, more seriously: "I like the fact that Sophia isn't just a good actress, but a real person. There's never been anything between us. A deep affection: it's too easy to compare it to that between a brother and a sister, because it's really something quite different."

I also got along very well with Marcello's mother, Signora Ida. She would often invite me over to their place for lunch because she knew I liked good cooking. "Sofi, I want to make rabbit cacciatore for you tomorrow, can you come over?" She had good common sense. She was proud of her sons—Marcello's brother, Ruggero, was a highly regarded film editor—but she had her feet firmly rooted to the ground. She had been born

155

poor, and she had refused to embellish her past or invent a false identity. She lived in the same two-room apartment where she'd lived all her life.

She was happy when Marcello was named a commendatore, or knight commander, a great honor in Italy, and she framed the diploma and his photograph with Aldo Moro, the Italian prime minister at the time, complete with a dedication so she could show it to her neighbors. But she was unhappy about her elder son's extramarital affairs, which she could never really fathom. She did, however, understand perfectly his close friendships, like his and mine, which were based on affection and loyalty.

I always had the feeling that she counted on our relationship; maybe it gave her a sense of security. Whenever she'd see him with a different partner in the movies, she'd call him up and ask worried: "Marcè, what's happened? Did you have an argument with Sophia?"

Even today I don't know where the secret of our success lay. What I do know is that we had lots of fun, and I think this came out in our movies. After making *Too Bad She's Bad* with Sandro Blasetti in 1954, our first job together, we put ourselves in the hands of De Sica, who understood us better than anyone else, and who knew how to get in on the fun with us. He was the one to show us the way, he was the key to our silver-screen love. When the baton was passed to Dino Risi, to Giorgio Capitani, and then to Ettore Scola, to Lina Wertmüller, and, lastly, to Robert Altman in *Ready to Wear*, we had adjusted to each other. So well did we know each other that all we had to do to play any role was just be ourselves. We didn't need to rehearse, we simply moved in unison. It came naturally to us, like two friends off to a spring picnic. "Sofi, how about it, should we go for it?" he'd say to me.

Now that I think of it, maybe our secret indeed lay in that

naturalness, which reflected our everyday lives, our common experiences. We understood the hopes and flaws of ordinary people. In Italy, as elsewhere, people are sometimes poor, other times petit bourgeois; some are snobbish, some pompous. The audience could see itself in our characters. Yet these relatable characters are not only Italian—they share a vast collection of human feelings, universal ones, which we drew on and which spoke to audiences the world over. We brought to our characters that Italian way of life that, with its sense of irony, succeeds in crossing every national barrier.

Marcello and I shared the same reserve, the same optimism. And maybe more than anything else, we shared a certain *joie de vivre* and the complete awareness of just how lucky we were.

"I believe in friends, the landscape, good food, and work," Marcello would often say with his marvelous simplicity. Work saved him from his laziness. Marcello was a born idler. When he wasn't acting, he felt like "a flag without pride." I, on the other hand, was always on the go, preparing every part diligently, organizing my life as if it were an assembly line.

"I know I'm a flash in the pan," he said one day in an interview with Oriana Fallaci, the famous Italian journalist and writer. "A spark that's goes right out if someone doesn't throw some gasoline on it."

He said he was superficial, yet few in his shoes would have revealed their inner feelings with the same degree of honesty. It's true, he let things slide along, he never faced things head on, he let himself be pulled along. Some say that, because of his absentminded air and his candor, there was always something of the child about him. For him, being an actor was a chance to hide behind someone else's feelings, while for me acting meant revealing my deepest feelings. In other words, it was a game, an escape route to slip down unobtrusively.

We both believed in the strength of kindness, we always ignored the gossip, and we never stuck our noses into other people's lives. His delicate soul was visible in every gesture, in every word he uttered. Maybe that's why being labeled a Latin lover always annoyed him. "There are land surveyors who've had more affairs than me," he'd say to defend himself from the mediocrity of commonplaces.

His early life had been hard, just as mine had been. Marcello was born in 1924 in Fontana Liri, near Frosinone. His family moved to Rome when he was still a child, to the San Giovanni quarter of the city. He'd experienced the war as though it were an adventure. To avoid the draft he'd taken part in a contest for illustrators organized by Todt, a large German company that built bridges and roads for the Wehrmacht. That way he got a job with the Istituto Geografico Militare in Florence, but after September 8, 1943, the company came under German control and was relocated to Dobbiaco. To avoid the risk of being dispatched to Germany, in 1944, Marcello fled Dobbiaco with a fake pass, and went to Venice, where he made a living selling a friend's artwork, until the Allies arrived. When he finally returned to Rome, with some money saved up for his family, he found out that his younger brother, Ruggero, had done even better than he had, bringing home leftover food every night from his job at the Hotel Excelsior.

Casa Mastroianni, just like Casa Villani, had experienced hardship and struggled to make ends meet. We were born into that life. That's the way Italy was at the time, and maybe that's another reason why we loved each other. Growing up in Rome, Marcello had to share a bed with his mother until he was twenty-seven because there was no room in the house. His brother slept on the floor on the other side of the bed, and his father, who was a carpenter, slept in the hallway.

When the war ended, life became a little easier, and there was new hope. There was also a place right across the street where you could dance. Marcello had fallen head over heels in love with Silvana Mangano, who lived in the same neighborhood as he did, but after a year she had a breakthrough in cinema and got engaged to Dino De Laurentiis. Although it had been a love of youth, he'd felt deeply hurt at losing her all the same. One day he even went to see her on the set for *Bitter Rice*, navigating the rice fields and defying the humidity and mosquitoes, but she pretended not to see him.

Marcello had wanted to become an architect, but times were hard, and you had to make do with what you could get. He worked as a building surveyor, and as an accountant in a film production company, but was fired after a couple of years. In the meantime, he'd started acting for the Centro Universitario Teatrale, where he'd been noticed by Luchino Visconti, so he shifted for himself, moving between theater and Cinecittà. Rising through the ranks wasn't easy, and the Count, which was how we often referred to Visconti, was capable of making even Marcello suffer—"Why don't you go drive a streetcar? You're like a gorilla!" he said to him during the rehearsals for the play *Oreste*, by Vittorio Alfieri. But Visconti did teach him a lot. Marcello never would use the informal "tu" to address Visconti—or, for that matter, with De Sica, despite their closeness.

One evening, while shooting *Marriage Italian Style*, Vittorio lashed out at him: "Last night I lost five million lire because of you."

"Who, me?"

"I looked for you, but couldn't find you. If I had, we could have gone to eat a nice pizza and I wouldn't have been forced to go to the casino."

"Commendatore, pardon me: but may I ask why you squander all that money at the betting table?"

In contrast, with Fellini, Marcello had a brotherly understanding that was born right away. It was the kind of immediate recognition and understanding that school friends have. As Marcello liked to say, jokingly, their friendship was very sincere because it was based on a complete lack of trust. They had fun loafing around; they'd lie just for the sake of lying. They were even more than brothers. Together, they went through life making some of the masterpieces of Italian cinema. Just think: *La Dolce Vita, 8½, Ginger and Fred.*

Marcello's affections were unwavering, and he never abandoned the people he loved. His marriage to Flora Carabella lasted until the day he died. He had loved other women, other companions, but he refused to divorce her. She was his wife. Not even when he met Catherine Deneuve, not even during his *amour fou* for Faye Dunaway did he ever come to that decision, which he felt would have brought about unjustifiable pain. Flora knew it; she loved him and she spent her whole life putting up with his affairs. He was a kind and loving father to both Barbara and Chiara, who would, sometimes, even comfort him over his lost loves.

The first thing that comes to mind when I think of Marcello is his bonhomie. In most of the stories we acted in together, he was always the accommodating good guy. I, instead, was the aggressive, raucous, bitchy one. After doing a scene in which I'd roughed him up, I'd say: "Sorry, Marcè, I didn't want to. This time I think I went overboard . . ."

And he, being a real actor, as well as a good person, never got upset. "You're a witch, Sofi, come over here. Let me give you a hug, *te voglio da' 'nu bacio* (I wanna give you a kiss)."

He'd end up consoling *me*, and I, to thank him, would make him one of my specialties, *fagioli con le cotiche* (beans and pig rind).

Our friendship didn't need many words. All it took was one look, a gesture to understand each other; we encouraged each other by staying close together. We would never scold each other, complain about each other, expect anything other than what each of us felt like doing. Sometimes, to ease the tension of a difficult scene, to needle each other, we'd say. "*Nun me piace come l'hai fatta*" (I don't like the way you did it).

But there was a smile in our eyes, and we knew right away that we were just trying to be funny.

FROM ROMAGNA TO BRECHT

Faith, faith . . . It almost sounds like a password. In time I learned that the real challenge in our job, and maybe not just in ours, lies in transforming other people's faith in us into self-confidence, self-esteem, a belief in ourselves and our abilities. That's where the experience begins, the moment you start believing in yourself, and you treasure both your successes and your mistakes.

That moment for me came in *Two Women*. After doing Cesira, I felt ready to handle practically any role. It was that success, a personal one before being a public one, that started a very intense decade, in which I was a recognized actress, and would ultimately become a wife and mother, too.

It was the Fabulous Sixties, which were to change the world forever. The years of the Beatles and JFK, of *8½* and James Bond, of the popularity of nightclubs and the nonviolent protests of Martin Luther King, Jr. I was often working on several fronts, on the international scene, but, also, whenever I had the chance to, I'd go back to playing Italian characters, in whom I could be myself completely.

Before appearing with Marcello again on the set of *Yesterday, Today and Tomorrow*, I traveled in time and space, adapting to very different worlds. After playing the part of Jimena next to Charlton Heston in *El Cid*, a sort of "Superwestern" in costume, I played Madame Sans-Gêne, a revolutionary washerwoman who became a duchess, in *Madame*.

In the fall of 1961 I left my historical costumes aside and let De Sica drag me into doing "La riffa" ("The Lottery"), one of the four episodes of *Boccaccio '70*. The others were directed by Visconti, Fellini, and Monicelli. The screenplay was credited to Ennio Flaiano and several others, including Italo Calvino, as well as the ever-present Cesare Zavattini, from whom it had all begun. Parading in front of the camera were great talents such as Romy Schneider and Paolo Stoppa, Peppino De Filippo and Anita Ekberg, who had just acted in *La Dolce Vita* with Marcello.

In my episode, De Sica used all the irony he could muster— which was always gentle and delicate even when it was just one step away from the grotesque—to stage a clandestine lottery during a rustic country fair in Romagna. I was the prize, Zoe, the queen of target shooting.

"People of Lugo, it's time for balloon shooting . . . pistol or carbine?"

To the rhythm of an irresistible *cha cha cha* by Trovajoli— "*Soldi soldi soldi tanti soldi, beati siano i soldi, i beneamati soldi perché / chi ha tanti soldi vive come un pascià, e a piedi caldi se ne sta . . .*" (Money money money lots of money, blessed money, beloved money because / when you have money you live like a king and your feet are always toasty), I sang cheerfully and also somewhat coarsely—wearing a flaming red dress, I had found another incarnation for the Pizza Girl, giving up wealth for true love.

I had lots of fun shooting the movie in that rural area, surrounded by cows and clouds of dust from the amusement park nearby. Hearing the Romagnolo accent always put me in a good mood, and by the time we'd finishing shooting I'd almost made it my own. I always seemed to be happy, and everyone was aware of it. I'd ride to the set on my bike, cook during the breaks, listen to jazz, sing. Sometimes my sister, Maria, would join me and we'd launch into Neapolitan duets and the whole crew would stay up late to listen to us. As if that weren't enough, the flower growers in Lugo named a rose variety after me. What more could I possibly have wanted?

My Zoe so resembled the Pizza Girl that it annoyed Marotta, who had written *The Gold of Naples*, causing him to good-heartedly accuse Zavattini of plagiarism. The movie was hugely successful with the public, and the producers were thinking of making an international *Boccaccio '71*, with Jacques Tati and Charlie Chaplin directing jointly with De Sica.

But the movie was never made, and in 1962—after working on *Le couteau dans la plaie* ("The Knife in the Wound") which came out in America as *Five Miles to Midnight*, a thriller directed by Anatole Litvak, and after receiving the Oscar for *Two Women*—I was back under Vittorio's wing with the drama *The Condemned of Altona*. The original play was by Jean-Paul Sartre, and we had some three Oscar winners on board: the actors Frederic March and Maximilian Schell and the screenwriter Abby Mann, backed by Zavattini. I played the part of a sophisticated Brechtian actress of the Berliner Ensemble, at odds with a Nazi brother-in-law and his shady past. The role was far from my personal experience, in a movie that didn't really work, despite the excellent names involved. It was a beautiful story, though, and we actors did what we could to interpret it in the best way possible. But the critics tore it to pieces, maybe because they were somewhat bewildered by it. These things happen. As you grow older you realize that failure is not a tragedy: tomorrow morning the sun will rise again and at breakfast your appetite will be back. In any case, for me it was an interesting experience, which won me another David di Donatello award and an extra pinch of know-how.

While we were shooting, Carlo called. From his voice I could tell he had bad news. We'd just finished shooting and I was back at the hotel.

"Sophia . . ."

"What is it? What's wrong?"

"Marilyn's dead . . . we just got the news. Barbiturates. They say it was suicide."

I hung on to the receiver speechless, not knowing what to say. I was so quiet that Carlo started to worry. He knew that behind my carefully controlled, determined façade lies an emotional woman.

"Sophia, are you still there?"

"Yes, yes, of course I am. Where else could I be?"

That death, so untimely, so ambiguous, caused me terrible distress. And it got me thinking. I thought about the meaning of beauty, about loneliness, about the need to feel love that's hidden in the heart of each and every one of us. I remembered Marilyn's seductive smile veiled with sadness. It wasn't enough to be the most beautiful woman in the world to be happy.

Marilyn had been a great actress, crushed by the weight of her own talent, by all the men who had asked her for everything without giving her anything in return, or by those who had wanted to transform her according to their own tastes. Marilyn's allure had ended up destroying her, reducing her to an ill-fated sex symbol. She hadn't managed to find her own way. I felt a shiver run up my spine, as if a shadow had been cast all around me.

The world is a cruel place, nourished by and satisfied with appearances, rarely concerned about what lies beneath the surface. This is why it's up to each of us to keep any fairy tale anchored to real life, so that we never forget who we are, where we come from.

YESTERDAY AND TODAY

"But, Vittorio, I've never seen a striptease before, *nun saccio proprio comme se fa*" (I have no idea how it's done).

"Sofi, don't worry, I've called in an expert on the matter."

I'd spent a long spring in Spain making *The Fall of the Roman Empire* with Alec Guinness and Omar Sharif. In the movie, Alec, probably the most accomplished all-around actor I've ever met, played my father, Emperor Marcus Aurelius. Whenever he started to say something, the world just stopped, and I would stand there watching him with dreamy eyes. From there I'd taken a short break to go to Hollywood and give Gregory Peck an Oscar. I'd come back to the set with Vittorio, who was in better shape than ever before, and was again pushing me to become better than ever. It was July 1963 and with us was Marcello, with whom we once again formed a magical trio.

Despite my reluctance Vittorio wouldn't let up.

"You'll see, Sofi, you'll see. We're going to prepare such a sexy scene that all that'll be left of Marcello is a pile of ashes!"

I looked at him, dismayed, but underneath it all I knew I was in for some fun.

Yesterday, Today and Tomorrow is also a film in episodes, like *Boccaccio '70*, but the main characters are always the same. Marcello and I portrayed in different cities and contexts. We started shooting the end of the movie first, then proceeded backward as we traveled up and down Italy.

My character, Mara, is a big-hearted prostitute who lives in Piazza Navona. Her balcony overlooks the rooftops of Rome and is adjacent to that of a young seminarian, who falls hopelessly in love with her and because of that runs away from home. The boy's grandmother is in despair and accuses Mara of having seduced him, but then the two women make peace and actually become accomplices. The unbelievable result of this is that Mara vows abstinence for a week so that the young man will come back home. She does, however, dedicate to her most passionate customer a striptease, which has become famous in cinema history.

The expert summoned by De Sica to help me was Jacques Ruet, choreographer at the legendary Crazy Horse cabaret in Paris. After a few "training" sessions, during which he taught me about the gestures, the rhythms, the moves, I was ready to do a striptease my own way.

Before doing the scene, I didn't sleep for a week. I must not have been completely at ease the morning of the shoot, either, because I made a request of De Sica that was unusual for me: "Vittorio, listen, how about clearing the set for this scene?"

So Marcello and I were left alone, with just the cameraman and De Sica's wife, who was often on the set. Marcello, lying on the bed completely dressed, was ready to enjoy the show. "Go, Sofi, full steam ahead!" he said with an encouraging smile. His sweet, amused attitude paved the way for me. As I disrobed to the notes of "Abat-jour," the original soundtrack for the movie, Marcello was curled up with his chin in his hands, watching me like a greedy child. Every once in a while, he'd mop his brow with a handkerchief. When I removed my garter belt, he let out a coyote howl of love, which summed up all the happiness a human being is capable of. This touch of genius won Vittorio an Oscar for Best Foreign Film in 1965.

I know I'm going to sound like a broken record if I say one more time that neither Marcello nor I could ever have made it without Vittorio. But that's the truth. Neither of us was prepared to be exhibitionistic, to flaunt sex in such an unabashed way.

"I remember that in old movies," Marcello said to Enzo Biagi during that same interview, "you'd be watching, let's say Marlene Dietrich; she and someone else might go behind a folding screen, and suddenly you'd see a corset. And you'd fantasize, you'd pierce that screen and imagine her naked as she got undressed." Instead, if there's a wall here at all, it's De Sica's irony, his way of never taking things completely seriously, his smile filled with affection and humanity. The striptease was probably one of the most amusing scenes I've ever had to do in my life. And I think it still works, even though times and customs have changed so much."

Omar Sharif, whom I'd met only recently then, told me, "For me that striptease wasn't at all a surprise, Sophia, I'd dreamed of you naked so many times that it appeared to me that I was seeing something I'd already seen before!"

As soon as we finished that scene, we moved on to Naples to shoot the "Adelina" episode, written by Eduardo De Filippo based on the true story of Concetta Muccardi. A seller of black-market cigarettes on the streets of the Forcella neighborhood, Concetta had figured out that if a woman was pregnant she wouldn't have to go to jail. So she had fourteen children, which for the movie had luckily been reduced to seven. In the movie version, seven children aren't enough to prevent her from being arrested. But they're a lot to deal with anyway: those kids are all over the place, in her arms, under the bed, outside the jail waiting for her to come out.

Marcello played the funniest part as her exhausted husband, Carmine, who can no longer fulfill his marital duties to his wife. The scene when they go to the doctor's to find a solution is hilarious.

"So you don't want children . . ." says the doctor.

"*No, tutto 'o cuntrario*" (the exact opposite), "*chisto non funziona cchiù!*" (he doesn't *work* anymore!).

"But when the horse is tired," the doctor warns her, "you have to stop whipping it, and put it back in the stable . . ."

It just so happened that while I was shooting the Neapolitan part of the movie I started feeling out of sorts. After a few days thinking that maybe playing Adelina had made me feel pregnant, I started thinking that maybe I really was pregnant. I went to see a local doctor who had me do some tests, but they all came back negative. However, the feeling wouldn't go away, so another big expert from Rome arrived, carrying a dark leather briefcase. When he opened it I jumped with fright. Inside it was a tiny green frog staring at me, his eyes bulging, scared to death.

"*E chisto che c'entra?*" (What does this have to do with it?).

The doctor was unperturbed and injected the animal with some of my urine.

"If the frog dies, it means you're pregnant . . ."

It wasn't long before the tiny animal started moving around erratically, as if it had been hit on the head. But it didn't die. I got rid of the doctor and went out to take a walk in Mergellina, releasing the poor creature into a pond.

"Too bad," I said to myself, "for a moment there I thought I was pregnant."

However, contrary to all expectations, just before the shooting ended, my pregnancy was confirmed. I was desperately happy, happier than I'd ever been before. I was twenty-nine, which at the time was considered old to have children, and my desire for motherhood had become an obsession. I loved children, and the idea of having one all my own gave me a sense of peace and fulfillment I'd been searching for all my life.

"Sophia was born a mother," said Vittorio, who was particularly sensitive to children, and had given them leading roles in many of his movies. I myself had met many child actors on the set, and stayed in touch with some of them for a long time. The little girl in *Houseboat* even wrote to me a few years ago to tell me she'd become a grandmother!

In *Woman of the River*, I had been a despairing mother, in *The Black Orchid*, a mother in crisis, and in *Two Women*, the embodiment of the great Mediterranean mother, a woman who will do whatever it takes.

In *It Started in Naples*, which was shot in 1959, I had played a happy, unconventional aunt and I had in fact become an aunt shortly before. On December 30, 1962, nine months to the day of her marriage to Romano Mussolini, a talented musician and the youngest son of Benito Mussolini, Maria had given birth to Alessandra. The little one was born too early and in the first days she gave us cause for concern. But she was christened on January 12, with me in the role of the proud, happy godmother.

In hindsight it seems impossible to believe, but even a joyous and innocent event like my niece's christening had its meddling gossips and detractors. Yes, because a sinner like me should never have been allowed to participate in a religious ceremony. Carlo's and my situation was far from being solved, and it continued to fuel the morbid interest of the well-wishers. We didn't let their unkind thoughts affect us too much. Anyway, after the initial scare, Alessandra grew strong and healthy and this gave us consolation for some of the upset. Now it was my turn to be a mother, and I couldn't wait to look my own child in the eyes.

But that's not how it went, and the following days turned out to be among the saddest and darkest of my life. Although I kept on working, I could tell something was not right with me, not up to par. In Rome I went to see another gynecologist, who reassured me: "Get a few days' rest and travel by train, rather than by car. But don't worry, everything's normal."

We were headed to Milan to shoot the last episode of the movie based on a short story by Moravia. Too bad, though, that "Anna," the title of the episode, almost entirely took place in a stage car that had been mounted on a hydraulic arm to simulate the bumps. It was much worse than any real car.

The first night in Milan I felt a terrible pain. The physician summoned by the hotel tried to reassure me, but a few hours later, the pain was so bad that I had to go to the emergency room. In order to avoid attracting attention we didn't call an ambulance, but as I was inside the elevator, going down I almost fainted. The doctors took good care of me, but the urgency and nervousness with which they moved around left me with little hope. I was afraid, and terrified at the thought of the tragedy that was about to hit me, shattering the beautiful dream I'd just started to believe in. I felt helpless, I asked questions, but no one knew what to answer me.

"Keep calm, Signora, we're looking into it, we're trying to understand. Don't be nervous, you'll see, everything will turn out for the best." The ocean of meaningless words left me desperate and isolated. I can still see myself lying on that hospital bed, surrounded by white walls, the neon lighting, the smell of disinfectant penetrating my every cell and piercing my heart.

The most painful recollection about that night was the scornful look on the nuns' faces, who seemed to want to blame me. They were insensitive, inhumane, devoid of feeling, their useless, gratuitous humiliation of me spurred by prejudice and ignorance. They thought they knew the truth, the real story, but they didn't know anything about me, my desires, my fears.

I lost the baby. After the D&C that was necessary, I went right back to work. I didn't want to keep the crew waiting—and it was really the only thing I could do.

I had to make a real effort. But I felt gutted. It was as if the world had been turned off forever. I tried, but I could see nothing ahead of me, nothing that could console me. Carlo was by my side and my sister had rushed from Rome to keep me company, but it was all useless. I felt desperately alone, as I had never in my life felt before. My life as a star was nothing compared to the happiness of the new mothers I'd glimpsed at the clinic, getting ready to breast-feed their newborn babies.

The morning I went back to the set I was sitting in the car, curled up in a corner, absently staring out the window at the gray cityscape of Milan that I couldn't make sense of. Marcello came up to me, shy and gentle.

"Has anything happened? Are you expecting?"

"I was."

"I'm so sorry."

He left without another word, with the same gentleness as he'd approached me. We never talked about it again, but I was relieved that he knew. And I knew that he was close to me, and that he loved me. At that moment I knew that I would always be able to count on his friendship.

TOMORROW

I would soon discover that the bumping of the car on the set had nothing to do with my miscarriage. It was all a matter of hormones. Before I discovered that, though, my life had a great deal more suffering in store for me.

Four years later, I lost a second child. I was making *More Than a Miracle*, a beautiful fairy tale directed by Francesco Rosi, also starring Omar Sharif. Although nothing can alleviate the pain of this type of mourning, I was more prepared this time. I knew my body better now, and knew how to interpret its signals.

At the first signs of pregnancy, although there were still three days before the shooting was to end, I called Carlo, happy and concerned at the same time: "Carlo, I'm pregnant . . . But this time I'm going to be careful, I don't want to take any risks."

He seemed to be even more nervous than I was, he couldn't stand the thought of seeing me suffer again like the first time. I was used to having total control over a situation, but here we were venturing into unknown territory, without rules and without certainties. To keep me calm he feigned confidence: "Of course, Sophia. I'll take care of everything. We'll finish the movie later."

I left the set and forced myself to stay in bed. I did nothing. I didn't read, didn't watch TV, I even spoke as little as possible so that I wouldn't disturb the baby. I wouldn't even touch my stomach for fear it might bother him. But a little voice inside was telling me the same thing was happening all over again.

My gynecologist, who was considered to be the best one around, was of little help. Actually, he was of no help at all. At the first signs of the pain I remembered too well, I was at home—we had moved to a beautiful villa in Marino, in the Roman hills—Carlo was in London for work, and my dear friend Basilio was there to keep me company. Since we'd met on the set of *Woman of the River*, we rarely left each other's side. His fraternal friendship made me feel safe even when I felt that tragedy loomed ahead. Ines, my assistant, was there, too, to hold my hand. Her sixth sense had already guessed, and maybe mine had as well, but we didn't utter a word.

Basilio called the doctor.

"Come quickly, please . . . As I told you before, she's having contractions, she's as white as a ghost, and she feels faint."

But the great and mighty doctor wouldn't be moved to pity, and, from the height of his arrogant self-confidence, declared: "It's nothing to worry about, have her drink some chamomile, we'll talk about it tomorrow." He thought he was a god, never had any self-doubt, and his passion was elsewhere. He was crazy about racing cars, and he went around wearing a car racing hat, like some ridiculous latter-day Tazio Nuvolari, the legendary racecar driver.

We rushed to the hospital, despite the doctor's indifference, and ran into him on his way out to a cocktail party. "It's just a passing crisis," he announced as he tried to shut the door behind him, his whitecoat fluttering about over his cashmere sweater. "Now, try to get some sleep. I gave you a nice strong sedative; we'll see what happens tomorrow."

The contractions were getting worse, as if I were in labor, and my face was as yellow as a lemon. My mother, who had joined us, pounced on him with all her strength: "Can't you see her face? She's having a miscarriage!" But nothing doing. His cocktail party could not wait.

When my pain ceased suddenly at four in the morning I knew it was over. It was Ines who telephoned the doctor, with all the details. He took his time coming, arriving at around six, and said: "Signora, you no doubt have excellent hips, and you're a beautiful woman, but you will never have a child."

His scathing words made me feel powerless, barren, deeply inadequate. They dashed any hopes I might have had. This was no fairy tale. My life was taking a sad turn and I saw no future. The press made everything even more difficult, and wasted no time parading the news of our pain to the whole world.

"Now I can go back to the set and finish the movie," I said to Carlo as soon as he stepped into my room, having come directly from the airport. I was trying to lighten the blow, to show him how strong I was. His smile turned into a grimace, it was obvious that he felt totally helpless. Only at that moment did I let myself go, crying my heart out.

In the desperate months that followed, a sense of failure spread to every corner of my soul, like a flood that washes over everything, houses, streets, cities. Even Carlo, a solid, concrete businessman, lost his step. He became depressed, could hardly work, talk, or smile.

Luckily, fate led us to an unexpected discovery. The wife of Goffredo Lombardo, who had invented my stage name, had gone through an odyssey similar to mine, but she'd chanced upon the right person, an internationally renowned expert who had helped her carry to term. His name was Hubert de Watteville, and he directed the gynecology clinic at Geneva Hospital.

Tall, very thin, de Watteville was about sixty years old, with a beaklike nose and a somewhat aristocratic, detached air. At the beginning I had been disappointed, having hoped to find a sympathetic, loving father more than an ascetic professional. But I was mistaken in my first impression. As I got to know him I found he was one of the most affectionate, sensitive men I'd ever meet in my life. He himself hadn't had any children, and he'd poured his desire for fatherhood into his work, so that the children he helped come into the world were in some ways his, too.

After studying my case at length, he had drawn conclusions that were more optimistic than even I had hoped for. "There's nothing wrong, you're a very normal woman. The next time you get pregnant we'll monitor you from up close to see if we can understand exactly how to step in. You'll see, things will go smoothly next time."

In early 1968, when I got pregnant for the third time, I moved to Geneva. I chose a hotel close to the doctor's office, took to bed, and waited patiently, under his authoritative watch, for him to perform a miracle. He examined me right, left, and center, and did every test imaginable. Afterward, he smiled at me and said: "The problem is you don't have enough estrogen, and this keeps the egg from attaching to the uterus. We can give you estrogens, with some good strong injections, and this child will be born in December. Just like the Baby Jesus!"

In the following months, I was anxious and calm at the same time. I stayed on the eighteenth floor of the Hotel Intercontinental for months of forced idleness. To distract myself. I started cooking with Ines. The kitchen spoke to me of my childhood, family, and whole life. We recreated recipes from my past, and used ideas I'd gathered while traveling around the world, as well as advice given to me by chefs, both great and unknown, I'd happened to meet. I diligently wrote everything in a notebook so I wouldn't forget anything about this extraordinary experience. It was actually Basilio who one day, years later, while leafing though it by chance, exclaimed, "This is a great cookbook!

IX

MARRIAG

Why don't we publish it?" And that's how my first cookbok, *In the Kitchen with Love*, came to be published. Love and cooking carried me along until the day—the one I had both greatly feared and desired—I was to give birth.

When the day came—a C-section had been planned so as to avoid any other complications—de Watteville came to pick me up secretly at five in the morning, actually driving into the lobby in his car. He wanted to spare me from the crowd of journalists thronging the front of the clinic.

The night before, lost in my thoughts, I hadn't slept a wink. The truth is, I didn't want my pregnancy to end. But as soon as I entered the clinic I heard the other babies crying, and I realized that I would soon be hearing my own child crying just like them. I wanted to stop time, dilate it to infinity. I was scared. I didn't want to share this child that was all mine with anyone else. I now know that this is a feeling that characterizes the first instant of motherhood. Separating from him meant delivering my son to his own life.

A few hours later Carlo Hubert Leone Jr. was born—Carlo after his father, Hubert after Dr. de Watteville, Leone after his paternal grandfather—offering me the greatest, sweetest joy I had ever experienced, equal only to what I was to get from Edoardo four years later.

Now my greatest dreams had at last become reality.

As I savor this indescribable joy once more, my treasure trove of memories again takes me by the hand and leads me back a few seasons.

"Dummi', o' bello de' 'e figlie l'avimmo perduto . . . Figlie so' chille che se teneno 'mbraccia quanno so' piccirille, ca te danno preoccupazione quanno stanno malate e nun te sanno dicere che se sènteno . . . ca te corrono incontro cu' 'e braccelle aperte dicenno: 'Papà.'"
(Dummì, we've missed the beauty of having children . . . it means holding them in your arms when they're little, it means worrying about them when they're sick and don't know how to describe how they feel, it's when they run toward you with their arms wide open and call you "Papà.")

Filumena Marturano's words from *Marriage Italian Style* reverberate in my ears like sweet music filled with truth while I use my fingers to try to smooth out a creased page of the magazine *Oggi*, an issue dated April 23, 1964, which announced that shooting of the movie was about to begin. Carlo and De Sica had decided to make a movie out of the comedy Eduardo De Filippo had written for his sister, Titina, a renowned actress who had immortalized the role on stage. Here I was again on the set with Marcello.

Carlo had been thinking about it for a long time, until one day he'd made up his mind, and just tossed the question at me, with carefully studied nonchalance:

"Sophia, could you see yourself as Filumena?"

I shut my eyes; before me was the parted curtain, the lights dimming, the red velvet of an immense seating area . . .

"Filumena? Filumena Marturano?"

Carlo had guessed I might be reluctant, and he looked at me with a smile.

Smiling back at him, I replied: "Do you think I could? I'd really like to . . ."

This simple exchange of words was enough for us to begin one of our happiest adventures.

Marriage Italian Style—the title chosen for Filumena's story, and a nod to *Divorce Italian Style*, directed by Pietro Germi in 1961—was one of my most important movies. It offered me a great role, an all-around one, which encompassed twenty-five years of Neapolitan life lived, and suffered, one year after another, by an intelligent, passionate woman, who was determined to use everything in her power to fight for her dignity and for that of her children. In other words, it was a role with which any Italian actress would have wanted to test her skills.

In the comedy, Filumena is middle-aged and worn down by life—but not defeated. Born in Vico San Liborio, in one of the city's poorest quarters, she ends up like many other young women her age, working in a brothel, where she is found by Don Dummì, a confirmed well-to-do bachelor who belongs to a completely different social class. The two of them love each other, and she fools herself into thinking that something might come of it. But Dummì has absolutely no intention of marrying her. Filumena becomes his kept woman. He hands over the management of his pastry shop to her, a job she does with all the air of being its efficient owner. Don Dummì takes her to his home, but he relegates her to the maid's room, and he cheats on her his whole life.

Over the years, Filumena gives birth to three children, whose father's identity perhaps only she knows. She keeps her sons hidden, raising them secretly, and making sure they get the right schooling, which she pays for with Don Dummì's money. But she's tired now, her children have grown up, and she's determined to give them a father, a name, to guarantee their future. How could anyone not agree with her? My sister, Maria, and I knew all about such things.

The performance starts right at this point in the story, with a splendid ruse. Filumena pretends she's on her last breath to get Don Dummì to marry her. She does not give up, even when he discovers her plan. There's no stopping her anymore. She's decided to show her cards, to play the game to the bitter end. "*Dummi', uno di chisti figli è tuo*" (one of these children is yours), but I won't tell you which one. Either all of them, or none of them."

The play on which the movie is based had been written by Eduardo in 1946 and had become a huge success. The character of Filumena had become so dear to the public in the late 1940s, that it had taken on a life of its own. One evening, Luigi De Filippo, the playwright's nephew, recalls, a group of women entered the dressing room of the Roman Elisio theater to say hello to Titina De Filippo and pressed her to tell them who the fathers of the three Marturano boys were.

"Brava, brava, Titina, you are truly a charming actress. But tell us, which of the three boys is Don Dummi's son? We're dying to know . . ."

Titina, being the actress that she was, played along with them, and replied: "My dear, dear ladies, I know which one it is, but I can't tell you because my brother Eduardo would be furious if I did!"

Usually, I can understand a person in a single glance, and the same thing happens when it comes to my characters: either I like them, or I don't, either I feel them, or I don't. Filumena belonged to me as much as my Pozzuoli accent. Maybe I liked her because she had always abided by her own personal motto: "Don't be someone who makes people cry (*chiagnere*), make them laugh instead."

After I'd agreed to play the part, Carlo hadn't wasted an instant. He'd sounded out Mastroianni's willingness to be in the movie, and assigned the screenplay to Renato Castellani, Tonino Guerra, Leonardo Benvenuti, and Piero De Bernardi. But it was De Sica, as usual, who cleared up any last doubts I might have had by finding just the right angle for my part.

The play had already been adapted for cinema in 1951 by the

De Filippo siblings. Just saying the name Filumena conjured up the image of Titina, as well as of the other great actresses who had played the same part, such as Regina Bianchi, the crème de la crème (*meglio del meglio*) of Italian theater.

De Filippo, on his part, was happy to pass on the baton to De Sica; he trusted his deeply Neapolitan spirit, his sensitivity. He also seemed curious to see how I would play the character he'd written to fit. "*Saccio ca 'a trattarraje bbuon'*" (I know you'll treat her well), he had said to me smiling one day. "*Ca nun 'a farraje manca' niente, ca 'a darraje quaccosa d' 'o ttuoje, e a farraje girá 'o munno.*" (I know you'll make sure she has everything she needs, that you'll give her something of your own, that you'll introduce her to the world).

Sometimes life likes to play nasty tricks on us. On December 26, 1963, after we'd already begun working on the movie, the phone rang at our home in Marino. We were all sitting around the table enjoying the Christmas leftovers—Basilio, Mammina, Maria, and little Ale, as we called Maria's daughter—wrapped in that snug atmosphere of the day after Christmas, when everything is so much calmer, the tension is gone, and you can finally enjoy the holiday spirit. On the other end of the line we heard De Sica's desperate voice: "Sofì, Titina's passed away." Her ailing heart had given up, taking away with it a sweet yet very strong woman, and a great actress.

I went to the funeral with Vittorio, which was held at the Sacro Cuore dell'Immacolata in Piazza Euclide. It was a cold winter's day in Rome, and hundreds of coats made a dark stain on the square. Boundless sadness hung in the air. Our hearts heavy with sorrow, we entered and sat down next to Totò and Eduardo. Eduardo and Peppino, his brother, had argued twenty years before, and since then they had avoided each other at all costs, although, until the very last of her days, their sister had done everything in her power to heal their relationship.

Just like Filumena's three secret children, Titina, Eduardo, and Peppino had been born out of wedlock. Their father was the great Eduardo Scarpetta, the unforgettable maestro of Neapolitan theater. Their mother, Luisa De Filippo, was the niece of Scarpetta's real wife, Rosa. The Scarpetta–De Filippo family was an extended one, which they say even included an illegitimate son that Rosa had had with Italy's king Victor Emmanuel.

Scarpetta had lived with both women at the same time, a bit here and a bit there. De Sica was doing the same thing: living with his wife Giuditta Rissone with Emi on the one hand, and María Mercader with Manuel and Christian on the other. Marriages Italian style? Perhaps. Meanwhile, for Carlo and me, our marriage seemed to be as unattainable as the moon itself.

It wasn't easy to adapt a comedy for cinema, to transform the power of theater without watering it down. Just as with Cesira in *Two Women*, Filumena was much older than me. Vittorio solved the problem in his own way and, as usual, with a touch of magic. He took this beautiful story with its monologues and dialogues and set it in the street, in the alleyways, on the slopes of Vesuvius. He took Filumena to Agnano, the racetrack built in a volcanic crater, to see the horse races. He took her to church in Piazza del Gesù Nuovo, the beautiful historic center of Naples, and to the elegant Pasticceria Soriano, which was so real on film you could practically smell the delicious food there. He tinted the story with images, he gave it movement, he made it travel in time. By taking Filumena out of the theater, he could free her from the confines of her mature age and tell the story of her youth in flashbacks, first as a young girl with close-cropped hair, terrified of the furious wartime bombing outside the brothel, and then as a young Neapolitan beauty with a mirthful, bubbly personality.

My sons' favorite scene is when Don Dommì sees me for the first time. The alarm has emptied the brothel, the girls and their clients have escaped to the shelters, while I, like a scared animal, stay in my room, hidden inside the closet, because I don't have the courage to go outside.

"*Quanti anni tieni?*" (How old are you?), Marcello asks.

"*Diciassset'*" (Seventeen), I reply, my eyes wide from fear. Throughout the movie, there's never a tear in those eyes, because "you can't cry if you've never known goodness."

And goodness is indeed something that Filumena has never known. Only at the end when, thanks to her tenacity, everything falls into place, can she abandon herself to tears that free her, tears filled with humanity.

It was hard to imagine a role closer to my heartstrings. At every moment I was being asked to interweave happiness and sadness, courage and despair, ugliness and beauty, placing them at the service of deeper sentiments. I was again in Naples, in my city, to give one of its women, a *malafemmina* (a bad woman) but only in name, a deeper identity.

I have to confess that, to make *Marriage Italian Style*, I got some help. And it's a good thing I did! The idea just came to me, one night, while I was chatting with Carlo and Enrico Lucherini, my press agent, on the terrace of the Hotel Excelsior in Naples. A light breeze was rising up from the sea; it swept away any feeling of tiredness and made room for new thoughts. Looking at the streets of my city, I went back a few years and let myself be overcome by the scent, that familiar air.

"Carlo, what do you think about inviting Mammina and Zia Dora to the set?"

"Of course, if it makes you happy. But how come? What are you up to?" Even though he was a man of few words, Carlo was interested in understanding motivations.

"Who better than Mammina and Zia Dora could get into the mind of Filumena, her psychology? Who better than they could show it to me the way it was, real, right before my eyes, with all the right gestures, the words . . ."

I wasted no time in calling them. They were both about fifty by then, which in those days meant they were just entering old age.

"*Zietta*, I'll have someone pick you up in Pozzuoli tomorrow morning early."

"Mammina, make sure you're ready, the car will be there to pick you up at seven."

"*Che staje dicenno, si' asciuta pazza?*" (What do you mean tomorrow morning? Are you crazy?), they answered almost identically, although I had made two separate phone calls. They had been living far apart for a long time, and yet they spoke the same language and had the same reactions. I was sure that my invitation had made them happy.

The crew welcomed them like two queens.

Mammina was convinced she was the right person in the right place, prancing up and down the set like a star, happy to lend us the artistic talent that life hadn't given her a chance to express. Zia Dora was a little out of place, precisely because she had never wanted to be an actress—which made her all the more precious. The two of them would take me aside when one of my lines sounded wrong, and say: "*Chest' 'o facess' accussì, chest' acculli*" (This is how you do this; that is how you do that). I followed the script, of course, but their spontaneity really helped me give my Filumena the naturalness she needed. Between one shoot and another, I would look at them, filled with tenderness. It was thanks to them that I was there, and that day they were my guests of honor.

Marcello, of course, courted them gallantly, playing his part as best he could. They hung on his every word, and fought over him as though he were the rooster in the hen house.

At long last, Marcello had a role in which he played less of a nice guy than usual. He turned his Don Dummì into an unforgettable character, with a pompous moustache, elegant clothing, and a somewhat theatrical superficiality—all in perfect contrast to the female character, whose drama is that of a woman who grows old without being noticed, without being seen.

The passion that Marcello and I conveyed on the screen worked, as it always had, and touched people's hearts. Because, once again, it told a story that was real, a story so filled with flaws that even the happy ending was profoundly human.

All of us working on the film were touched by it, too, besides having loads of fun making it. The first scene, in which Filumena pretends she's in agony, had to be shot ten times, because, each time we heard the word "Action," Marcello and I would burst into laughter, and simply couldn't stop. That day Vittorio got really angry with us. He was tired, his feet were aching, and we were making his life impossible. Even when the priest came to the house for the last rites, we tried to be serious, but all it took was one look and we'd start laughing all over again, spoiling everything. Vittorio felt powerless before our laughing fit. He thundered like Zeus annoyed by the pranks of mortals: "You're two actors, not two children! Aren't you ashamed of making fun of all of us like this? What are you even doing here? That's enough now, get a grip on yourselves!"

Marriage Italian Style was nominated for an Oscar for Best Foreign Film, despite the recent victory of *Yesterday, Today and Tomorrow*, and it also earned me a nomination as Best Actress. It was a huge satisfaction, a confirmation that my award for *Two Women* hadn't been just a decision made on the wave of emotion.

Filumena won me many other important prizes, too, from a David di Donatello to a Golden Globe nomination, from a Moscow International Film Festival Award to a Bambi Award. And I also won an award as most popular actress in Germany, which I would continue to receive each year from 1961 to 1969, the only exception being 1966.

Carlo and Vittorio, Marcello and I had won our bet, just as Filumena had won her own by getting her marriage Italian style. But in real life, things seemed to be much harder for us.

My sister's very Italian wedding, two years before, had been to Romano Mussolini, in Predappio, famous for being the birthplace of Benito Mussolini. Romano devoted himself heart and soul to music and was a talented jazz pianist. His passion may have been what won Maria over, she being naturally musical herself. But back when she'd decided to marry Romano, I was concerned about her choice, and I tried telling her as much. We were, we are, sisters in the true sense of the word, and we've always told each other everything. Our closeness is one of the most wonderful things in my life.

"Marì, are you sure? Are you really in love with him?"

"What are you saying, Sofi? Of course I love him. Did you hear how he plays? Did you see his hands? His smile?"

But Romano lived in a world of his own, filled with trips, concerts, and women. He'd come and then disappear, and then come back, you never knew when or why. But she loved him, or at least she thought she did. And there was no convincing her otherwise.

At the wedding on March 3, 1962, the crowd of guests filled the church and spilled out into the square. There were paparazzi everywhere, cameras held above heads just to get a piece of this strange event. I couldn't see a single thing, not even when the groom, who had been inauspiciously late arriving at the altar, fainted, and had to be resuscitated.

"What? He isn't coming? There he is! Romano, Romano . . . Are you all right? Has he fainted? It must be the heat, the crowd, the emotion . . ."

Everyone had an opinion about what happened, based on his or her narrow point of view. In the throngs, it was almost impossible to have a complete view of what was going on.

I left as soon as the ceremony was over, my head in a daze from the chaos.

Horribly, the car that was taking me back to Rome collided with a Vespa, and killed the young man riding it. It was one of the most terrible moments in my life. There are no words to describe it.

Romano and Maria's marriage lasted long enough to bring my goddaughter Alessandra into the world, late in 1962, and then Elisabetta, in 1967. Their troubles were different from Carlo's and mine, however, since we were still fighting our uphill battle to have our marriage recognized legally.

MARRIAGE FRENCH STYLE

"What do I have to do with it? You know I don't like to be photographed with you on the set, Sophia."

"*Jamme*, come on, Carlo, *nun te lamenta'*" (don't grumble), you know how much I want this. Tazio says that in this vanilla-scented lighting we'll come out great!" I answered with my most cunning look, the one I would flash at him when I wanted to get something at all costs.

I trusted Tazio Secchiaroli—my invaluable photographer—with my life. He was completely free to do as he pleased because I was sure he'd do the right thing. Marcello was a friend of his and had recommended him to me, and I'd gotten along with him right from the start. Fellini adored him as well, and they often worked together. He'd been the first to immortalize the nightlife of Via Veneto, inspired not just by the character of the paparazzo in *La Dolce Vita*, but by the whole atmosphere of the movie.

He became like family to me, accompanying me all over the world, from set to set, and from event to event. His son David, who was the same age as Carlo Jr., often came on vacation with us. Tazio was thoughtful, an outstanding photographer, in love with life. But when his wife left him years later, he couldn't stand the pain and let himself die.

One day, on the set for *Marriage Italian Style*, Tazio took some beautiful pictures of me and Carlo in the back room of the Pasticceria Soriano, where Don Dummì—behind Filumena's back—plots his marriage to the young and respectable Diana, the pastry shop cashier. The pictures were great, but none of the newspapers wanted to publish them. Matteo Spinola, who, along with Lucherini, was my press agent, couldn't figure it out, and neither could I. "Have we gone out of style?" I kidded around, to sugar-coat the disappointment. But we soon understood what the problem was and found a way to get around it. The first shots had been posed, and so no one had been interested in them, but when Tazio reprinted them to make them look out of focus, Matteo could sell them as "the secret photos of Sophia Loren and Carlo Ponti!" That was it! The fake scoop rekindled people's morbid curiosity about our adulterous and sinful love. And to think that we'd been together for years, that Carlo's first marriage had ended a long time ago, and that only the law—and the Church—refused to admit it.

We were legal abroad but still not in Italy. The whole thing would have blown over if a housewife from Milan, a prisoner of her own prejudices, hadn't interfered by deciding to report us in order to defend the sanctity of marriage soiled by Carlo's and my love for each other. I still wonder what the real reasons for her actions were. We asked ourselves the same question back then.

We were charged with bigamy. Then, in 1959, the mayor of a small town in Abruzzo, filed another complaint against us. Now, Carlo risked a five-year prison sentence, and I a sentence for complicity—and for being a concubine.

During the early years, until 1959, we'd stayed abroad because we were really afraid we might be arrested. But you can't live in limbo, far from home, forever. And so, tired of our exile, after our Hollywood years, we decided to go back to Italy at our own risk.

It wasn't easy. We always felt that we had to be careful. We tried not to be seen in public together. Whenever we went out to dinner we'd go and come back separately. We'd avoid people's gazes like two lovers caught in the act, like two students who'd escaped from boarding school, like prisoners on parole.

The real irony was that Giuliana, Carlo's ex-wife, also wanted her freedom, and as a lawyer she had been examining the situation carefully in search of a way out. Three times the Pontis applied to the Sacra Rota, the highest appeals court in the Catholic Church, to have their marriage annulled, and all three times their request was denied. It seemed that the only way to get around the bigamy charge was to annul our Mexican marriage, something that in any case represented a step backward more than a step forward.

I suffered terribly, but I knew in my heart that I had done nothing wrong. However much I had been upset by all the public and private accusations that rained down on us, I knew I was in the right. I felt married, and that should have been enough, but it was painful to be pilloried and branded with infamy. Notices that banned my movies and invited the faithful to pray for our sinful souls were put up on the church doors. We were inundated by letters that were often ferocious, the worst of which came from a group of women in Pozzuoli. Being attacked by my own town, by the very heart of my childhood, my native land, hurt me deeply, and it took me a long time to get over it.

Italy was divided between those who were for us, and those who were against us. It was the Italy of famous love affairs, including that of Roberto Rossellini and Ingrid Bergman. But this bigoted Italy wasn't going to last much longer. In about ten more years everything would be taken care of thanks to the

1974 referendum on the divorce law. But it was still a long way off, and all we could do was put up with it.

In late August 1960, Carlo and I were called before the judge. We got there right on time, and Carlo stopped at a café for a cup of coffee, as if everything were normal and it was all just a formality.

"Sophia, do you want something?

I couldn't speak at all, I shook my head, turning it slightly to one side. My eyes were too tearful to be able to look him in the face.

We walked up the court steps briskly, short of breath because of all the emotion we were feeling. For the first time since I'd become an adult I was afraid. I felt naked and helpless, the world seemed to be turning in the opposite direction, any rules there might have been had been thrown out. Not even having Carlo by my side reassured me. As he knocked on the door to the judge's chambers to let him know we'd arrived, I sat down on the edge of an old leather armchair in the waiting room. Luckily it was August, and there was no else around, just the dust, the long corridors, and the filthy windows. I was as tense as a bowstring. I looked out the window at the summer sky, which was as clear and as blue as a children's drawing of it. The sun, the small white clouds, the birds chirping.

"How can a morning like this possibly change my life? How can a person go to jail for love?" The Middle Ages seemed dangerously close.

"Come, Sophia, the judge is waiting," said Carlo softly, encouraging me with his eyes.

I went in alone and in my hazy memory the whole thing lasted just a few seconds.

"Are you married to Carlo Ponti?"

"No, I am not."

"Thank you, Signorina, you can go now."

Then it was Carlo's turn. He was inside for five minutes, but it seemed like forever to me. When he finally did come out, his face dark and strained, I got up to meet him. He brushed my back gently and pointed to the way out. We walked back down the stairs without saying a word, the only sound the clicking of my heels on the cold marble floor, which seemed to mimic the beating of my broken heart. Once we were back in the car, he told me that the judge had again asked him if we were married. That he had answered no, that the marriage celebrated in Mexico by proxy was actually illegal for several reasons, including the fact that the two witnesses required by law had not been present.

But for the judge to be able to reconsider the case, he needed the certificate from Ciudad Juárez, which we couldn't find anywhere. It was as if another obstacle between us and our happiness had been written into some lousy script. While he drove us home, Carlo took his hand off the stick shift and laid it over mine: "It will all work out, I'm sure of it. We just need to bide our time."

We eventually did find the certificate—it had been stolen by an Italian journalist—and the hearing was postponed to February of the following year.

The situation, from one postponement to the next, remained the same, and gradually all the attention focused on us faded away. What can I say? It was your typical Italian farce. And Giuliana found us a solution: if all three of us were to become French citizens, she explained to Carlo, this conundrum could be solved instantly, and would melt like snow in the sun.

So that's why, in 1964, we moved to Paris, to a fabulous apartment on Avenue George V. France awarded us honorary citizenship, for our contribution to French and international cinema. And Giuliana was given citizenship by marriage. It was a complete joke: an Italian woman was given French citizenship because she was married to a Frenchman, which was the only way she could get a divorce from him.

Not much more than a year later, on April 9, 1966, the mayor of Sèvres, a suburb of Paris, was ready to join us in matrimony. I made two phone calls in advance.

"Basilio, take the first flight out without letting anyone see you. And don't forget the wedding bands."

"Marì, we want you here with us tomorrow morning. Don't let anyone see you. What? Your hat? Wear whatever pleases you, it's going to be a simple ceremony, just the family. "*Sì, chillo verde, me piace assaje*" (Yes, the green one would be perfect). Mammina? It's useless, she'd never come, she's too afraid of flying. We'll tell her when it's over. And anyway, with no church and no white dress, she'll say it doesn't really count . . ."

The evening before the wedding, Carlo slept in a suite at the Hotel Lancaster, while I went to my friend Sophie Agiman's house. Besides sharing the same name, we also resembled each other physically. The following morning, when it was time for me to leave the house for the ceremony, I saw a photographer lying in wait in front of the main door. The news had gotten out, I don't know how. Sophie put on my raincoat and my sunglasses, and walked briskly toward my car. The poor photographer fell for it. While he followed her, I left with her husband for my wedding.

How long had I been waiting for that day? It didn't even strike me as real anymore.

The ceremony was quick and solemn, and felt both old and new. Life is never exactly as you might expect it to be. Dreams make way for reality, which often surprises you.

According to the local custom, it was the mayor and not Carlo who placed the ring on my finger. *Je vous déclare unis par les liens du mariage.* Wearing a yellow dress and holding a bouquet of lilies of the valley, I felt strange, tired, and happy.

And then I burst into tears and couldn't stop.

Interlude

Outside my apartment, the snow has shrouded everything in silence as I've gone through my treasure trove of memories. What time could it be? Memory is a strange friend. At times it carries you away, without your even realizing it. It's wonderful to go back, to let yourself be transported. Memory can play kind little tricks on you, too, wiping out the pain or the love that was too intense. Maybe you'll get a date wrong, mix things up. But if you're patient enough to follow it, memory takes you to where you really lived. To the place where you really were, not where you thought you were. You have to resist the temptation to take shortcuts. Let yourself be guided along longer pathways. Sometimes, hidden right around the corner, is a surprise.

Tonight my bed is covered in memories—in the lines of a letter, in the look and colors captured in a photograph, in the voices that come back to life. They all invite me to browse through my past like a book, as though it were someone else's story.

I've often had the chance to see myself from the outside, to watch my success as though it were someone else's. It's a peculiar feeling that, when I was younger, bewildered and annoyed me. I would suddenly go outside of myself, observing myself and all that was going on around me. Today I'm not afraid anymore, I'm used to it. Sometimes I think this distant perspective I get doesn't just happen randomly. I think it's meant to help me see something that's bigger than I am, to catch sight of a direction that is possible even where there seems not be one.

Now, I make myself comfortable and treat myself to one of those crescent-shaped chocolate cookies that Ninni left with the tea. Its round flavor caresses and consoles me. If I eat it without anyone seeing me, it won't count, I think with a smile. I pull up the blanket. Winter in Switzerland is merciless.

I'm tired, but all my senses are alert, ready to capture everything that emerges from my box of secrets. Having relived the birth of my children, the wedding I had so desired, Marcello's and Vittorio's cheerfulness, support, and friendship, I feel excited about what I will discover next. A name shows up among the papers, more real, more alive than ever, just as I can hear his words echoing inside me, more real, more alive. "Sophia, the time has come for you to learn to say 'No.'" I read this short note on a piece of paper and I feel bigger, stronger. That's what happens when you're lucky enough to be touched by a genius like Charlie Chaplin: the light that resonates from that person's heartstrings enlightens and transforms you.

X

STARS

"Signora Loren, there's a phone call for you."

"Who is it?" I shouted down from the top floor, where I'd gone to get my shawl.

"Charlie Chaplin."

I was sure I'd misheard, so I tried again.

"Who? Speak louder, I'm upstairs!"

"Chaplin! Charlie Chaplin!"

It must be another one of Carlo's or Basilio's pranks, I thought. It had to be a mistake, I had to be hearing things. Then I picked up the receiver and uttered a timid "Hello?" The maestro wanted to come and see me. He was asking me when that might be convenient.

As soon as I'd hung up, I dialed Carlo's number at his office in Champion's in Rome. "Carlo??? Carlo??? Are you sitting down? You have no idea, you can't possibly know or imagine who's just called me!" He listened to me touched by my excitement. But at bottom I could tell he was very proud of me.

On the morning Chaplin and I finally met, in that faraway spring of 1965, I was alone at home. Even Ines had gone out. Outside, a typically English rain was falling, an invitation to stay in and rest. The cottage we'd rented was near Ascot, a few miles from the studios where I was making *Arabesque*, a spy movie in *007* style, with a gorgeous Gregory Peck. The plot was too complicated for anyone to really understand it, but we were having loads of fun with it, what with dangerous escapes, kidnappings, horse races, and Christian Dior's wonderful fashions. When the doorbell rang, I slowly got up from the sofa and moved toward the entrance. I was hoping that if I took my time I might be able to control my emotions. When I opened the door, before me was Chaplin's round face, wearing what seemed to be a quizzical expression, under his mop of white hair.

"Good morning, Miss Loren," he said, in English. "Pleased to meet you!"

I smiled at him, stood to one side so that he could come in, and showed him into the living room, without saying a word. Charlie Chaplin was dressed in dark clothing. He had on a tweed jacket that was slightly worn, a pair of gray trousers, and a blue polo shirt with three buttons fastened all the way to the top. As he handed me a bunch of violets, I noticed that under his arm was something that looked a lot like a script. I couldn't seem to get a single word out. He looked at me patiently, the way you look at a child who freezes up out of shyness. He was in no hurry.

Finally, almost in a whisper, I asked him: "Can I get you something to drink? Tea, coffee, a glass of water . . . ?"

"Please, don't bother, thank you," he said. Then, having become aware of my impasse, he started talking. He skipped all the formalities and went straight to the point.

"I've had a story on the shelf for a long, long time. When I saw you in *Yesterday, Today and Tomorrow*, I realized how perfect it was for you. I'd really like . . ."

"Yes," I interrupted him on impulse, regaining control of my voice, conquering my fear. "Yes, Mr. Chaplin, of course, whenever you wish!"

He had written *A Countess from Hong Kong* for Paulette Goddard, one of his many former wives, the unforgettable star of *The Great Dictator* and *The Diary of a Chambermaid*. And now he wanted to adapt it for me.

Acting alongside Charlie Chaplin was every actor's dream, in every corner of the Earth. It was like being summoned to court, hailed by the king, invited to the prince's ball. It was the fairy tale to top all fairy tales, the complete fulfillment of a trade, a vocation, a career. Under his guidance, I would even have been willing to recite the telephone directory.

He gave me a rundown of the story, which was set on a boat on its way from Hong Kong to America. Natasha, a Russian countess and refugee sneaks aboard and stays in the cabin of an American diplomat, wreaking havoc in his life.

Chaplin acted out a few of the parts, doing all the voices himself. He mentioned Marlon Brando as a possible partner and invited me, along with Carlo, to Vevey, where he lived with his family.

I had a contract to honor at the moment, I said, but that as soon as I finished shooting *Arabesque* I would be at his complete disposal. He got up and, bowing imperceptibly, said: "Well, then, we shall be in touch soon." I was about to ask him for his phone number, an address where I could contact him, but then I bit my tongue. Geniuses never have a phone or an address, I thought to myself. Their address is always "somewhere in the world," and they seem to exist just to make it more beautiful every day.

We said good-bye like two people who had a common goal, something to become excited about together. We felt comfortable with each other, and if we had been speaking Italian we would no doubt have been using the informal "tu" form.

As soon as we could, Carlo and I went to Vevey, where Charlie, who was seventy-six, was living with his very young wife, Oona, Eugene O'Neill's daughter. They had so many children it was hard to keep count. Together they were both an odd and beautiful couple, a couple whose every gesture was thoughtful. Despite the warmth of our first encounter, I felt tense and emotional, my heart was pounding. There's nothing you can do about it, you can never get accustomed to geniuses.

The Chaplin home was close to Lake Geneva. All around it was an enchanted garden, more like a park than a garden, the silence broken by the cheerful shouting of children. I didn't know what to do, to think, or to say. I didn't know where to begin a conversation that would make any sense at all. Carlo, who might have been more relaxed than I was on an occasion such as this one, was hampered by his shaky English. Oona was gentle and shy, used to living in the shadow of that extraordinary man whom she looked after with love and affection. So Charlie Chaplin took it upon himself to entertain all of us, with his marvelous elegance. He would be talking about the script, but then suddenly tell us something about himself, about when he was a child in the poorer quarters of London. Then he'd go back to talking about the movie, but suddenly, without warning, walk over to the piano, sit down, and pick out a movie theme he'd started composing. He was a whirlwind—a great, imaginative storyteller, absorbed by his own magic.

As proof of his affection for us, he had prepared his favorite dish himself. He had us sit down, then he raced into the kitchen, and came back smiling triumphantly. "And here, specially for you, is my famous recipe for potatoes with caviar!" he exclaimed with the sweeping gesture of a magician as he set the tray down in the middle of the table. He served us himself, and he showed us how to eat them.

"You see," he said solemnly as he removed the tin foil around the potatoes, "this is how you cut them, lengthwise. Then you thinly spread them with some butter, and set them on top of the caviar, with a drop of lemon . . ." He was meticulous about every detail. There was never anything slapdash about what he did or said. If he didn't think he was capable of doing something perfectly, he preferred not to do it at all.

I went back to Vevey a second time, this time with Marlon Brando, when Chaplin had finished writing the script and wanted us to see it. He welcomed us with an embrace, accompanied us to see the lake at the other end of the garden, then invited us into his study. When it was time to get the show on the road, he read the script straight through, reciting every single part, every single line. It was sheer ecstasy: I listened to his words, trying to grasp every inflection, every nuance. I watched him as he became each of the characters one by one, from seductive Natasha, which was supposed to be my part, to the handsome and somewhat grouchy ambassador, concerned about his career, from the old bed-ridden heiress with a chronic cough, to the commander of the ship, a halfhearted man who strutted about.

Like Vittorio, Chaplin was a director but also an actor, and he put his talent at our disposal to inspire us, to show us, with his body and soul, what he expected from us.

And what about Brando? Despite his charming looks, his great talent, he was a man who seemed to be ill at ease in the world.

The first day of shooting, I arrived on the set as I always did. I arrived early, all my lines learned by heart, my heart in my throat. The first scene was to take place in the ship's ballroom, where all the couples were ready to dance. I was wearing a white evening dress, which I would actually wear for most of the movie. All of us, the extras, the stagehands, the director, were ready to begin. But something was missing. *He* was missing.

"Do you know where Brando is?" Chaplin asked me nervously.

"I have no idea, Charlie, I'm sorry," I answered, slightly embarrassed. It wasn't my fault, but I felt responsible all the same, I don't know why. There I was, standing before this living legend of world cinema, and I just couldn't bear the idea that something could go wrong, that someone might be disrespectful. Chaplin was quiet, intense in his vexation, almost scary. He kept pacing up and down, like a father-to-be, and every three minutes he'd look at his watch, knitting his eyebrows. I looked around, trying to find a place where I could rest my eyes. The others, too, didn't know where to look anymore, the tension was so thick you could cut it with a knife.

After three quarters of an hour Marlon finally waltzed in, as fresh as a daisy. Perhaps he hadn't even realized what he'd done. For sure he wasn't at all expecting what was about to happen. Chaplin slowly walked over to him, sternly, warlike. He glared at him, from the bottom up, looking straight at him without an ounce of compassion, in front of the crew that was standing at attention all in a row.

"If you're planning on arriving late tomorrow, and the day after tomorrow, and the day after the day after tomorrow, well, as far as I'm concerned you can leave the set right now and not come back at all."

Brando deflated like a balloon and mumbled his apologies. He took his place, his head hanging, and at last he was ready to start. But just as he was about to say his first line, his voice wouldn't come out. It had vanished, along with his brash facade.

Brando never arrived late again, but things didn't improve much all the same. It didn't take long for me to see that he was an unhappy person, wrapped up in his own problems. He didn't know where his place was, what to do with or make of his immense talent, his body. At the start of the shooting he was in great shape, as handsome as only he knew how to be. But this malaise of his tormented him, it wouldn't leave him alone. I don't know why, but at a certain point he decided he was only going to eat ice cream. And, of course, he put on a huge amount of weight, to the point that his role was compromised.

He had absolutely no qualms about ruining our working relationship. One day, just before shooting one of the most romantic scenes in the movie, he suddenly reached out and grabbed at me. I twisted around and very calmly hissed in his face, like a cat when you pet its fur backward: "Don't you dare. Don't you ever do that again."

As I gave him my dirtiest look, I suddenly saw how small and harmless he really was, almost a victim of an aura that had been created around him. He never tried anything again, but it became increasingly difficult for me to be near him.

Chaplin had his own problems. He hadn't made a film in a long time, and the first week he found it hard to get behind the camera. As if he didn't dare take control of the situation. What helped him through his difficulty was the gentle patience of a marvelous cameraman who, little by little, persuaded him to once again take over his command post. I think he was also reassured by the silent presence of his wife, Oona, who was always on the set, ready to come to his aid if need be.

However, a few days later, Charlie gave me the biggest compliment I'd ever had. The script said that after listening to Brando's words I was to respond with a look, without saying a word.

"You're like an orchestra answering its conductor," he said, almost moved. "If I raise my hands, you go up, if I lower them, you go down . . . Outstanding."

From those words, which were sown inside me, a strong, green plant grew, which continues to bear its fruits today.

Working with Chaplin was an unforgettable experience. He was a meticulous filmmaker, fussing over even the smallest details. He could spend hours on just one scene, suggesting intonations, gestures, and, most importantly, moods, using the most remarkable images to evoke them. But it was when he stopped explaining and started acting that the world suddenly changed. Those were the moments when he forgot he was the director and he would leap around like a ham actor, despite his age. And you'd find Little Tramp right there in front of you. It energized you, but could also inhibit you. We all knew that he was one of a kind, and that everything started and ended with him.

Chaplin was very demanding, he wanted things to be exactly

as he had imagined them, and he refused to budge. He was always very straightforward. If he liked you there was no ulterior motive, he just liked you and that was that. He always spoke his mind, and if someone gave him the impression of being disloyal, he'd turn his back on them and erase them from his life.

His teaching marked my thirties in a significant way. I had been working for more than half my lifetime, but in some ways I was still vulnerable, inexperienced in certain ways. Being thirty-something, for a woman, isn't easy. Her youth is behind her—or at least it was in my day—and even if you do something amazing, no one will ever again say: And to think she's so young!

I was starting to understand that what lay before me wasn't necessarily more new beginnings, that by then I, too, had a past I needed to come to terms with, for better or for worse. The time had come for me to face up to my shortcomings, and to either accept them, or overcome them. It was Chaplin who identified my weak point, and pointed it out to me with his proverbial frankness.

"Sophia, my dear, you have one imperfection which you must overcome if you wish to be a truly happy woman. You have to learn to say 'No.' Enough with always trying to please everyone, enough with trying to satisfy everything and everyone. 'No,' 'No,' and again 'No.' You still don't know how to say that word, and this is a serious drawback. Learning to say 'No' is of essential importance to being able to do as you please with your time. It was hard for me, too, but from the moment I got it, nothing was ever the same again: my life became much simpler."

A Countess from Hong Kong was Chaplin's last film, and also his first one in color. I will never forget his face peering through the cabin door, in a cameo appearance as the old ship steward. A small, humble appearance that comes back to me every now and again to keep me company.

LADY LOREN

Charlie Chaplin and Marlon Brando had entered my life after a series of movies that, over the course of the 1960s, had me working beside some of the most glamorous international stars: Gregory Peck, Paul Newman, Alec Guinness, Omar Sharif, Charlton Heston, and the marvelous, unforgettable, Peter Sellers.

Also in 1965, Paul Newman and I did *Lady L* together, an important, difficult movie directed by Peter Ustinov, adapted from a novel by Romain Gray, the Russian-French writer who also wrote under his pseudonym, Émile Ajar. He is the only author to have won two Prix Goncourts, one under each name. Working alongside us were David Niven and Philippe Noiret, both brilliant actors. I had the complex role of the main character, an eighty-year-old duchess who recollects her life back to the Napoleonic era. It forced me to work on myself a lot. Having to age like that was a huge challenge, because, in addition to the makeup, my voice was key. I don't remember how I managed to find it, where I got it from, but I do remember that I was very proud of the results, because I had to speak in a perfect British accent. And of course I enjoyed traveling in time, and imagining myself fifty years older.

In my treasure trove of memories, I find this beautiful letter to my mother, which I wrote at the time:

Dear Mammina,

Yesterday I rehearsed the part of an old woman and they took these three Polaroid photos of me. I'm sending them to you because when I saw them I was very moved to see how much I looked like the portrait of MAMMA in the living room.

Kisses, see you soon Sophia

(Three hours of makeup, and glue used to pull my skin.)

Life and cinema play strange tricks on you. Lady L was the same age as I am now. And yet, even today, I often feel as young as I did back then. And sometimes even younger. Perhaps it's because time is subjective, and depends on the peace you feel inside. Aging can even be fun if you know how to spend your days, if you're satisfied with what you've achieved, and you're still curious about the world around you. I wake up in the morning and try to think optimistically. I do things I can appreciate, that make sense to me. Even small things—they may not be important, but they give my days a touch that pleases and suits me.

When I was working with Peter Ustinov, he had just won an Oscar as Best Supporting Actor for *Topkapi*. He was an excellent director, strong, charismatic, and funny although his humor could be somewhat coarse. It wasn't always easy to keep up with him. Paul Newman, on the other hand, was gentle and sensitive, rather shy, but at peace with himself. He was as handsome as can be, with those eyes that gave him such a great screen presence. He was very fortunate to have had a long, peaceful, fulfilling marriage, which always kept him rooted in real life. He never put on airs, never blamed others for his own problems. He knew himself very well.

Paul always came to the set with a pile of towels. "*Chi 'o ssape' pecché?*" (Who knows why?) I'd wonder to myself.

One day I couldn't resist the temptation and I just came out and asked him, maybe a tad too impertinently: "Paul, what do you need those towels for?"

He looked at me with a big, unabashed smile: "My hands sweat, Sophia. They're always moist."

He was an adorable man, who didn't feel any need to hide his vulnerabilities.

When Omar Sharif and I worked together on the set of the very beautiful fairy tale directed by Francesco Rosi, *More Than a Miracle*, we put together a cooking contest. As I think of the food today, it still makes my mouth water.

Omar was full of life, overflowing with ideas. We had been born on the opposite shores of the Mediterranean, so we shared a love of the same fragrances, the colors, the wit. We had already made *The Fall of the Roman Empire* together, with Alec Guinness, and now it was 1967. In those days, the production company offered actors a rancid "brown bag" lunch. One day, after we were faced with another bag, Omar looked up at me with his beautiful deep, dark eyes and sighed:

"How can anyone eat this rubbish? How I'd love to be eating some of my mother's eggplants right this minute."

It was something I might have said. I burst out laughing, and raised the stakes: "You can't imagine how good *my* mother's are . . . They're the most delicious eggplants in the world!"

"Oh no, Sophia," he replied. "I'm sure that everything else you tell me is true, and Romilda might even be an excellent cook, but there's no contest when it comes to eggplants. My mother's are unsurpassable!"

"Do you want to bet?" I asked, giving him a cunning look.

So Omar called his mother in Egypt and suggested she come visit him in Rome, without telling her why. She was more than willing to do so, happy to spend some time with her son, whom she rarely managed to see. When she arrived, he showed her around, showered her with kindness, and introduced her to his Italian friends. And then, in between the lines, he launched his final attack: "Mother, next week we're having dinner with Sophia, her mother and the crew. How about cooking some eggplants?"

The woman took the task very seriously, and checked out all the stands at the market, buying an eggplant here, another one there . . . only the nicest ones. As for Mammina, she was playing in her own backyard, so it didn't take much to convince her to participate.

On the evening of the contest, we summoned the two cooks and put them to the test. We improvised a makeshift jury, one that had a healthy appetite, and it wasn't easy to choose a winner. Their recipes for eggplant parmesan were very similar. Both the Pozzuoli and Egyptian dishes melted in your mouth, with a crisp crust that tickled your palate. After having subsisted so long on leathery sandwiches, we wolfed down everything. In the end, after a long debate, Mrs. Sharif won by a slim margin. But Mammina wasn't at all upset. She'd found a friend in that likeable, warm Egyptian mother. That night she confessed to me, laughing: *"Amm' parlato sulamente 'e vuje. Pecché ogni star è bell' a' mamma soja"* (We only talked about the two of you. Because every star's a beauty in their mother's eyes).

Food makes people happy, it takes you back home, it says so many things that words can't say.

I first met Peter Sellers in 1960 on the set for *The Millionairess*, and we'd hit it off right away. A man of outstanding intelligence, Peter always knew how to surprise and overwhelm you with his charm. He never once played a scene the way you would have expected him to. He was outgoing, unpredictable, incredible fun. He could make me laugh like no one else. He had grown very fond of me and we loved working together. Our friendship would last a very long time.

The movie was freely inspired by a comedy of the same title by George Bernard Shaw. By the terms of her late father's will, the heiress Epifania cannot marry unless her husband can turn £150 into £15,000 within three months. In a melodramatic attempt at suicide, Epifania plunges into the Thames and meets an Indian doctor (played by Peter), whose mother has made him promise to marry a woman who can survive on 35 shillings for three months.

A week after we finished shooting, Peter and I holed up in

With Vittorio, to whom I owed so much.

An affectionate note from dear Audrey, congratulating me on my Oscar.

LA PAISIBLE
TOLOCHENAZ
VAUD

There are no words to tell you how happy I am for you both — the whole world rejoices for you — Brava! brava! brava! — you have had so much courage and now you have your beautiful reward — I send you three all my love.... and happiness — Audrey

1961. But there's more work to be done. Me making a funny face on the set of *Madame Sans-Gêne*.

In the fall of the same year, while making "The Lottery."

March 3, 1962. Maria's wedding, a moment of happiness for our family.

And less than a year later, in January 1963, my niece Alessandra's christening.

1963. The year we made *Yesterday, Today and Tomorrow*. I had to learn how to do a striptease. In this picture I'm with an expert from the Crazy Horse.

The original 45 rpm of "Abat-jour" by Henry Wright, the movie's striptease theme.

OGGI

ANNO XX · NUMERO 17 · 23 APRILE 1964 ★ **SETTIMANALE DI POLITICA ATTUALITÀ E CULTURA** ★ SPED. ABB. POST. GR. II · LIRE CENTO

A PAGINA 43:

Quanto costa davvero farsi una villa?

A PAGINA 24:

Dodici bambini chiedono una mamma

IN ESCLUSIVA PER "OGGI"
LE PRIME SCENE A COLORI
DI "FILUMENA MARTURANO"

Napoli. Sofia Loren ha posato per il nostro giornale coi costumi di scena del film *Filumena Marturano*, le cui riprese sono iniziate in questi giorni a Napoli con la regia di Vittorio De Sica. Sofia interpreta il personaggio di Filumena, Marcello Mastroianni quello di don Mimì. Ecco i due attori come appariranno nelle scene iniziali del film: lei con una grande chioma rossa e riccuta, lui coi baffetti e i capelli imbrillantinati. «La commedia di Eduardo De Filippo mi aveva sempre affascinato», dice Sofia Loren nell'intervista che pubblichiamo dalla pagina 52 insieme con i provini a colori in esclusiva per *Oggi*. «Fui io a suggerire a Carlo Ponti di portarla sullo schermo». All'inizio del film, Sofia ha diciassette anni; alla fine, quarantadue: cioè la versione cinematografica della commedia abbraccia tutto il doloroso cammino della vita di Filumena Marturano.

The April 23, 1964, issue of *Oggi*, launching *Marriage Italian Style*.

An article in the magazine described how I was made to look older to play the part of Filumena . . .

. . . and in this note written during the same year, I tell Mammina how I had been aged even more for *Lady L* ("three hours of makeup, with glue used to pull my skin").

A portrait I made of Carlo on the letterhead stationery from a Paris hotel . . .

HOTEL LANCASTER
7, RUE DE BERRI
CHAMPS-ÉLYSÉES
PARIS

Télégr. OTELANCAST-PARIS
TÉLÉPH. ÉLYSÉES 90·43
5 Lignes groupées
INTER. ÉLYSÉES 192

. . . and a self-portrait.

Carlo and me.

England, 1965. An image from the set of *Arabesque*, directed by Charlie Chaplin, and also starring Gregory Peck.

1964. With Vittorio while we were shooting *Marriage Italian Style*.

With Charlie Chaplin, before
appearing in a scene from
A Countess from Hong Kong. I had
to stay completely motionless so I
wouldn't wrinkle my dress.

At the press conference
for the movie.

April 9, 1966. My wedding day.

1967. With actor Vittorio Gassman while shooting *Ghosts, Italian Style* by Eduardo De Filippo.

Soon after the birth of Carlo Jr.!
The two of us are pictured here with
Alfred Eisenstaedt, our photographer.

Our friends share our joy. Among the many congratulations,
we received a telegram from Vittorio, a lovely letter from
actress Giulietta Masina, and a note from Joan Crawford.

Telegramm Télégramme Telegramma

von - de - da | No | Wörter | Aufgegeben den Consigné le Consegnato il | Stunde Heure Ora

ZCZC 27/173 ROMA FONO 27 29 1420

Erhalten - Reçu - Ricevuto

64910B ROMA I | Heure - Ora | Name - Nom - Nome | nach - à - a | Befördert - Transmis - Transmess | Stunde - Heure - Ora | Name - Nom - Nome

6357 29 16:14 No

SOHPIA PONTI

HOTEL INTERCONTINENTAL GENEVE

L

SIAMO FELICI PER LA NASCITA DEL TUO BAMBINO SPERANDO DI
ABBRACCIARVI PRESTO TUTTI ET DUE TANTI BACI   MARIA
VITTORIO MANUEL ET CHRISTIAN

PTT 740.12 XII 66 30000 A5 O 65   Auf Wunsch werden die Telegramme zutelephoniert Sur demande, les télégrammes sont téléphonés A richiesta, i telegrammi sono telefonati

Roma 9-1-'69

Sofia cara
    ho voluto scriverti,
dopo che un po' si pace ha
finalmente restituito il clamore,
e Tu puoi goderti Tuo figlio, Tuo
soltanto e di tuo padre, e non
di qualche centinaio di milio-
ni di persone -
      Tanto contenta con Te-
Il vostro incontro è stato
breve, ma io ho provato per
te subito una vivissima sim pa-
tia umana - So che cosa
significa quale incredibile
emozione di vederlo, eh, appe-
rire veramente finito, comple-
to, totale, bello, forte, così
come chi Ti vuol bene voleva
folle - Se posso invidiare un
istante della Tua vita, quello è

l'istante -
Dagli un bacio, e a Te e
a Carlo un abbraccio sin-
cero assieme a Federico
        Giulietta Masina Fellini

JOAN CRAWFORD

December 31, 1968

Darlings Sophia and Carlo,
        I am so happy to hear of the
birth of your Carlo Junior. My congratulations to all of you. Your
baby has already shown discretion in
choosing you for his parents.
        Bless you, and my love to
all of you.

        Joan

With Carlo Jr. on the set of *Man of La Mancha*.

1970. With Marcello and director Dino Risi, while shooting *The Priest's Wife*.

1973. Another year of bliss: Edoardo is born.

Chère petite maman
comme un papillon tu voltiges
d'un androit à l'autre et
comme lui tu remplis de joie
les yeux et le coeur de ce qui
te regardent mes quand en
rintrent chez, nous tu refermes
la porte derrire toi tu es
seulement à moi.
Ma chère petite maman Carlo eli

A note with a poem that Carlo Jr. wrote for me when he was at elementary school.

Here I am with my beloved Cipi & Edo.

Memories from my dear friend Richard Burton.

+ 14 NEWYORK PUB187 26 19 1525===

DEAREST SOPHIE CONGRATULATIONS ON REACHING 29 STOP GREAT SHAME
YOU ARE TOO YOUNG FOR ME STOP DOST LOVE = RICHARD ++++

Richard Burton

Dearest Dost and Divine Ashes,

Have read script. What on earth ever persuaded anybody
to do it without me? Incredible impertinence. I shall
see you in one week from today. I love you, of course,
but it's also a fine piece for much as I love I wouldn't
do it otherwise.

The metteur-en-scene seems very nice but very nervous.
Is he alright to work with? I expect there'll be some
nonsense with the "Churchill" people but we'll let
Frings and the other idiots work that out. I love you.

Im completely recovered from my recent madness and have
rarely felt so content. Elizabeth will never be out of
my bones but she is, at last, out of my head. Such love
as I had has turned to pity. She is an awful mess and
there's nothing I can do about it without destroying myself.
I love you.

I'm looking forward to seeing you with immense eagerness.
And Cipi and Eduardo and Inez and Pasta and Carlo and
even England. It's quite a long time since I've been
there. I was surprised at how long.it's been.

This time I shall be a good actor for you. I was a bloody
idiot last time.

See you in a week.

            Love, Richard

I forgot to mention that I love you.

The photograph that Richard dedicated "To my beloved Cipi."

To my beloved "Cipi." This is Uncle Richard when he was a bit younger and you and Eduardo and E'en So were not even born! Que cosa incredible!

Richard.

A note I wrote about the charm of his gaze: "Eyes are an actor's most important tool because they have direct emotional control over an audience. Burton would hypnotize you with his eyes."

Two images from the set of *The Voyage*, also made in 1973, my last movie with Vittorio.

1977. Marcello and I, together again in *A Special Day*.

The letter I wrote from prison to the then president of the Italian Republic, Sandro Pertini.

1991. Gregory Peck presented me with an Honorary Oscar for "a
career rich with memorable performances."

FRANK SINATRA
1041 N FORMOSA AVE
HOLLYWOOD CA 90046 26AM

WESTERN UNION | MAILGRAM®

1-017253S085 03/26/91 ICS IPMRNCZ CSP LSAC
2138502444 MGMS TDRN HOLLYWOOD CA 24 03-26 0639P EST

▶ MS SOPHIA LOREN
1151 HIDDEN VALLEY RD
THOUSAND OAKS CA 91630

BRAVA...SOPHIA...BRAVA...
AM DELIGHTED FOR YOU AND I SEND YOU MUCH LOVE.
FRANK SINATRA

18:38 EST

MGMCOMP

The telegram I received from Frank Sinatra congratulating me.

Paris, le 5 Mai 1993

Madame Sofia LOREN

COMPAGNIE DE MIME
**MARCEL
MARCEAU**

Chère Amie, *chère Sofia Loren*

Ayant été élu en 1991 à l'Académie des Beaux-Arts au fauteuil de Germain Bazin, je dois suivre les traditions de cette vénérable institution.

L'une de mes obligations est de constituer un "Comité de l'Epée" parrainé par des personnalités de mes amis, et j'ai pensé à vous qui avez joué un rôle important dans ma vie artistique. J'aimerais que vous répondiez très simplement à ma proposition de devenir Membre d'Honneur de ce Comité.

Je n'ai pas interrompu mes activités depuis mon élection et ai déjà du retarder de plusieurs mois mon installation sous la coupole. La date étant irrévocablement fixée au 27 Octobre prochain, mon bureau apprécierait une réponse rapide à cette lettre, afin de mettre en place l'organisation de cet évènement.

Dans l'attente de votre réponse, que j'espère favorable, je vous prie de croire, Chère Amie, à mon amitié fidèle.

Et avec toute mon admiration
Je reste votre fidèle
ami

Marcel Marceau

32, RUE DE LONDRES - 75009 PARIS
TÉL. 42 80 48 32 - FAX 48 74 91 87

A letter, including some illustrations, written by Marcel Marceau in 1993, inviting me to enter the Comité de l'Épée, the Society of the Sword.

1994. With Marcello on the set of *Ready to Wear*.

With Giorgio Armani.

At a fashion show
with my dear friend
Roberta Armani.

1999. I presented Roberto Benigni with his Oscar for *Life Is Beautiful*.

Two scenes from *Human Voice*, my latest movie, thanks to Edoardo.

My most beautiful portrait, as a grandmother.

the Abbey Road studios—yes, the very same studios of Beatles fame—to record *Goodness Gracious Me*, a single conceived by George Martin, their legendary record producer, to promote the movie. It rose to the top of the charts in just a few weeks, which encouraged us to do another. The next hit was *Bangers and Mash*, which told the amusing story of the marriage between a British soldier and a Neapolitan woman. Food joined us and divided us in this duet. Whenever Peter/Joe wanted his mother's cooking, sausages and mash in Cockney sauce, I would, instead, cook minestrone, macaroni, tagliatelle, and vermicelli. It was one improvisation and laugh after another, resounding in the song's every note.

Ironically, while we were shooting *The Millionairess*, my path crossed with that of The Cat, a notorious thief, or, rather, The Cat's path crossed with that of my jewelry. *All* of my jewelry. After spending a night at the Ritz, where I had been able to leave my black jewelry box in the hotel safe, we moved into the Norwegian Barn, a cottage located inside the Country Club in Hertfordshire. A small world followed me everywhere from set to set, including Basilio and Ines, Livia, the cook, and a hairdresser. Basilio, who was worried about the jewelry, had asked for a night guard, but the club secretary had confidently replied: "This is England, not Naples, you have nothing to worry about!"

We took possession of the cottage, and each of us settled into his or her own room. My room, which was on the upper floor, had a large, brightly lit wardrobe adjoining it. That's where the thief hid, while we were all still inside the house, like some subtle, silent gust of wind, lying in wait for the right moment to blow. That evening, when I went to pick up Carlo at the airport, while Basilio and Ines were watching TV and chatting, The Cat slipped out of the wardrobe upstairs and took away all the precious pieces of my life.

When we got back, at around eleven, we went up to the bedroom. It was late, and we had a hard day's work ahead of us. As soon as we got in I could tell something wasn't right and looked around, trying to figure out what it was. When I saw that the dresser drawer was open, and so was the window right next to it, at last, I understood. I felt faint. "*Uh maronna mia!* (Holy Mary)," I managed to blurt out. "I can't believe it . . ." My diamonds, my sapphires, my pearls and rubies, my fondest memories, had all of them taken flight through the window.

I had become able at last, thanks to my work, to buy jewelry for myself, and Carlo would give me a present each time I finished making a movie. Behind each pair of earrings, ring, necklace, was a story. Each piece represented hard work, a new achievement. The pieces of jewelry were my medals that signified my victories.

We called Scotland Yard and the police came right over, but the thief had taken off, and they never did manage to catch him. (A long time later, when, the crime was described publicly, The Cat actually wrote me a letter signing it with that name. And that was how I imagined him, a cat moving around stealthily, all dressed in black, one of Cary Grant's stand-ins in *To Catch a Thief*.)

At first, I could hardly control myself, my head was spinning, I felt like I'd been violated. I knew in my mind that there are far worse things in life, but it was as if someone had entered my head, my heart, to rob me of my accomplishments and above all the hard work I'd done to achieve them. Each piece had reminded me not only of the movies I'd worked on, but of all the emotions at the time. I could relive everything by wearing a necklace around my neck or a ring on my finger.

When I finally went to bed, it was almost dawn, but the next day I went to the set, as if nothing had happened. I had a sense of duty and it was important to honor my commitment, and to show my respect for my colleagues and their time. And in my work I could find the order that the robbery had stolen from me. By doing what I knew how and had to do, I had the impression of regaining control.

That morning, during a break from the shooting, the crew gathered all around me.

"What is it?" I asked, a little frightened at the small crowd. I was still very much on edge.

Peter Ustinov handed me a small silver package with a gold ribbon around it. Inside it was a beautiful brooch, which my fellow workers had decided to give me as a sign of their affection, to let me know they were with me. Their generous, thoughtful gesture made me realize that nothing is ever really lost, that there were going to be lots of other movies to make, celebrate, remember. And to wear.

But once more it was De Sica who had the last word about this episode, and who offered me the most precious gem of all.

Vittorio was in London for a few days to do a small part with us. As soon as he heard about the theft, he came to visit me and to see how I was. He found me in tears in the privacy of my bedroom. Still upset, I was sitting on the bed, and I kept looking at the dresser, the window, the emptiness that The Cat had left behind. Vittorio sat down next to me and handed me his handkerchief.

"Donna Sofi, don't shed your tears in vain. We're both Neapolitans, born in poverty. Money comes, and then it goes. Think of all the money I gamble away at the casino . . ."

"What are you saying, Vittò? *Nun aje capito* (You don't understand). Those jewels were a part of me . . ."

"Sofi, listen to me. Never shed tears for something that cannot shed tears for you."

XI

COMINGS AND GOINGS

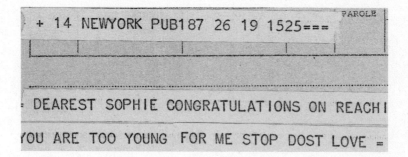

+ 14 NEWYORK PUB187 26 19 1525=== PAROLE

= DEAREST SOPHIE CONGRATULATIONS ON REACHI

YOU ARE TOO YOUNG FOR ME STOP DOST LOVE =

THE MIRACLE

As my memories skip from one to another, they take me back to January 1969 to the Geneva hospital where Dr. de Watteville brought about my own new life as a mother.

I can safely say that I was born a second time on the day my first child was born. I was completely overcome by emotion when I held him in my arms. For years, this had been my greatest wish. In order to enjoy that long-sought feeling as much as I could, or maybe for fear of waking up from this marvelous dream, I shut myself up in my room at the hospital. It was warm inside, and I felt safe, me and him, alone together, in a soft cocoon of endless gazes, nursing, and caresses. The nurses pampered us, took care of us, and calmed my concerns.

We were still in the very middle of the star system, and Carlo Jr. was being treated like a royal baby. So the outside world was greedy for a show. A sea of photographers and cameramen had arrived from every corner of the planet, and crowded the area all around the hospital, but couldn't really touch us inside. Of course, keeping that world at bay was no simple task, but Carlo was able to give them what they wanted while keeping the rest private for us.

A press conference was organized, to please them all in one go. The records show that the noisiest of all the paparazzi were the Italians, of course, the most determined the British, the most organized the Germans, who had two helicopters and a private plane, the best informed the Americans, the cleverest the Japanese, who had chosen a woman as head of the crew, someone who would find it easier to "penetrate" this mother's heart.

I made my entrance into the crowded room, carried there on the bed I'd given birth in, holding my baby in my arms, my eyes tired and at last happy. Next to me were my defenders: on one side Carlo, on the other my sister, Maria, who had flown in from Rome for the big event.

The reporters barraged me with questions. They seemed almost as excited as I was. After all, emotion is contagious, and wherever there's a newborn baby everything exudes the scent of a miracle having taken place.

"Who does he look like?"

"Whose eyes does he have?"

"What about his mouth?"

"How much does he weigh?"

"Sophia, Sophia, how do you feel?"

"Were you afraid?"

"Has your milk come in?"

"Was it more or less exciting than winning an Oscar?"

"When do you think you'll be heading back to the set?"

I looked at them smiling, but then I'd bow my head over Cipi—as I had started calling him. "*Quanto si' bbello*" (You're so beautiful), I thought. His face was round, his tiny hands grasped one of my fingers. He was a bundle of warmth that felt like heaven. Everything else was a blur—it lost its importance, as if it really didn't have anything to do with me.

While holding a child in your arms, you can feel both strong and vulnerable at the same time. It's an intoxicating feeling, one that makes your head spin, and that you keep within you forever.

My existence had unexpectedly taken on a deeper meaning, a kind of stability that was both fragile and fulfilling. I was afraid to go out, worried about my little one catching cold. And I simply didn't feel like going home yet. And so, day after day, I grew increasingly rooted to my clean white room, shielded from all danger, refusing to think about tomorrow.

My doctor, de Watteville, gently prepared me and pushed me back out, after fifty days, which seemed to go by in a flash.

"Sophia, you can't stay here forever, life is waiting for the two of you out there . . ."

At first, I just looked at him, terrified, but little by little, I gave in.

After nine months of not being able to move, and almost two months of cocoonlike postpartum, the time had come for me to go forth and face reality. But this reality, unlike a story in a movie, had no script. My story as a mother, Cipi's as a son, were entirely to be invented.

I realized that I needed someone who could help me emerge from my shell so that I could go back to the world, but I found all the young women that were introduced to me to be unsuitable. My son's potential nannies were all too showy, or else they seemed to be half-undressed, all lace and trimmings, like improbable bathing beauties. "Just where do they think they're going? This isn't an audition for Cinecittà," I said to myself, incredulous at their exuberant displays. I needed someone who was reliable, calm, who understood my happiness and could focus on the baby completely. And above all, someone who wasn't impulsive.

One morning, looking out the window in my room, I caught sight of a baby carriage in the garden, shrouded in the winter fog, being pushed by a nurse who I thought was imprudent, to say the least.

I thought to myself, "How can anyone take a newborn baby out for a walk at this time of day, in such cold weather? Has she gone out of her mind? I wouldn't dream of placing my child in the care of someone like that."

The following day Dr. de Watteville came into my room triumphant. He had found someone who could accompany me out into the world and give me the courage to vacate the room. After all, there were other women who had babies about to be born.

Peering in from behind him was Ruth Bapst, a nurse with an experienced, kind air about her, but as soon as I saw her I recognized her as the crazy woman pushing the baby carriage in the fog . . . I was somewhat aloof when I greeted her, because in my mind I had already crossed her name off the list.

Ruth wasn't discouraged, though, and she held out her hand, competent and professional. I looked at her sincere smile, her simple manner, her direct gaze. In her eyes I could read her love of children, her desire to work. My inner magnet, that mysterious ability I've always had to attract and recognize the right people, those most suited to me, started vibrating, contradicting my earlier judgment. "We can give it a try," I managed to say, a little hesitant.

Ruth came to be known as Ninni in our family, and she is still with us today, after forty-six years. She helped me raise my children, and now she dotes on their children, with the same enthusiasm as ever.

With her by my side, I was able to leave the hospital for our villa in Marino.

THE TWO SIDES OF PARADISE

In 1962, we had bought Villa Sara, a sixteenth-century estate lost amid the olive trees of the Castelli region. Half an hour's drive south of Rome, it appeared to be an oasis of tranquillity and silence that wiped away all the confusion of the city, the set, public life, and gave back to us peace and quiet. Wherever I laid my eyes I was intoxicated by beauty. Floors covered with Roman mosaics, luxurious gardens with marble fountains, antique furniture, and precious furnishings decorating the many rooms.

The frescoed walls gave me dreams with their depictions of great banquets, hunting scenes, decorative garlands bearing fruit and flowers, and more animals, trees, stars—all set within Italy's gentle landscape. This was so much better than the movies! Looking at everything around me was always cause for celebration.

After two major refurbishments of the villa, we moved out of our apartment in Piazza d'Aracoeli, where we'd spent the night of my Oscar, and into the Villa Sara. In 1964 we moved to Paris, but went back to the villa for short periods as often as we could. The villa's magical interweaving of art and nature offered a beautiful environment.

Nothing, of course, compared with the miracle of Carlo Jr., who was growing and starting to smile his first smiles. He lifted his arms whenever he wanted to be picked up and watched the leaves in the trees shaken by the wind with a sense of wonder.

At last I was happy. For the first time in my life I had everything I wanted. If I could have stopped time I would have chosen that very moment, at Villa Sara, sitting around the edge of the swimming pool as my son splashed water everywhere in his duck-shaped life preserver. The pool had been built in an asymmetrical shape so that we wouldn't have to sacrifice a beautiful apricot tree that Carlo had fallen in love with. At the end of my deck chair lay a script, which reminded me of my duties. Comforted by two artificial waterfalls I'd had installed to keep me company, I could lose myself in thought.

I want to make it perfectly clear that it hadn't been easy for me to get used to so much magnificence. At first, I'd felt intimidated by the splendor of the villa, and I would often seek refuge in my bedroom, surrounded by my magazines and my movies. Carlo helped me get over it.

"Sophia, houses are like people, you have to approach them nice and slowly, get to know them well . . ."

And he was right. Soon afterward the villa and I began to understand and love each other.

Like every paradise, the villa had its dark side, too. It was isolated, and therefore not without its dangers, a place that attracted petty criminals and even some people who were delusional. One in particular had scared us. After escaping from a psychiatric institution, a man crept into the garden one morning and almost made it to the patio around the swimming pool. He was holding some papers and wanted to set fire to everything. He was shouting at the top of his voice that Cipi was his, and that he'd come to take him away. "I want my son, I want my son!" he ranted. He got as far as the door to the house, which he struck with an ax.

It was fairly easy to calm him down, but he fell prey to his obsession once more and showed up again. He escaped from the psychiatric hospital on several occasions and bombarded me with letters. We kept an eye on his whereabouts, without letting ourselves be overwhelmed, but the fear stuck with me, a profound feeling of uneasiness that was hard to live with. During that period many kidnappings were being committed in Italy. And they often ended in tragedy.

Besides riding out various empty threats, Carlo himself risked being kidnapped on two occasions, and only managed to save himself thanks to his quick reflexes and the timely intervention of the police. One evening he was on his way home from the office, driving down the Appia Antica. Suddenly, a car cut him off, forcing him to stop. Glancing quickly into the rearview mirror, he saw that another car had blocked him from behind. The car door suddenly swung open and a man, whose face was covered, jumped out, running in his direction and pointing a rifle at him.

Carlo was always very sure of himself and had fast reflexes. He was accustomed to making quick decisions in emergency situations. He slammed on the accelerator and took off, burning rubber, almost hitting the car that was blocking his way. From behind, the man started shooting, but Carlo, bending down over the steering wheel, refused to be frightened. When he finally got home, his Alfa Romeo was riddled with bullet holes, looking like something out of the war.

The only thing the police could do was warn him for the future.

"Doc, don't hesitate to call us when you know you'll be going home late."

And that's how it came to be that the second time, again on Appia Antica, when Carlo saw a strange fire blazing not too far away he started worrying. A few minutes later a car drove up beside him and tried to run him off the road, but a police car came out from nowhere and put the kidnappers to flight. Because that's exactly what they were. At Villa Sara, hidden among the shrubbery, the investigators found a van without a license plate and the engine running. Inside the trunk were ropes, packing tape, syringes, and chloroform. Everything that was needed for a kidnapping in grand style. It was simply too much for us. So in 1974 we decided to move to Paris with both of our sons, because by that time we had our second, Edoardo.

I had had a terrible scare like Carlo's, myself, a few years earlier in New York when Cipi was still very small. It was October 1970 and we were staying in a suite on the twenty-second floor of Hampshire House, in the heart of Manhattan, whose large windows overlooked Central Park all dressed in its blaze of fall colors. Carlo's son Alex from his first marriage lived there, as did Greta Garbo, who, unfortunately, I never ran into. We were in the United States for the launch of *Sunflower*, which I'd made with Vittorio and Marcello. Carlo had had to rush back to Milan because his father, to whom he was very close, was dying. I had stayed on alone with Ines, Ninni, and Cipi.

The morning after Carlo's departure I was awakened by some strange noises that sounded like stifled screaming. I couldn't understand what was happening, and, still drowsy, I thought that maybe I was dreaming. I took out the earplugs I was accustomed to sleeping with and heard the screaming again. This time it was much clearer. As I tried to figure out whether I was really awake or still sleeping, two men barged into my room: one was the hotel concierge, who was holding a huge bunch of keys, looking like someone who'd just come back from the dead—he'd obviously been forced to open the door to my room against his will; the other man, standing behind him, was holding something that at first sight I thought was a stethoscope. *Oh, my God, my son's not well,* was my first thought. But in fact, it was a real gun, not a stethoscope.

"This is a robbery," the man with the "stethoscope" barked at me, like in some third-rate detective movie.

I pretended I couldn't understand what he was saying, but this made him even more nervous.

He held the gun to the side of my head and screamed: "Quit fooling around!" The situation was unreal. The thief looked like he was dressed for Mardi Gras, with a wig, a fake moustache, and sunglasses, but the weapon didn't look like a fake at all. His eyes were even bluer than Paul Newman's. A few feet away, in the other room, was my fragile, helpless child.

"Move it and start getting the jewelry out," shouted the thief, as he searched everywhere for the loot. Van Cleef & Arpels had lent me a set of jewelry to wear to the Rockefeller gala that evening. *"How could he possibly know?"* I wondered, confused, overcome with fear, but the thought of Cipi encouraged me to tell him everything: "They're in a bag in the bottom dresser drawer." The blue-eyed thief frantically followed my instructions, found the diamond and ruby bracelet, with the matching necklace and earrings, and stuffed them into his pocket. But it still wasn't what he was looking for.

"All this is peanuts . . . I want the ring, the ring, the one you wore on TV . . ."

I finally realized what he was talking about and cursed myself for my vanity. During the long interview Marcello and I had done with David Frost a few nights before, I had shown off a gorgeous diamond, also from Van Cleef & Arpels, which I had given right back right to them. Worth more or less 500,000 dollars, it was now putting both my life and the priceless life of my son at risk. I tried to explain, but he grabbed me by the hair and threw me to the ground.

"Where's the kid?" he shouted, making my blood freeze.

I panicked, but his partner, on the lookout in the next room, was even more frightened and yelled, "Let's get outta here!" As they ran off with the jewelry from Van Cleef & Arpels, I threw a bag with all my own jewelry at them. I don't know why I did it, maybe it was a form of catharsis, maybe a provocation. Or maybe it was a kind of plea, hoping that they would take the whole situation far away from us as soon as possible.

I ran to Cipi and hugged him tightly, collapsing in tears. I swore to myself that from now on the only precious jewels I'd wear would be my son's embrace.

THE (IM)POSSIBLE DREAM

When Edoardo was born, he doubled the happiness that I thought could never be repeated. It is yet another unfathomable mystery of motherhood.

I got pregnant with Edoardo while I was shooting *Man of La Mancha* with Peter O'Toole. Adapted from Dale Wasserman's huge Broadway success, it was the first and last musical of my life (except for a small part in *Nine*). It's the story of Miguel de Cervantes, the great Spanish novelist and author of *Don Quix-*

ote, who has been thrown into a dungeon by the Spanish Inquisition, and distracts his cell mates by putting on a play about Don Quixote and his love for the servant Aldonza, whom he imagines to be the noblewoman Dulcinea.

An extraordinary actor, Peter had an uncontainable, nonconformist intelligence. He was as funny as a great comedian and as intense as a character in a tragedy. It was wonderful working beside him. I hung on his every word, filled with admiration. When he acted it sounded like he was singing. And yet, when he really did have to sing, he had trouble. Neither one of us was a professional singer, and we were perfectly aware of this. To be honest, we were scared out of our wits.

Most of the movie was filmed in the studio in Rome, but we had to sing on the set, too, because, as in every self-respecting musical, the songs were part and parcel with the action. One morning, just as the shooting was about to begin, I found myself completely voiceless, unable to utter a single word, worse than Marlon Brando standing before Charlie Chaplin's icy rage. Peter took me aside and declared: "There's no point in getting worked up, Sophia. This is clearly a form of psychosomatic laryngitis . . ."

I tried to defend myself but his sly smile wouldn't let me off the hook. However, when the nurse gave me a thermometer and we saw that I had a temperature of 102 degrees, I found the courage to argue again.

"You see, Peter, there's nothing psychosomatic about my laryngitis, I have the flu!" I managed to whisper, in some ways reassured about my mental health.

But he wouldn't back down: "What are you saying, Sophia, it's fear, the fear of having to sing in front of all these people."

Peter was right, of course, although two days later, in the familiar atmosphere of the set, I managed to make it to the end of the song smoothly. He, on the other hand, couldn't shake off his nervousness after playing around with Freud. When the time came to sing "The Impossible Dream," the recurring theme of the film, a famous standard sung by Frank Sinatra, Elvis Presley, Jacques Brel, and Plácido Domingo, among others, he wanted me by his side. We were companions in glory and misfortune.

During breaks on the set, I would challenge him to a game of Scrabble. Ironically, even though he was the erudite Shakespearean and I just a Neapolitan on the visiting team, I thrashed him. Maybe it all depended on the fact that, although I'd quit school early, I'd had enough time to get a feel for the rudiments of Latin, and this allowed me to invent words that I often got right. We had so much fun! Or maybe I should say, I had so much fun at his expense!

My most vivid memory, however, is focused on a very clear, precise image. One evening, he knocked on the door to my suite, where I was staying with Ninni and Cipi. When we got to the door we found him wearing an outlandish green tunic, his arms outstretched like some Christ figure on the cross. "Can I come and keep you company?" Peter was totally mad, in that creative, affectionate kind of madness that changes your way of seeing the world.

When we finished shooting, I found out I was expecting Edoardo. The news found me much better prepared than the first time. The stage dressmaker gave me the estrogen injections I needed and I didn't stop working until I was in my fifth month. In September 1972, I took a plane to Geneva to be near the clinic and wait out the remaining months in peace. I read, cooked, and watched TV. And I made room inside my heart for the arrival of another great love. Although the context was much more serene than before, the many emotions I went through were exactly the same as the first time around. De Watteville chose to perform a C-section again, because he didn't want to take any risks, given my history. I felt the healthy fear that affects every mother before giving birth, a fear composed of excitement and amazement before the greatest miracle of nature. Just like Carlo's, Edoardo's birth was the most wonderful gift life could offer me. Until the arrival of my grandchildren.

When Edo came into the world on January 6, 1973, as beautiful as any baby can be, my Don Quixote came to see me with an extraordinary ostrich egg, signed: "With all my love, Peter." I kept it on my nightstand for a long time, the surreal memory of a dear, eccentric friend.

UNCLE RICHARD

Speaking of dear, somewhat eccentric friends, that same spring of 1973 a special guest arrived at Villa Sara, who brought cheer to our daily routine, and in some ways complicated it. Richard Burton had been chosen by Carlo to act with me in *The Voyage*, directed by De Sica. It would be Vittorio's last movie.

One morning in April, I had just finished breast-feeding and was sitting on the balcony enjoying the timid arrival of the spring. Edo, finally satiated, had fallen asleep, while Cipi insistently demanded my attention to make up for the presence of that little brother. It was then that Ines handed me the phone.

"Sophia? Is it you? This is Richard speaking."

"Richard?"

"Yes, Richard, Richard Burton!"

We had not yet met, and I wasn't expecting his phone call, but his forthright manner, his openness pleased me. *And what a voice.* It made you forget everything else and concentrate on what he had to say.

I couldn't wait to meet one of the gods of my Olympus, but had expected that it would be when we began to work together. Richard, instead, took one step further.

"If you agree, I could come and stay with you before we start shooting. You know, I have to get back in shape and I don't really feel like living out of a hotel . . . They wouldn't leave me be."

Burton's tormented relationship with Elizabeth Taylor had been filling the gossip columns, and the reporters and paparazzi weren't going to leave such a juicy prey alone. Villa Sara, on the other hand, had lovely guest quarters, which allowed us to host friends and relatives so that we wouldn't get in each other's way.

"You're welcome here, Richard," I answered without hesitating, happy to be of some help.

He arrived with a whole entourage, including a doctor, a nurse, and a secretary. He was trying to quit drinking, as well as to get over his love for his beautiful violet-eyed Cleopatra. He could talk of no one and nothing else, and I listened to him patiently. He often ate with me and the children on the patio around the swimming pool, and we soon became friends. Cipi had absolutely fallen in love with him, and together they were an odd pair.

In my treasure trove of memories—which is starting to empty out—I find a lovely photograph of Richard dressed for the stage, which he sent to his young friend a few years later.

> To my beloved "Cipi,"
> This is Uncle Richard when he was a bit younger and
> you and Edoardo and E'en So were not even born! Que
> cosa incredibile!
> Richard.

These few words are enough to bring back his voice, his warmth, his intelligence.

Born in Wales, the twelfth of the thirteen children of a coal miner, Richard had made it to Oxford University where he had studied drama. Always torn between cinema and theater, and being a womanizer and heavy drinker from youth, he'd fallen in love with Elizabeth Taylor on the set for *Cleopatra*, and a few months later, in 1964, left his wife to marry her. But in the early months of 1973, their marriage had reached a crisis that would lead to their divorce a year later. They remarried in 1975, only to divorce once more, for good this time, in 1976.

During his stay with us in Marino, Richard was a bundle of nerves, maybe because of the detox diet he had subjected himself to. But all the same he was very likable, brilliant, affectionate, always pouring out ideas and quotations. His love and profound knowledge of literature always came through and made him unique company.

And yet he, too, fell victim to my skill at Scrabble. I know, it's hard to accept. Despite his immense knowledge and huge vocabulary, he succumbed to my supremacy, just as Peter had. He'd look at me in dismay when faced with the evidence and I'd chuckle with satisfaction.

We'd play to while away the time, as we waited for the first "Action!" But shortly before we began shooting *The Voyage*, De Sica's health got worse and he was forced to have surgery, which postponed the start of everything for a month. By then, Richard had become one of the family, Cipi called him Uncle, and Edoardo would look at him with his mouth wide open and the wonder typical of toddlers. Although we were both very worried about Vittorio, we nurtured this domestic friendship of ours, which consisted of games, pranks, and sharing secrets. Richard seemed to have found a balance, although it wasn't to last long.

On the Friday before we were about to resume shooting, he got a phone call, a fateful one, from Liz in Los Angeles.

"I'm being operated on tomorrow, Richard, you must come."

"You have to be joking," I wanted to say, but I held my tongue. After all, it was his life and it was better if I kept out of it.

He probably read my mind when he saw my face, and just gave me a helpless look, as if he were saying, "What can I do? Of course I can't say no."

Carlo understood the situation, and, as usual, settled things once and for all. "Go on, go ahead, as long as you're back on the set on Monday morning."

Richard left, flying fifteen hours on the way over, and another fifteen back, just to hold her hand for a few minutes. But he fulfilled his duty, was at peace with himself, and made sure he was there for the first "Action" on Monday.

Liz joined him in Rome a few weeks later to spend some time with us, and the rest of the time in a hotel. She was a rogue wave, a loose electron, an arrow aimed straight for his ailing heart, that's what she was for him.

When we started shooting *The Voyage*, although Richard was there, his mind was wandering elsewhere, in search of a solution to his problems.

He finally found one, albeit temporary, a while later, and he wasted no time letting me know. We were getting ready to be together once more on the set for *Brief Encounter*, the remake of a famous movie directed by David Lean that we were to shoot in 1974 under the direction of Alan Bridges, when he wrote me this letter. In it he's as always facetious, but he also knows how to talk about himself in an authentic, profound way, and rejoice in the friendship that united us:

> *Have read script. What on earth ever persuaded anybody to do it without me? Incredible impertinence. I shall see you in one week from today. I love you, of course, but it's also a fine piece for much as I love I wouldn't do it otherwise . . .*
>
> *I'm completely recovered from my recent madness and have rarely felt so content. Elizabeth will never be out of*

*my bones but she is, at last, out of my head. Such love as
I had has turned to pity. She is an awful mess and there's
nothing I can do about it without destroying myself. I love
you.*

*I'm looking forward to seeing you with immense
eagerness. And Cipi and Edoardo and Inez and Pasta and
Carlo and even England. It's quite a long time since I've
been there. I was surprised at how long.*

*This time I shall be a good actor for you. I was a bloody
idiot last time.*

See you in a week.

Love,

Richard

I forgot to mention that I love you.

CIAO VITTORIO

Four years before *The Voyage*, when I had just become a mother,
I had gone back to the set for *Sunflower*. It was the fall of 1969,
and while the world was being rocked with protests, we were
traveling between Milan and Russia to make a movie. However,
for me it was like being back with the family again, in the garden
of my home. The three musketeers were together once more:
Vittorio, Marcello, and me. Special guest Carlo Jr. playing himself, my son, in real life *and* in the movie. So small, he was the
ideal travel companion. I could take him everywhere with me,
and in any case, I couldn't stand to be away from him for long.

Sunflower went back to the war we'd known in Italy, and then
broadened its horizons as far as Russia, to the great retreat, to
a soldier named Antonio who, almost frozen to death, is saved
by a local girl with whom he builds a new family. His Italian
wife goes looking for him and, eventually, finds him. There's a

heartbreaking scene between the two women who are overcome by the same pain. In the middle of it all was Marcello Mastroianni who, once again, did his best to personify a man without qualities. Like Dummì in *Marriage Italian Style* and like Adelina's husband worn out by too many children in *Yesterday, Today and Tomorrow*.

Vittorio wasn't well; lung cancer was slowing spreading through his body. Yet he hadn't lost his eye for detail, his love of children—whether Russian or Neapolitan, little did it matter—his skill at describing the everyday toil of women, the heartbreak of farewells said at the station, the tragedies of love frustrated by life's violence.

Cipi—and I'm not exaggerating—acted perfectly, and the film was a hit, especially in the United States. Watching it again today, the bright yellow color of the sunflowers, fertilized by the bodies of millions of soldiers, Russian, Italian, German, sent off to die who knows why, it seems like a final appeal to life, a glimmer of hope, a touch of color in a world that slowly grows dimmer before the last great journey.

And indeed the title of Vittorio's last movie was *The Voyage*, shot between October 1973 and January 1974, starring Richard and me. The movie was inspired by a short story by Pirandello, played out between Sicily, Naples, and Venice at the dawning of the First World War. It's a story of love and death, the classic Italian melodrama. Vittorio was sick, Richard had other things on his mind, and I was more of a mother than an actress. And yet it was a lovely story that moved its audiences, and was once again a hit abroad.

Two days before finishing, while leafing through the set photos with Vittorio, I came across a beautiful shot of him.

"Vittò, what a beautiful picture. Write something nice for me!"

He looked at me tenderly, and complied: "Sofì, Sofì, when you were fifteen you said yes to me."

This is one of the pictures that persuaded me to take this long journey down memory lane.

When the shooting ended in January 1974, I kept working hard, going from *Verdict*, with Jean Gabin, to the TV movie *Brief Encounter*, with Richard Burton, until I met Marcello again in *Sex Pot*. But my thoughts were always with Vittorio.

On November 13, Carlo called me and, upon hearing a tone in his voice, my first instinct was to hang up. I didn't feel like listening to what he had to say to me, something that I already knew deep down inside. And that was it—De Sica had died, in Paris, just a few miles from my house. We were close and yet very far away, on opposite shores of the same river where our story had flowed together.

He died in the American Hospital and his family gave precise orders that their privacy be respected, which meant that even his dearest friends were not to intrude. I felt helpless, frozen in my pain. I didn't know which way to turn, what to do, how to find relief. One thing was sure, however, I couldn't stay home like that without saying good-bye to him before he left for Rome.

I called the hospital once, a dozen, a hundred times, and the answer was always the same: "I'm sorry, Signora, it's impossible."

After countless attempts to make contact, I finally found an opportunity to sneak into the hospital. A compliant hospital worker escorted me to the morgue, but it was locked. From the window, I could see his coffin, which had already been sealed. Next to it was a cot, where his body had lain until shortly before. Where his head had rested I noticed a stain from the pomade he always wore. Suddenly, I could smell its fragrance in my mind, and I started crying, harder than I'd ever cried before.

NEITHER A SOLDIER, A HUSBAND, NOR A FATHER

Without De Sica, I was convinced that I would never work again. Or rather, I thought that though I might act again, I would never again find a role that would win me over and make me soar. If Vittorio had still been alive, I'm sure that seeing me in *A Special Day* would have made him proud. After all, I could never have played Antonietta if I hadn't first played Cesira, Adelina, and Filumena.

In 1977, Ettore Scola, a great filmmaker, rigorous, eloquent, idealistic, presented Carlo with the screenplay for *A Special Day*. The story sounded like it had been written specially for Marcello and me. Delicate and profoundly human, it spoke to us of our lives, about those of us who had experienced the war.

That "special day" was May 6, 1938, when Rome, disguised as the capital of an empire, and Mussolini welcomed the Führer with a huge carnival parade. The whole city flocked to the streets. Everyone or almost everyone. There were a few who preferred not to go out, who chose to stay indoors in the building on Via XXI Aprile, a large tenement building that spoke of conformism and normality. There, stuck in the folds of the regime, are Gabriele, a radio broadcaster who has just been fired for his anti-Fascist ideas and his homosexuality and is about to be deported to the border, and Antonietta, a weary housewife, a mother of an army of young *ballila*, the name for the members of a Fascist youth organization, consumed by a solitude she isn't even aware of.

When Antonietta follows her mynah bird that has escaped from the balcony, she and Gabriele end up on the rooftop, in between the sheets drying under the sun. Their encounter is intense but reserved, and lets us glimpse that, behind the dark circles under their eyes, a few steps of the rumba, the coffee beans scattered on the floor, there is a desire to explore different emotions, to emerge from stereotypes, to change their lives even by a fraction.

While Gabriele and Antonietta brush past each other, confessing their own limits and weaknesses, the radio, the third character in the movie, broadcasts the pounding noise of the parade, and the custodian of the building watches over everything in a permanent rage to make sure that nothing changes. And yet she, too, this embittered person left in charge that day, realizes that their timid encounter, like any encounter, will break rules.

Aging and despondent, Antonietta falls in love with her gentle neighbor. Previously, her only hobby was to paste pictures of Mussolini in a photo album, and Gabriele tells her that he doesn't match any of the Fascist models she thinks she believes in. He whispers to her that he is neither a soldier, a husband, nor a father. He's just a man.

Carlo found it hard to finance the movie, but managed to find backers in Canada, so we could start shooting. But Marcello and I had come to symbolize youth and beauty, so playing the parts of two deliberately marginalized and subdued characters was a huge challenge. Scola was a good friend of Marcello, and had no doubts about him, but he did have some about me. He was afraid that my exuberant physique wouldn't be able to fit into the role of a demure woman without makeup who wore a faded cotton housedress.

I instantly felt his lack of confidence, and the first few days of shooting weren't easy. I felt that the character belonged to me, but I still needed the director's trust to be able to find the key to enter her mind and body.

After a few days, without my knowing, Carlo called Ettore.

"Scola, ciao. It's Ponti. What's going on? You made Sophia cry."

"Who me?" he answered. "How's that?"

"Maybe she feels uncomfortable, maybe the clothes . . ."

Scola wouldn't back down an inch.

"Sophia is a great actress, she's the one who has to find a way to fit into those clothes. It's not the clothes that need to be changed."

Carlo had to agree. He had been the first to picture me wearing Antonietta's housedress, and he wasn't the kind of man who sought compromises where they weren't needed. He believed in the story, in the filmmaker, and in me.

Maybe the phone call helped to give us some breathing space anyway, to help all three of us understand that an actor's identification with a character is a delicate process, one that takes time.

A few more days went by and I finally fell in love with that very normal, but very special woman. I will forever be grateful to Ettore. The movie was a huge success, raking in lots of awards, winning over the public and the critics and a very special place in my heart.

While we were shooting *A Special Day*, Riccardo Scicolone, my father, passed away.

One morning, my sister called me while I was on the set. She was in tears. "Sofì, hurry, Papà's not well."

I rushed to the hospital to find the women in his life standing around his bed. Mammina, Maria, and his latest companion, a woman from Germany. I went up to him and squeezed his hand. He stared at me. I stared back, as if paralyzed. I smiled at him and then moved toward the window where Maria was weeping. I looked out. Seen from up there the cars, people, bicycles looked like nothing more than toys. I tried to cry, too, but I couldn't.

XII

SEVENTEEN DAYS

THUNDERBOLTS

One morning in February 1977, two police cars drove through the gates of Villa Sara, in Marino. The officers were members of the Guardia di Finanza, the Italian law enforcement agency that deals with financial crime and smuggling. They searched the entire house, and made a detailed list of all the furniture, paintings and other valuables. A similar search was being done at the very same moment at the Roman offices of Champion, Carlo's production company. The investigation had been initiated by Public Prosecutor Paolino Dell'Anno, who accused Carlo, as a resident in Italy (despite the fact that Carlo had been a French citizen and a foreign resident for many years), of unlawful currency dealings concerning the sale of movies on the international market. He was also accused of having coproduced movies with foreign businesses, and of having taken advantage of concessions provided by Italian law to do so. According to the charges, he'd no right to do that, because they were movies that had been entirely funded abroad.

It was a bolt from the blue, and it robbed us of our peace of mind and sense of security. All our lives we had always been law-abiding citizens, and we were in no way prepared for what was happening to us. We tried not to panic and to preserve our family's equilibrium, but it wasn't easy and we had to muster all the moral strength we had.

A month later, on March 8, I was in Rome working on the release of *A Special Day*. When I got to Rome's Fiumicino Airport to take the last flight to Paris, I was stopped at customs and held overnight for questioning. The officers asked me questions I didn't know how to answer. "I'm an actress, not a businesswoman," I said, trying to defend myself, to no avail. It was only thanks to my lawyer's intervention that I was able to get my passport back and take the first dawn flight to Paris, where we were living. Waiting for me at the Paris Charles de Gaulle Airport, besides Carlo, was a crowd of reporters on the warpath. It was a very unpleasant experience, and I fooled myself into thinking it would end there.

Instead, by that time we had entered what seemed like a Kafkaesque castle, where everything appeared to be the exact opposite of everything else. Paolino Dell'Anno's investigation led to Carlo being put on trial for smuggling money abroad and being sentenced to four years in prison. He was later completely cleared of the charges. Carlo was later also cleared of the charges that concerned his international coproduction of films. Although everything worked out in the end, those were difficult years, years when we felt vulnerable and helpless.

There seemed to be no end to our problems with the law. We were next accused of the crime of offshore relocation (the sham relocation abroad of a company's tax address that, instead, actually does its business in Italy), charges that were without grounds, wholly unfounded. This led to one of our collections of paintings being sequestered and later confiscated. These were paintings that we had been fortunate to be able to collect over the years, thanks our hard work. The confiscation (which took several years to sort out and several wearisome trials) wounded us deeply. On top of what it ended up costing us, it touched one of the passions of our life. When the paintings were returned to us, that happy ending would never completely wipe out the bitterness it had caused.

THE SENTENCE

But of all the things that happened to us, there was one that was even more traumatic for me personally. During that same period, I was hit by a sentence for alleged tax evasion (something that I never did) from earnings made many years before.

I couldn't believe it. The court's decision caught me completely off guard. It stunned me.

Between the late 1950s and the early 1960s I had lived abroad, which meant that my tax residence was abroad as well. That's why my accountant from that period hadn't made me file an income tax return. Years later, however, another accountant (who obviously wasn't aware of his predecessor's decision) encouraged me to present a fiscal agreement for that very same period of time. By so doing, I was contradicting the fact that my residence was elsewhere during that period. Practically speaking, I was accusing myself of not having filed an income tax return.

The result of this was that charges were brought against me.

The first guilty verdict was appealed, and in 1980 the Court of Cassation sentenced me to thirty days in prison, because my lawyers had forgotten to declare mitigating circumstances. In a comedy of errors, I now had to choose between exile (in other words, never being able to come back to Italy, which meant never seeing my mother again) or going to prison.

We had been living in Paris for a while and I wasn't sure what to do. In the end I chose to go back to Italy and face prison. It was a decision I made slowly, by myself, following my instinct, listening to that voice inside me that has always pointed me in the direction of the straightest and narrowest path, refusing to take shortcuts or accept easy compromises.

I felt weary and confused and I fooled myself into thinking that, by handing myself over to the magistrates, I would find justice and be able to prove the truth of the matter. I have never wanted to cheat my country, and I felt oppressed by the shadow of accusations over me. I had already tasted the bitter flavor of exile during the years when Carlo and I were struggling just to get married. Now, close to my forty-eighth birthday, I couldn't stand the thought of it anymore. I wanted to be free to go back home, to embrace my family, my friends, to be able to gaze at the sea next to the town I had grown up in. A bureaucratic mess had smeared my name and my reputation in the eyes of my fellow citizens. And yet I still felt Italian, just as I do today, and I wanted to be at peace with my conscience, with my people, and to prove that my record was clean.

The Sunday before returning to Italy, on May 16, 1982, Carlo Jr. and Edoardo, at ages fourteen and nine, received their first Holy Communion. The four of us celebrated. It was a special moment of warmth and intimacy before I would take the great leap. On Tuesday night, before I packed my bags, the boys came into my room to say good-bye. As I looked at them with all my love and tenderness and tried to memorize their expressions, I finally understood what had driven me to take this difficult step. The fact is, I could never have allowed my sons to have an equivocal image of their mother, an image veiled with dishonesty and cowardice. I had always tried to teach them, ever since they were very small, the value of responsibility, the power of bravery. I couldn't disappoint them now that they were growing up and getting ready to head out into the world.

So the following day I left for Italy with my head held high, although I was worried sick and my heart throbbed with sadness. I didn't know exactly what lay in store for me, and perhaps, yes, I admit it, I hid my fear behind my big dark sunglasses. When my plane landed in Rome, a white police car, an Alfetta, was waiting to take me to the prison in Caserta, just a stone's throw away from where I'd grown up. The police car zigzagged in and out of the sea of reporters and photographers lying in wait for me, and took me to the small prison—twenty-three female inmates, I was the twenty-fourth—located in a small building in the historic part of the city, which was soon to become famous across the world. Crowding around the entrance was a flock of people who greeted me warmly, almost as though it were some kind of celebration. In spite of every-thing, the people still loved me, and their applause gave me the strength to face my difficult fate.

Despite the flowers, the letters, the telegrams, the visits from Zia Dora and the affectionate presence of my sister, Maria, who stayed in Caserta the whole time I was in custody, spending every night under my window to keep me company, I experi-enced the pain of solitude and isolation. Nothing is more hu-miliating than the denial of freedom. Nothing is more painful than not being seen.

I will never forget the morning they called me in for ques-tioning.

"Where's inmate Scicolone?" the officer asked from behind his desk.

I was standing right there in front of him, and had been for five minutes.

I had been given a single cell—which even had the luxury of a TV, as the president of the Republic, Sandro Pertini, was care-ful to point out—and I was advised not to fraternize with the other inmates. It was in fact a delicate situation that could get out of hand. Nevertheless, I tried to transmit some affection, kindness, and hope to those unfortunate young women, and when I left I said good-bye to each and every one of them. I had experienced firsthand, albeit not for long, what some of them would be forced to experience for years and, with the help of the nine marvelous nuns who took care of us, I wanted them to know that I would never forget them. And I haven't.

In prison I learned that time has a different pace. It swells up with gloomy thoughts. It becomes bitter. I tried to tame it by reading, observing, sometimes cooking. And, above all, writing.

In my treasure trove of memories I find a plain red notebook of the kind Swiss children use at school. It's the diary of my short yet traumatic prison experience. It contains my thoughts, reflections, and intense, fragmentary notes. It contains my deep anger, a feeling that is unusual for me to have. And it also contains a letter to Sandro Pertini, president of Italy, whom I had asked for a pardon, and who denied my request. Much better than many subsequent reconstructions of my imprisonment, my diary expresses the sense of my experience there.

I want to make this diary known to others, just as I wrote it during those days filled with darkness. Because prison changed—for good and for bad—my way of living in this world.

NOTES

> *Fame is a vapor, popularity is an accident, riches take wings, those who cheer today may curse tomorrow and only one thing endures—character.*
>
> —*Harry Truman*

My diary begins about halfway through the time I spent in custody. After the first days of settling in, I began to attempt to put things in order, to control my emotions, to take heart. I also tried to resist the attacks of the press that, as always, seemed to enjoy seeing its popular subjects fall to the ground, people who just before had been up on pedestals. Rereading these pages, which emerge from so far away, I feel a shiver of fear, of despair, and a sense of vulnerability that nothing will ever be able to erase again.

> *I try to react to the sadness with a rage and a fury that keep me watchful and active.*

> *Saturday*
> *I'm in prison. My cheerfulness is hollow and even my sadness mechanical.*

Sunday

Eleven days have gone by, I'm very sad, melancholy, completely cut off from the world. It seems hard to believe that all this has actually happened. It's grotesque, and it truly lends itself to philosophical considerations on just how low human beings can go, on vanity, on the frustration of the common man. . . . The so-called reporters who've gone wild these past few days: their envy, moral poverty, constant frustration. None of them has sought the source to explain to their readers where the truth lies, and how grotesque the situation is . . . Well, it's best if I don't think about it anymore, actually, I'll try to learn something from it for the future.

Fortunately, every situation, however difficult, can provide special encounters with people who have the strength to look beyond appearances and shun easy, superficial judgments. These people can make a difference and enrich even the worst situations. They arrive like manna from heaven to nourish you. They recognize your humanity behind the prejudice and the commonplace beliefs about you.

The Mother Superior is caring and affectionate, like a real mother, in the moments of pain. God Bless her for the goodness she knows how to offer.

What would this terrible experience have been like without her?

Surrounded by so much sadness it's the only precious experience I'll take away with me, an experience that has enriched me, and that will no longer make me despair about whether or not human kindness exists.

Prison should not be a hell without hope. In the heart of the person carrying out her sentence, however grave it

247

may be, there's always a spark that can become a flame of redemption. I have spoken to my dear Mother Superior at length, I have watched her, I have admired her. She harbors great wisdom in her soul.

Reliving those terrible days moment after moment, thirty years later, I ponder the meaning of freedom. Real freedom does not consist in doing what you want to, but in being able to share your thoughts and reasons with others. As I reread the diary now I realize that my suffering was caused by a feeling of abandonment, of being cut off from others, of a lack of acknowledgment of my point of view. Under the spotlights, I felt invisible, completely transparent. It was as if the world could see nothing behind my image of a star fallen from grace.

The absence of freedom is hell. All you can think of are the things you'll do when you get out. You become more selfish.

At this very moment my imprisonment might be to someone else's advantage.

You need to be strong, humble . . . Those who might have helped me promised me the world, but after the initial fervor they didn't follow through—like so many of the things that happen in Italy (it's almost normal for me to be an innocent person in prison). They've all disappeared—some of them, scattered here and there, do speak up to comment on the matter with indifference and irony . . . I hope that when I get out and get my freedom back they'll all vanish from my heart.

Without freedom I feel useless. I'm a piece of driftwood, my only purpose is to be discarded.

They're all there staring at me, they can't wait to condemn me for even the smallest gesture. It's so hard to make them understand that I'm capable of having real feelings.

I try to muster some strength inside me, but I can't count on the law. I have to try to get past this terrible experience, this scene . . .

I've never enjoyed writing, but I'm writing like crazy now. It's the only thing that keeps me busy for a few minutes, the only comfort in this moment of blackout. It's also a way for me to keep myself company, I feel less alone, it's like talking to myself and, with a bit of imagination, I feel better.

My days spent in prison were broken up by reading, talking to the nuns, sometimes around the comforting warmth of the stove in the kitchen. And by the awareness of being in a place where the level of pain is inversely proportional to the level of hope. It was a passing pain for me, but for many of the inmates it could be permanent.

Tuesday

I spent the morning in the kitchen today.

Basilio hasn't written to me at all. They've all forgotten me. Here, justice is slow and the paperwork very laborious. I can't see the end of it all. I hope Basilio writes to me soon.

Meanwhile, here in prison the heavy atmosphere has been made worse by the attempted suicide of one of the women, and another one cutting her arm.

At last, at 6:30 p.m. I receive a letter from Basilio.

Tragic evening. Another inmate cut herself and was taken to the hospital. I can't sleep. So many thoughts crowd my mind.

Wednesday

I think, I read, I write, I observe. I console myself thinking that every experience should be put to good use and in a few days freedom perhaps? I also think about those who will remain in prison. Who knows for how many years, and maybe even unfairly.

I'm feeling very blue, my dominant color. I have to appeal to all my resources of vitality and irony to avoid falling into despair—which is so easy when you aren't free.

I wasn't sure of anything, and when the end of the nightmare was close at hand, I wasn't told the day or time I'd be released from prison. Nothing depended on me, except for the strength to withstand this test with dignity.

Thursday

I didn't sleep a wink. Last night, as I carried out those routine, everyday gestures I said to myself: I'm closing the windows for the last time, I'm hearing the key in the lock and the metallic sound it makes when it shuts for the last time, I'm sleeping in this bed for the last time, and this morning I started over again: I'm sleeping in this bed for the last time . . . I'm beginning to look around carefully so that I won't forget any of this. The orange closet, the two beds with military blankets, a very small washbasin and a square they call the balcony surrounded by tall glass panes with iron bars. If I lift my head I can see a tiny patch of sky that's always blue where the sun comes out for about two hours each day.

The room is light colored, a table covered with checkered plastic, a basket filled with violets and fruit and lots and lots of flowers. Messages, fruit that arrives each day. This is the first time I mention my room. Could it be because the end is drawing near?

In the diary, I also wrote in French and English. Using a different language probably helped me to overcome my feeling

250

of claustrophobia, to see things from a different point of view, which made me feel less compressed, paralyzed, less of a prisoner.

Friday

It's very tough, naturally. I am facing a world that I have never been acquainted with. The pain, the suffering, the frustration. I think that being locked away is the worst form of punishment that any human being can ever be forced to bear.

And here finally is my farewell and a special thought for the Mother Superior, to whom I will forever be grateful.

Saturday

The last looks, the last gestures in this cell which has been my torment for 17 days.

A last farewell to the nuns who are emotional, the last embraces for the guard. In the farthest corner of the corridor a tiny, sad figure, that of the Mother Superior. She is waiting for me, she avoids my gaze, she is the only one who doesn't accompany me downstairs, leaving me, instead, at the elevator, the corners of her mouth trembling. I turn quickly and go, leaving behind a world filled with pain and human misery.

LETTERS

At the back of the diary I find, written in my handwriting, a "letter from a friend," an anonymous and very precious gift that comforted me in my darkest moments.

If I had been one of your advisers or friends I would have prevented you from making such a difficult decision.

A single day in prison in Italy is a terrible and useless experience. More than out of a feeling of solidarity, I'm writing to you out of a sense of gratitude for what you have represented and continue to represent in world cinema, and for your great courage, which sets an example for us in each of the choices you make . . .

But now be careful. You will have to cope with emptiness and solitude. Face them by finding within yourself the huge pool of humanity and reaction that you no doubt have. Alienate yourself and let this violence slip past you without harming you.

With great friendship.

I also find a letter I wrote to a Neapolitan journalist who understood perfectly, while many others passed judgment on me and turned the events into a show.

Letter to a Neapolitan journalist

Thank you, and allow me to use the 'tu' form. How could I possibly, from a place such as this, consider using the ceremonial 'lei' form . . . Thank you, you can't imagine what balm, what blessing your words have brought to my heart. And that flavor of truth when you say "one reaches the depths of the bowels of the earth . . . of humanity wiped out and tinted with madness, that cannot find peace, that cannot sleep at night . . ."

You have understood and been brave enough to write it down, refusing the facile arabesques of those hack writers who have attached themselves to my case simply to show off their decidedly questionable morality. But you are a real writer, and the others will vanish, as do fashions, vanity, exhibitions "whichever way the wind blows."

I want to thank you for your honest, civil voice, which

*echoes not in the circles where pseudo-intellectuals meet,
but in the places of the ordinary people, the ones who love
me and know that injustice and mortification are right
around the corner at every moment in their lives.*

*Please forgive my outburst, but the hours, minutes here
are long, eternal. Your heart beats faster, but your mind
slows down. You lose any sense of rhythm and sometimes
you have a hard time putting your thoughts in order.
When I at last succeeded in rearranging my thoughts, the
first thing I wanted to do was write to you, who, with
Neapolitan simplicity and passion, managed to bring so
much sweetness to my bitter experience. Perhaps being
understood, while intolerance and bad faith spread out
all around you, is one of the most beautiful gifts that a
human being can receive. You gave me this gift, a sincere
and real one, in Neapolitan style, and for this I am
grateful to you.*

Lastly, my letter to Sandro Pertini, which perhaps better than
anything else sums up my thoughts and my feelings.

Dear Mr. President,

*The solitude of prison forces the mind to grapple with
many things, to seek out many whys and wherefores, and
to try to get to the heart of certain truths.*

*When the journalists reported to you about my case and
my imprisonment, you received the news by recalling your
own incarceration, and I felt tiny, almost ashamed of the
comparison. I envied your great faith, the ideal passion
that supported you in that dark, anxiety-ridden tunnel
that is life in prison. But in my case there cannot be any
moral support. I entered prison almost innocent, embroiled
through no fault of my own in the meanderings of legal*

bureaucracy. My only impetus was my invincible nostalgia for Italy, I couldn't give in to the idea of not being able to take my place among the free citizens of my country.

Prison, Mr. President, is not just an individual cell, or the work that's done there, or a television. You have personally experienced this same pain, so you should know that it is total isolation, being shut up in a place where the locks and keys are in someone else's hands. It is the cries of anger, the outbursts of rage of the other unfortunate people also locked inside. The sleepless nights, the soul reduced to a primitive state.

One's mind is muddled, one's heart beats madly on its own.

Mr. President, is it really true that I deserve all this? And do I deserve it because I am who I am? My career, my fame, are these things I am to blame for? Shouldn't the idle gossip, the sadistic frenzy to stone idols be seen as aberrations to be judged and condemned when they are carried out solely for the purpose of character assassination?

Do forgive me, Mr. President, I've wasted a few minutes of your precious time which you know how to spend so well for our country, and for which you are beloved by all like an affectionate and loyal father. But the minutes and hours I have spent inside this place have helped me to overcome my shyness, and I wanted you to participate in this moment of deep emotion and personal unhappiness, which I am sure you will understand.

My sincerest regards

On June 5 at 6:20 a.m. I left prison to serve the rest of my sentence under house arrest, at my mother's home in Rome, according to the law. I was thinner, disillusioned, much wiser. I was free again, ready to embrace my children, my heart unburdened at last. And I hoped that the truth would eventually prevail.

Almost thirty years later, in October 2013, I finally saw the end of another judicial matter, dating back to 1974, when, according to the charges brought against me, and that were once again unfounded, I had omitted something from my income tax return. This was followed by years of appeals and defenses before the Tax Board, at every level, until the Court of Cassation finally did justice by upholding the correctness of my application of the law and the payment of my taxes. Another memorable example of the slowness of the Italian justice system.

XIII

THE MONA LISA SMILE

A MORNING AT THE MUSEUM

By the early 1980s, my career had been dazzling, and yet before then I hadn't had a chance to really look back. Now, at last, I could stand back and reconsider the meaning of my success, and the relationship between appearance and reality. I'd always felt beautiful, but it was a restless kind of beauty, that had never been enough in itself. And beauty, no doubt, can turn into a drawback if you attach too much importance to it. It trips you up when least you expect it. It makes you soar higher, and then suddenly it lets you go and you tumble—a disastrous thing if that's where you've focused all your attention.

I thought about the meaning of beauty and charm. What exactly is charm? If we could define it, then it would be an ingredient anyone could have. But charm is actually a natural gift. It's a mystery, which, unlike physical beauty, has the advantage of not fading with age. Mother Teresa of Calcutta, Rita Levi-Montalcini, Katharine Hepburn, and Greta Garbo come to mind. And so does Mona Lisa.

On a chilly winter morning in the early 1980s, I visited the Louvre, which was unusually quiet. In the rooms that are almost always crowded with tourists, a gentle, soothing tranquillity hung everywhere, in which the visitors and the paintings on the walls were free to have a conversation with each other like old friends. That is how I suddenly caught sight of that modest poplar wood panel, surprisingly small given its fame. There is almost always a crowd of admirers in front of the *Mona Lisa*, but that day I was alone and I could finally enjoy her company with no need to hurry.

I looked at it for a long time, searching for an answer to my questions in its enigmatic smile. Time was passing for me, too; my experience in prison had left in its wake a feeling of exhaustion and pain, in spite of the fact that my children were growing up strong, handsome, bursting with energy, making me prouder every day. I was approaching the age of fifty, and the beauty that had been my companion in life, ever since the days when I was crowned "princess of the sea," posed questions of me now that required deep reflection.

That morning, Mona Lisa herself didn't seem as beautiful as before. There was something masculine about her. She'd put on a few pounds, and she would never have passed a screen test at Cinecittà. And yet, at that very moment I understood why she had seduced all of humanity with her magnetism. Mona Lisa's gaze revealed a secret that was to change my life: this lady's charm arose from her inner serenity, her profound self-knowledge. And, as George Cukor once said, there is no beauty that can compete with the knowledge and acceptance of who we really are.

By that time I knew perfectly well who I was, and I felt complete when surrounded by my loving family. Cinema was my passion, but I had other interests as well. I was at peace with myself, comfortable in my own skin, at ease in my life. I knew how to spend my energy and where to find joy. And, thanks to Charlie Chaplin's precious advice, I'd even learned to say "No" once in a while. Only age can offer you this sense of self-confidence. And only this self-confidence can nourish the beauty within each one of us.

True beauty, besides being its own expression, is a gift for all those around us. Cultivating beauty is a form of respect for those we love. Of course, as you get older it's slightly more difficult, and really becomes a question of discipline. Our body demands patience, care, and attention. To all those who have asked me what my secret is over the years, I have always tried to answer with plain common sense: each one of us must strike the right balance between rest and movement, activity and sleep, the pleasures of food, and the taste for a healthy and well-balanced diet. But the real fountain of youth is hidden in the imagination you draw upon to face everyday challenges. It is in the passion for what you do and in the intelligence with which you exploit your own capacities and accept your own limits.

Life isn't an easy game to play, it calls for earnestness and good spirits, which are two natural gifts I have, and have been training, for some time.

LITTLE MEN

In 1980, Carlo, Carlo Jr., Edoardo, and I had all left Paris to settle down in Switzerland, where we would be safer and could live more peacefully. Whenever I wasn't away for work I took care of the children as much as I could, I'd pick them up at school, supervise their schoolwork and other activities, and watch admiringly as their talents blossomed.

Carlo Jr. had started playing the piano at the age of nine and gave himself heart and soul to music. In long conversations with his father, who had a unique instinct for discerning a person's abilities and natural talents, he had started imagining his future.

"Why don't you think about becoming an orchestra conductor?" his father had suggested. "It's a more complex and complete approach to the music you love so much . . ."

As always, his father was right. Years later, after graduating from Pepperdine's Seaver College and earning an M.A. from the University of Southern California in Los Angeles, Carlo Jr. indeed attended an orchestra directing seminar in Connecticut, which paved the way for his career, after further study at UCLA and the Vienna Music Academy.

Edoardo, instead, had been dreaming of cinema ever since he was a child. We tried to leave him free to decide, encouraging him without being pushy. Precisely because he was following in his father's footsteps it was important that he be given time to understand the realities of his vocation.

In 1984 the two of us appeared together in a road movie called *Aurora*. Edoardo was eleven, I was fifty on the nose. He played a blind child, I his mother, who traveled up and down Italy telling all her past lovers that he was their son so that she could gather the money she needed for the surgery that would restore his eyesight.

Edoardo's role wasn't at all easy and I, as a mother and actress, tried to give him some advice.

"Edo, do you think we should talk? It might help . . ."

But he, with the presumption that comes naturally at that age, answered drily, almost resentfully: "No, thanks. I can take care of myself."

I left him alone, but kept an eye on him from a distance.

It didn't take long for him to come back to me, after running up against the first obstacles.

"Mamma, you were right. I can't do it without you, I need your help . . ."

I welcomed him with a smile, and took him for a little walk.

"You have to forget you're blind, Edoardo, you just have to *be* blind, that's all."

In the days that followed we went over his part, we tried to understand how he should move, how a child who can't see feels. He overcame his difficulty, did a good job, and won the Young Artist Award. He would always treasure the experience and keep it in mind when he was on the other side of the movie camera.

Adolescence is like that—it swings from being big to being little, from depending on others to being independent, between leaving and wanting to come back. As I busied myself in my children's everyday lives, I suddenly realized they'd grown.

"Now what am I going to do?" I asked myself. "What am I going to do now that they don't need me anymore?"

I knew it wasn't completely true that they no longer would

need me, but I needed to change my pace, to adjust the balance in the life that had guided us until then. After having taken care of them, down to the smallest details in their lives, the moment had come for me to watch them from the shore as they swam out to sea. It was a sensitive time, one that every parent goes through, one of satisfaction and nostalgia. Mothers will always be mothers, but they have to allow their children to choose a path for themselves.

Carlo Jr. left for Aiglon College, an English boarding school in Switzerland. When the time came for him to go to college, he chose a school in California. So Carlo and I moved to our ranch, La Concordia, in Hidden Valley, near LA, where we all had been spending our summers. It was a passage in our life together, an oasis of serenity where we could stop to ponder just how far we'd gotten, and where we wanted to go. Edoardo was also accepted at Aiglon and would join us for vacations, for which we'd often return to Europe. Although we lived far apart, we loved each other with the same love as always, and we'd often gather together to give one another support, happiness, and fun.

Michael Jackson's ranch was right next to ours. Our kids couldn't wait to meet him, and they did everything they could think of to make it happen. Finally, one morning Michael phoned to invite us to lunch and we happily accepted.

With his cascade of curls, wearing dark sunglasses and a black hat, he gave us a royal welcome.

For lunch we ate some delicious shrimp, then, with his delicate and somewhat childlike bashfulness, Michael showed us around his mansion, which was really an immense imaginative amusement park. It was like being at Disney World. Carlo Jr. and Edoardo couldn't believe their eyes—they were deliriously happy. And to make sure they weren't disappointed, Michael crowned the visit by taking them to his rehearsal room and improvising a legendary moonwalk just for them.

The boys lived between Europe and California, their lives filled with music, cinema, literature. I continued to work, but I had become selective and would only accept parts I was sure about. At ease in my maturity, I could look at younger women not with envy, but with a tender understanding and indulgence.

Each stage in life brings with it its whims and its pitfalls. When you're thirty you're young and insecure, when you're forty you're strong and often tired, at fifty you're wise, and maybe somewhat wistful. And when you approach eighty you often yearn to start over again from scratch. You're reborn in your memories, and you fall in love with the future.

If my age today doesn't frighten me, it's thanks to my children. Ever since I became a mother I have led a forward-looking life, and I continue to do so today, following both my own and their passions. You never stop learning. Everything depends on self-knowledge and self-love.

MOTHERS

After I became a mother, I was asked to play the role of a mother more often. Not that I hadn't before, but as a mother, I brought with me to the set all the range of emotions that Carlo Jr. and Edoardo had kindled in me.

The most intense of such roles was the one I played for *Mamma Lucia*, a movie made for TV aired on Canale 5 (Channel 5) in 1988. The story was adapted from *The Fortunate Pilgrim*, a novel by the great Mario Puzo, who wrote *The Godfather*. At my side was John Turturro, who plays Larry, my eldest son. An Italian-American, John was perfect for the part, and in time his ties to Italy grew even stronger. (It should come as no surprise that he chose the title *Passion* for a documentary on Neapolitan music, released in 2010, which was quite successful.)

Anna Strasberg, Lee's widow, was also a member of the cast

for *The Fortunate Pilgrim*. A good friend, she had welcomed Carlo Jr.'s and Edoardo's first steps in the world of art at the world-renowned Actor's Studio, which she'd inherited from her husband. We'd spent a lot of time together during the long periods we lived in the United States, even before she moved there permanently. When we were at the ranch, I'd take the boys to the Studio on Santa Monica Boulevard, to pass the time in the afternoons, and also to see if anything in our business might interest them. They played and acted in small improvised performances under Anna's knowing guidance. Besides having fun, they also built up important experiences for their future careers.

When organization is at its best, the longer periods of time involved in television, as compared with cinema, make it possible to really recreate an environment, a wholly genuine atmosphere. *The Fortunate Pilgrim* is set in New York's Little Italy in the early twentieth century, reconstructed in Yugoslavia, a country soon to be devastated by war. In this neighborhood, in the city but also somewhat apart from it, lives Lucia. Independent and courageous, twice widowed, she struggles each and every day to raise her five children "the way she says they should be."

In one of the scenes, John Turturro takes a bath in a tub. I, in the role of his mother, was standing at the window lost in my sad thoughts. During the shooting, I turned around suddenly, as called for by the script, and John was standing in front of me stark naked. I was flabbergasted! I don't know whether it was an accident, or a lack of modesty, but such things usually didn't happen. I instantly turned back around to give him a chance to cover himself, wondering to myself about male vanity.

Lucia pursues her dream, which was once an Italian dream, and is now becoming an American one. On Tenth Street, bisected by the tracks of a steam engine that invades the scene by puffing out tension from start to finish, Lucia ages and her children become men and women. She risks and eventually loses almost everything and yet, in keeping with her nature, stays hopeful, managing to preserve the sense of family, gathering everyone together on Long Island, in a clean white house where she can nurture her desire for a new life and preserve the memories of her loved ones.

One of Lucia's children, her kindest and most vulnerable son, kills himself. In a terrible coincidence, while we were shooting a scene with coffins that are understood to hold the bodies of American soldiers killed in the war, a young man who was passing by the studio outside pulled out a gun and shot himself. It was terribly tragic, and left us speechless, with a terrible weight on our hearts.

The Fortunate Pilgrim is an intense and moving film. When the plot of a movie is the work of a great writer, as in the case of this movie, the filming can be easier and it is likelier to be a hit. And when you have a soundtrack based on a song composed by a great singer-songwriter like Lucio Dalla, success is guaranteed.

One morning, a few months before the shooting was to begin, I was in the car with Edoardo who, as he always did, was singing softly. He had always liked to sing, and was good at it. Maybe he takes after his Zia Maria.

"*Qui dove il mare luccica e tira forte il vento*" (Here, where the sea shines and the wind howls . . .).

"What are you singing?" I asked him, curious.

"*Te voglio bene assaje, ma tanto tanto bene, sai*" (I love you very much, very, very much, you know), he crooned with a wide grin, fully aware of the fact that he was amazing me with his rendering of the Neapolitan song, "Caruso," by Lucio Dalla.

That was when I fell in love with Lucio Dalla. Later, when Carlo and I discussed the soundtrack for *The Fortunate Pilgrim*, I was adamant: "We absolutely have to use Lucio Dalla's song 'Caruso,' it's perfect!"

A tribute to the legendary tenor, Enrico Caruso, the song is about the longings of a dying man. Caruso himself had had a hard life and in the end died in the Hotel Vesuvio in Naples.

Carlo listened to it and was just as enthusiastic as I was. But as usual, never satisfied, he gave it his own special touch, and chose the best possible musician, the most suited to the genre and atmosphere of the movie—none other than Luciano Pavarotti.

Pavarotti knew well how to interpret this song to fit the ancient and very touching breadth of this grand family saga.

While he was cutting the record, one morning Luciano phoned me.

"Sophia, I have a confession to make . . ."

"What is it?" I answered, noticing his embarrassment.

"I'm so sorry but I have to stop here . . ."

"What are you saying, Luciano? Why, what's wrong?"

"I'm here singing this song, but I'll *never* sing it the way Lucio Dalla does, ever!"

I was taken aback and moved by his humility, his insecurity. I played all my cards to try to convince him, to encourage him: "How can you say that, Luciano, with that voice of yours . . . Dalla sings his own version, which you can't and mustn't imitate. You'll do your own, adding to it the way you feel, the person you are . . ."

Only truly great people nurture doubts about themselves. And it is precisely when they have doubts that they can outperform themselves and become even greater.

Just a few years before, I had made *Courage*, the story of a woman who, all by herself, fights to tear her children away from drug use, exposing a billion-dollar narcotics ring. The TV movie, which was aired on Canale 5 in 1987, was inspired by the real-life story of Martha Torres, a Latin American mother who had immigrated to Queens and who, for the love of her children, infiltrated the ring and succeeded in bringing fourteen

Colombian drug dealers to trial. Unfortunately, for security reasons, I wasn't able to meet with her, but I tried to do justice to the character, offering her all the love that I usually reserved for my own children. It was a kind of love that, in some mysterious way, encompassed all the children of the world. Any mother will understand what I mean.

I had experienced deeply how motherly love can spread when I was sent to Africa by the United Nations as a goodwill ambassador during the Somali crisis. The unspeakable suffering and poverty that I saw from close up were shattering. I really would have liked to gather all those children in my arms, feed them, and give them love, but all I could do was play my very small part, a necessary one that I hoped might alleviate someone's pain even if for just a moment.

The last mother I played in the 1980s was Cesira (from *Two Women*), again—the role that had won an Oscar for me. Dino Risi, a filmmaker who had already directed me years before in several comedies that had become classics, had decided it was time to bring her back. He asked me to instill new life into that great character. She had been tailor-made for me by De Sica, so naturally, I had to rise to the challenge of honoring the greatness of the movie that had changed my life and to give another worthy performance.

While the shooting was taking place, I had the distinct feeling that watching me from behind the camera was the Cesira from the past. My early fears, as well as my youthful determination, resurfaced in my mind. Guided by Dino's sensitivity, with the memory of Vittorio to inspire both of us, I brought all my experience as a mother to this new version, experience I hadn't been able to draw upon the first time around.

Running Away was aired in two episodes in April 1989, again on Canale 5. It was successful and it moved me deeply, just as it had the first time. Drawing on the different seasons of my life gave new meaning to my years of experience as an actress and gave me the strength to look forward. The past lives in the present, and it constitutes our future more than we might believe.

HAPPY BIRTHDAY

When Robert Altman invited us to the set for *Ready to Wear (Prêt-à-Porter)*, I was sixty and Marcello seventy. It was 1994 and we were happy to celebrate our birthdays this way. These were my words to him:

> *Dearest Marcello,*
>
> *We've reached a point in our lives where our birthday wishes surprise us: me 60? You 70? Have we gone crazy? For me, time must stop, let's not be silly. The only injustice in human destiny is that of spending half our lives regretting the other half (the first half, of course), pursuing the sweetest dreams of youth. But it's precisely in the balance of what we have behind us that we can find the joy of our more mature years.*
>
> *Dear Marcello, my friend and companion in so many stories, we have behind us a gallery of characters, feelings, emotions that can richly nourish us our whole lives. I imagine the emptiness and squalor of those who can no longer find a moment of joy, the thrill of love in their past.*
>
> *On this day, thinking about all the work we've done together, and proudly measuring the time that has passed, I want to tell you once more how grateful I am for having had you as an irreplaceable companion in a long adventure filled with characters that—allow me to be presumptuous just this once—the public will never forget.*

Marcello's reply arrived shortly afterward.

> *Dearest Sophia,*
> *I was moved, touched by your words. But most importantly I'm grateful because they made me see my gripe about these days from a different angle: people can say what they like, but as the years start to pile up, you can hardly believe it when a birthday like this one comes around, and you start looking around for a line of defense. "Have we gone crazy? for me, time must stop, let's not be silly." In this passion-filled alarm your words are like a balm, and they have prepared me to enjoy such a difficult role. On the other hand, these past few days, we've gone back to working together on Altman's set. It has all the air of a benevolent sign of fate. Who knows, maybe there's some wise god who metes out surprises and joys . . . It's hard to accept the idea that everything will end with us, that this marvelous concert of feelings and passions will suddenly be arrested and no longer expand throughout the universe. Yes, I believe that some part of us will remain rooted to the earth, to the world.*

Unfortunately, Marcello's end was not long in coming. Neither he nor I could ever have imagined that he would pass away only two years later. But meanwhile, rooted to the earth, to the world, we experienced our last, fabulous adventure together.

"ABAT-JOUR"

As soon as I read the script for *Ready to Wear*, I knew we were in for a lot of fun. The plot had all the flavor of the thriller, but actually it was a merciless cross section of the fashion world, assembled in Paris for Fashion Week.

In the movie I play the part of Isabella de la Fontaine, the widow of the head of the Chambre de la Mode—who has just been assassinated—and the ex-wife of a Russian dressmaker played by Marcello, named Sergei, who turns out not to be Russian after all, and whom I meet again after forty years.

The production was huge, the cast star-studded: thirty-one main characters, in addition to famous singers, models, and fashion designers in the flesh. Julia Roberts and Rupert Everett, Kim Basinger and Tim Robbins, Ute Lemper and Anouk Aimée, Lauren Bacall, Jean-Pierre Cassel, and many, many others shared the scenes with Cher, Harry Belafonte, Nicola Trussardi, Gianfranco Ferré, and Jean-Paul Gaultier, who played themselves. In the meeting between these splendid characters, the three-ring circus of haute couture, with all its neuroses and perversions, reflects like a mirror the passions and frailties of our lives.

During the shooting, I always stayed close to Marcello. In that whirlwind of film cameras—five, six at a time, you never knew which of them was filming you—his familiar face made me happy and gave me a sense of security. As did Altman, who understood my deepest needs.

The first day, when I got to the set and he didn't come up to greet me, I felt hurt.

"Sophia, what's the problem, you're not going to succumb to these small formalities, now, are you!" he said, with an embarassed smile when he noticed my disappointment.

"Bob, we're all different. I'm here to to support you, but to be able to do so, I need you, your smile, your trust."

From that day on, he never forgot to come over and say hello first thing in the morning. As for trust, he gave Marcello and me lots of it, leaving us totally free to do the scene that was to be the throbbing heart of the movie.

"How do we want to do this?" he asked us, with a crafty

smile, the morning it was our turn. "You can speak Italian, if you wish. Of all the movies you've done together, which scene would you like to do over again?"

We needed to be alone for moment, somewhere where we could talk that was far away from the spotlights. There, in that sheltered corner on the set, Marcello had such a mischievous look in his eyes, like a little boy who knows he's up to no good.

"What do you say, Sophia, how about doing our striptease again?"

"You're a real scoundrel . . ." I answered, pretending to be shocked. The truth is, I was tickled by the idea. The insecurity of the past was behind me, I no longer needed a choreographer from the Crazy Horse to guide me. De Sica's lesson had become a part of me. As for my age, experience had taught me to make time my biggest ally: I neither fought against it nor subjected myself to it passively. I lived each day for what it was, letting my beauty mature peacefully, just as the Mona Lisa has.

Marcello and I went back over to Altman sure of the fact that we were on the right path. He looked at us, understood, and shouted out: "Action!"

Although fate had separated us in our work, the places of our lives, our habits, all of this vanished as if by magic when the shooting began. For a few hours we were young again, ready to embrace life and to love each other.

Mara's striptease in *Yesterday, Today and Tomorrow*, remade thirty years later to the same languid notes of "Abat-jour," welcomes the passing of the years with a smile, and discovers in the vulnerability of each and every one of us the real essence of life.

As I performed, my heart went back to Vittorio, to his sensitivity and his amazing talent. And besides Vittorio, to María Mercader, his second wife, who was on the set the day we shot our first striptease, in that faraway summer of 1963. As she watched me get dressed again, having left behind the hardest part of the movie, she'd said, "You're a real beauty!" Her sincere, somewhat masculine remark, struck me, and it still brings a smile to my lips today.

While watching Mara, Marcello had howled with pleasure, but in *Ready to Wear* he looks like he's on the verge of yawning. At the climax of the act, in the split second it takes for me to twirl around, he's fallen fast asleep in his soft white terry-cloth robe. Even De Sica would have admitted it was a brilliant idea.

A TIMELESS STYLE

Ready to Wear's fashion princes and geniuses revolutionize the way its characters see the world. And in the real world Giorgio Armani is the king of kings of fashion, the wizard of beauty. He has been interpreting, dressing, and renewing me for years.

The worlds of cinema and fashion are very close, the one constantly communicating with the other. Richard Gere knows something about this, having been the first to introduce Giorgio to the world by wearing Armani fashions from head to toe in *American Gigolo*. From that moment on—it was 1980—Hollywood could no longer do without Giorgio. And he has continued to dress the stars, bestowing his touch on newcomers as well. With the same generosity he welcomes the younger generation of fashion designers, whose debut shows he hosts in his theater.

Maybe he chooses to be like this because he hasn't forgotten the arduousness of his own first steps, just as he hasn't forgotten the public at large, believing that the passerby encountered just round the corner may conceal a more authentic and natural elegance than the VIP. We can all be chic as long as we don't surrender to the latest fad styles and don't let ourselves get wound up in the desire for something new at all costs, which is a way of thinking that's devouring our world nowadays.

I met Armani when he was still working for Nino Cerruti, in Paris. He was so handsome, with sharp, blue eyes, and a presence that made you feel at home, and that abounded with class. As a young man he had wanted to become a doctor, but during a military leave he had by chance ended up working at the Rinascente department store in the clothing department.

Giorgio and I have many other things in common, apart from being exactly the same age.

We both love our work passionately. And both of us have evolved out of our shyness. In spite of our success, we are still introverts, who prefer a small group of real friends to a huge number of acquaintances. We're both terribly stubborn, always out to achieve the goals we set for ourselves.

We both scorn hypocrisy and pretense, we can't stand approximation and negligence, we live encouraged by the desire to find the substance behind the appearance. Maybe that's the secret of our great, indissoluble friendship.

Over the course of my career I had met and come to appreciate other designers before Giorgio: the bubbly Emilio Schuberth, who dressed my debut on the red carpet, and the very talented Valentino, with whom I shared a long period of my life. I just can't part with some of the dresses he designed for me. And then the prince of milliners Jean Barthet, and Pierre Balmain, who made the costumes for *The Millionairess*, and Christian Dior, Cristóbal Balenciaga. Yet entering King Giorgio's universe was like landing in the peaceful eye of the storm, in a perfect calm, in a style that can't be ruffled by sensationalism.

Giorgio's line has an indefinable soul to it; all you can say is "How wonderful!" and nothing more. It's pure creativity, to be worn, to be used for life. Phillip Bloch, one of Hollywood's greatest designers, says that when you slip on an Armani outfit you feel rich, you feel good. You don't even need a mirror: you know it fits you like a glove, and it enables you to express your most beautiful side.

That's it: what keeps Giorgio going, besides the fear of stopping, is the dream of offering men and women the discovery of their own beauty.

For me, just as for him, fashion hides a deeper dimension that triumphs on the catwalk, a dimension beneath its exterior, which is often exaggerated and ridiculous. It's the sum of certain fundamental elements and the natural laws of good taste, which never change. Fashion has nothing to do with shocking images that expose or disguise more than dress a person. It is not only that often perverted system that for years has imposed the images of dangerously anorexic models on the imaginations of young women and girls who contradict the concept of elegance.

Not Giorgio. Each and every day Giorgio interprets what's classical, simple, and natural: it is there, in this lightweight and creative operation, all played out on nuances, details, that he expresses his genius. And turns his life into a sublime work of art.

All that I've said is true. But King Giorgio gave me an additional gift named Roberta. Born and raised in beauty, Roberta is Armani's niece, a remarkable woman, with an amazing and original sense of style. She's the great soul who welcomes me every two or three months in Milan, when I drive down from Switzerland. Together, we go over all the latest collections and I choose the clothing most suited to my needs. We have lunch together at the Hotel Armani restaurant, surrounded by flowers, chocolate candy, and champagne. We sit at the most secluded table and pretend to put on airs, like two little girls playing grown-up ladies.

With her, everything is always a game, as serious and as amusing as the most successful of games.

"I love your necklace, Roberta!" I whisper to her admiringly.

Without a moment's hesitation, she takes it off and gently slips it around my neck, as if she were adorning a queen. There has never been a time I haven't left with something of hers: a piece of jewelry, a coat, a scarf. It's as if I were taking away with me a lived-in sign of our friendship.

SECRETS

Friendship is one of the most precious gifts that life can give, yet from them each of us has secrets that we don't want to, or can't, reveal. However juicy and ripe a piece of fruit may be, at its center is a seed that can't be shared. Mona Lisa understood this.

For years I've kept a personal diary, a shelter in which I could be myself completely. It acted like a small inner movie camera before which I could finally play my whole part. I started keeping it after going to prison, and haven't stopped. In the solitude of writing I found comfort and companionship, and I discovered aspects of my voice I wasn't aware of. I felt safe in my intimacy, as if only there could I truly, finally, be home again.

But life, we all know, doesn't flow smoothly; rather, it moves along in steps, and one spring morning, all of a sudden, I looked in the mirror and was afraid. "What's going to happen to my diary when I'm gone?" I asked myself.

Although I may be emotional, I do know how to make my own decisions.

"If anyone asks for me, tell them I'm not here!" I said to Ines and to Ninni, and then I went into my bedroom. I stared at that hardcover black notebook for a while. It had been my companion through so many thoughts and emotions. I thumbed through it lightly, slowly. As I turned the pages, I could smell the fragrance of the years. I could see when my mood changed by the differences in my handwriting, at times sharp, at other times edgy, sometimes relaxed.

Finally, I went into the bathroom with a box of matches, struck one, and burned the diary. All my words turned into fire, and then ashes. I never regretted it. Only now and again have I felt a bit of nostalgia. And I've never stopped writing. Since then, however, when the end of the year comes around, I take out another match, the magical instrument that lights a small ritual between me and myself.

XIV

GOING HOME

Chère petite maman
mme un papillon tu vol
un androit à l'...

MAMMINA

"*Chère petite maman . . .*" The round, fussy handwriting of Carlo Jr. when he was a child matches the blue butterfly wings that the teacher had him glue to his letter to me. It's one of those prefabricated poems for Mother's Day that the little ones proudly bring home after having struggled to overcome their messiness and inexperience. I come across letters such as these all over the place, in every drawer of every one of our homes. So there simply had to be one in my treasure trove of memories, which has by now dwindled down to the very last of its surprises.

As I look at it tenderly, I glimpse other sheets, written by me as a young girl.

Has anyone ever told you that you're the dearest mother in the world? Happy Birthday! Sophia

The letterhead in gilt italic lettering from back in 1961, or maybe 1962, reads Piazza d'Aracoeli 1, Palazzo Colonna, Rome. It's one of the many letters I wrote to my mother during my life, one of the many daily thoughts I sent to her from every corner of the world.

And now I find another one, written a few years earlier:

Dear Mammina,
I wish your letters were slightly longer and a bit more fun to read . . . Why don't you describe your days to me, the things you do? What's happening at home? Things are fine here and, please, Mammina, if you read anything in the newspaper that concerns me put it in an envelope and mail it to me. The movie is going well and here in America everything works like a well-oiled machine. I

miss Italy and you're the main reason for that. I adore you Mamma."

And there's another one, dated January 27, 1958:

Dear Mammina,
    you know the letters I write at the beginning of a movie always say the same thing. Filled with concerns, torment, and especially so for this movie . . ."

I wonder if it was *The Black Orchid*, as I continue to read.

It's a particularly difficult movie, a very dramatic one, it requires my undivided attention, so don't be upset if I don't write to you quite as often. I can't say the same for you because I'm sure you could devote 10 minutes a day to me if you wanted to. You know how happy it makes me to read about what you're all up to there, and especially to have news from Italy.

Mammina and I were always close, in spite of the thousands of miles that separated us time and time again. And, thank God, we were close even at the time of her death, which happened quite suddenly. This is the only thought that has lessened the pain over the years. A thought that now forces me to stop, along my journey through memory, and take a step backward. Death, especially the death of a mother, disrupts the chronology of one's existence. It interrupts the timing of the plot and leaves you suspended in an empty space made of darkness and silence.

It was early May 1991 and I was on my way back from a trip, I may have been returning from Carlo Jr.'s graduation ceremony at Pepperdine's Seaver College. I was to fly into Zurich, and go home from there. But that's not how things went. There wasn't anything urgent for me to do, and something inside me made me phone Mammina in Rome. I really wanted to see her. "What's wrong with that?" I thought to myself. "It only takes a minute to change flights."

I called her, happy to be able to surprise her.

"Mammina, it's me, Sophia! How are you feeling?"

"How can I possibly be feeling when I never see you . . ."

"Get my room ready, put the peppers in the oven, I'm on my way!"

She was so happy she started crying, and I knew I'd made the right decision.

After I arrived there, we spent two days sitting on the couch and talking. I slept a lot to make up for the jet lag, and in between we ate all the delicacies she cooked for me, seasoned with all her love: *salsa genovese*, meat slowly cooked in onions, stuffed veal, eggplant Parmesan, a staple in her kitchen. The hours we spent together were peaceful ones, almost as if fate had allowed me to become a child once more before the end.

That evening I was already in bed when she suddenly appeared at the bedroom door. Leaning up against the doorjamb for support she stared at me, her eyes unfocused.

"Mammina, what is it?" I asked, half asleep.

"Sofi, I'm not well."

I could see right away it wasn't just a whim. I got up quickly and rushed over to her.

"I feel peculiar, let's go to the bathroom, please."

With one hand on her shoulder, and the other one under her arm I slowly led her along the hallway, step by step. It seemed to take forever. I opened the door for her, she went in, stared at the washbasin, and then she started spewing blood. She kept her eyes on me, terrified, as if she were asking me to explain what was happening to her. I tried to reassure her, to smile, but I was scared to death.

"Help me to my bed," she said breathlessly.

I walked her back to her room and helped her to lie down. She closed her eyes, as if to rest.

"Mamma?" I said.

I called the concierge: "Come up, come up right away!" He arrived, looked at her, and shrugged helplessly.

"Signora Sophia, I think you need to call someone . . ."

I phoned Maria, who was in her car on her way to the countryside with a friend. She came racing back, waving a white handkerchief out the car window. But it was too late.

When my father died, fourteen years earlier, I tried hard to feel something, but had felt nothing.

Mammina, instead, had taken a part of me with her.

The more time passes the deeper the wound left by her death is. I miss our daily phone call. I miss her sudden fits of anger, her combative, exclusive love. Often when I'm with my sister, and especially when we're alone, we look at each other and, without saying a word, we're overcome by the same feeling of loss, the same irreparable absence.

My mother's story always interested me, as both an actress and a daughter. She was emotional, naive, dramatic, hysterical, and deeply loving. Nineteen years after her death, in 2010, I played her in *My House Is Full of Mirrors*, a TV miniseries broadcast by RAI, adapted from Maria's autobiographical novel. I'd actually already brought Mammina to the small screen thirty years before with the TV movie inspired by *Sophia: Living and Loving*, the book in which A. E. Hotchner, the author of *Papa Hemingway* and a close friend of Hemingway and Paul Newman, had collected my memories along with those of my family and friends. In that first movie the challenge had been even more exciting, because I had to play her part as well as my own. It was an exciting and at times distressing exercise of having to be two people at once. Looking back at our lives, maybe she, not I, was the real star.

When we made *My House Is Full of Mirrors* the emotion was even greater, because Mammina was no longer with us. It wasn't easy to get things straight in my heart so that I could give her a voice and a credible guise. I wanted to do more than that, though. I wanted to pay tribute to her, in the only way I knew how.

I don't know whether I succeeded. But playing her part forced me to relive our life together, our very close relationship, which was more like the relationship between two sisters than between a mother and her daughter. By embracing her point of view I understood things that had escaped me before. In some ways, it took me back home.

THE IMMACULATE

For me, going home today means staying with my sister Maria. Our lives, however different, are intertwined. Little does it matter that we live far apart, that we have different jobs, that we were born under two different signs of the zodiac—she's a Taurus, exuberant and determined, I'm a Virgo, determined and reserved. We've always helped each other out, supported each other, and have always been present during the critical moments. Whenever I arrive in Rome and enter her home, I can smell the scents of our childhood again, as if time hadn't passed at all.

Maria lives with Majid, an Iranian physician she has been happily married to since 1977. She had met him, years and years before, in a Roman hospital, where he was a young doctor, about to go back to Iran, and she was a gutsy journalist with a marriage behind her, out to rediscover herself. As soon as she saw those fabulous Middle Eastern eyes, Maria promised herself she wouldn't let him slip away. She courted him and won his heart. In her handsome Persian prince I find the brother I never had. And in Maria I find all the affection of my original family rolled up in one long, strong embrace.

The first thing I can see as I cross the threshold is the "queen" of their home, *L'Immacolata*, a painting of the Immaculate Virgin Mary. It's a small painting that, a long, long time ago, lay inside the drawer of a mirrored wardrobe in Pozzuoli, one of those drawers that contain a huge variety of things: spools of thread and handkerchiefs, letters and dried flowers, train tickets, photographs, hairpins, elastic bands, medals, receipts . . . *The Immaculate Conception* had belonged to Mamma Luisa's sister, who had moved to America in the early twentieth century and left it behind. Maria saved it from oblivion and has never parted with it. Now that they live together, Maria honors her with the eternal flame of a candle and fresh leaves, and she entertains her with games, tiny paper angels, stuffed toys.

"Sofi, see how well *L'Immacolata* is? With all her hard work to protect us she's aged, and she needs to take her mind off things . . ."

"Maria, what on earth are you saying?" I pretend to scold her. But I understand her perfectly. Each one of us harbors a spiritual, enchanted dimension that we nurture in mysterious ways, letting ourselves be guided by our heart.

Whenever we get together, Maria and I spend our time chatting and cooking. Actually, to be precise, she does all the talking and I listen, she cooks and I eat . . .

"Remember that time in Spain, you were sleeping and I . . ." she said, pausing.

"You what?"

"And I went out with the crew. As soon as you dozed off, I'd go dancing. I absolutely loved dancing the Sevillana . . ."

"Oh really? If only I'd known! But maybe you did the same thing in America, now that I come to think of it . . ."

"That's right, as soon as you fell asleep I'd get up, get dressed, and go downstairs where Frank Sinatra's car was waiting for me . . . I'd go hear him sing in the clubs, and sometimes I even sang along with him."

"You don't just live life, Maria, you steal it!" I say to her, smiling, "You're like a thief!"

And just like a thief, sometimes, she tries to find out some of my secrets . . . She taunts me, she circles around me, she asks me trick questions. And I, like any true actress, try to lead her astray with a gaze, a gesture, a line. But I know it just doesn't work with her, and in the end I give in to her clever directing.

"It's no use acting with me, Sofi, I know you too well," she exclaims, amused and proud of herself. These skirmishes between sisters keep us alive, they give us joy, and we feel tender toward each other. And they reach a peak when we're cooking something.

"Maria, do you put garlic in *friarelli*?"

"If you don't want me to, I can make them without garlic . . ."

"How can anyone eat *friarelli* without garlic?"

"Sophia, please decide, do you, or don't you want me to add garlic?"

It's wonderful to know that there's nothing in the world that can separate us, just as nothing has ever separated us in the past. And that, for as long as she's around, I'll always know the way home.

Whenever I'm in Rome, when I'm not on Maria and Majid's sofa, I have a home at the Boscolo Hotel, where the fabulous owners, Angelo and Grazia, reserve a suite for me. For me it's a peaceful oasis, where I can spend days of serenity, sheltered from curious onlookers . . . pampered by the impeccable, warm staff. Signor Giuseppe has become my friend, and every time I leave we say good-bye to each other with great affection, as if we were already missing each other.

THE GAL WITH THE WHITE GLASSES
AND CONTAGIOUS LAUGHTER IS
ALWAYS IN A GOOD MOOD

In the early 1990s, there was another great Italian filmmaker who brought me back "home." That filmmaker was Lina Wertmüller, the gal with the white glasses and contagious laughter. I hadn't experienced anything as intimate, as familiar on the set since my days working with Vittorio. I trusted her and let her tell me what to do, and it was the right decision. Today I think the fact that it was a woman who directed me in my mature years was no accident.

And you have to admit, Lina is an outstanding woman. She's extremely sophisticated, but she knows how to stay close to the people. She has a great imagination, she's a warm human being, she's positive. She's beautiful inside and outside. She reminds you of a child, with her desire to live life to the fullest, to be joyful. Even though we don't talk very often, we have a marvelous relationship.

We had already worked together in the late 1970s on a movie whose title I dare any Italian to remember: *Fatto di sangue fra due uomini per causa di una vedova (si sospettano moventi politici)*, more simply translated *Blood Feud* in English. Producers generally prefer short titles like *Senso* and *Sciuscià*, so Lina would tease them with long ones and be amused when they were mispronounced.

Lina has a Neapolitan street urchin side to her that makes her irresistible. I hope Lina likes the title of the section I've devoted to her.

In *Blood Feud*, as she tells us in her lively autobiography,

Tutto a posto e niente in ordine (Everything's Fine and Nothing in Order), she played around with my makeup so that my more tragic Mediterranean side would come out. The movie was set in Sicily, in the 1920s, when the island was barbarous and there were frequent clashes between the people. That's how she wanted me to be, too.

When Carlo and I were at our home in Paris, Lina came to see me with the script, which had just been written. While we were talking about the movie, she started fooling around with my face.

"Let's bring these eyebrows down, down, like the pediment of a Greek temple!" she chuckled, using an eyebrow pencil to torment me in front of the mirror.

She wanted to be sure to erase any trace of the international movie star so that she could stage a real Italian woman, a typically Southern one.

"Lina, Lina, what are you doing?" I tried to back her off, but ultimately my heart told me to trust her. And so I let her do what she wanted, with the acquiescence you might use with enterprising children—the ones everyone considers pests, but can actually be quite delightful.

As she prepared us for *Blood Feud*, Lina didn't just have it in for me. She forced Marcello, who was also in the movie, to wear a very long beard, the kind the Socialists wore in those days, which bothered him for the entire movie.

We'd started out with a comedy and ended up with a melodrama, to the heartrending notes of "Casta Diva" sung by Maria Callas. And we had so much fun.

In 1990 Lina was back, with Eduardo De Filippo this time, with *Saturday, Sunday and Monday*. The set always took me straight back to Mamma Luisa's kitchen in Pozzuoli, because *ragù*, meat sauce, "the holiest event on Sundays," was always simmering in the kitchen.

The whole movie revolved around the preparation of ragù in Rosa Priore's majolica kitchen, a great family woman busy restoring her honor, on which doubts have been cast owing to her husband's jealousy. All the members of the crew—myself included, as well as Luca De Filippo in the role of Peppino, Luciano De Crescenzo, and Pupella Maggio, on down to the technicians, the electricians and the stagehands—were convinced they knew the only real recipe for meat sauce. We continued to challenge each other to duels fought over unforgettable spaghetti dinners. All you have to do is watch the beginning of the movie, which is set in a butcher's shop, to understand that, against the backdrop of that ungraspable, chaotic Neapolitan anarchy, everyone has an opinion on the matter and it's impossible to reach an agreement.

"*Donna Cecì, ve voglio bene*" (I love you, I'm in a rush), says Donna Rosa. 'I need one and a half kilos of chopped meat, three kilos of tender veal, a piece of rump, some shoulder, and two kilos of hindquarter and bone."

"No sweetbreads, no beef brain?"

Line after line, each woman tries to impose her way of doing things:

"My mother-in-law, who's famous for her meat sauce, taught me to sauté the meat before cooking it, without the onion . . ."

"*Madonna signo'*," Rosa lets slip imprudently, "what you're saying is blasphemy!"

"Excuse me if I butt in, but the lady's right, because if you cook the meat and the onion separately, the meat sauce will be more delicate, fancier . . ."

"Oh, so you're saying that meat and onion cooked together is low class . . . ? Sorry to have to ask this, Signora, but where are you from?

"What does that have to do with anything? I'm from Afragola, so what about it?"

"Aha . . . that explains it."

That "Aha" is what triggers the fight, and the glorious weekend is about to begin.

Fortunately, on the set we were much tamer, although, to be honest, we weren't really that different from Rosa and the other women. Whatever the case may be, we worked really hard on that meat sauce, and the results were excellent.

Lina likes to recall that the delicious aroma of meat sauce even drew Al Pacino, who was also making a movie at Cinecittà, to our table.

"What's for lunch?" the great actor inquired as he stuck his head inside the sliding door of our field kitchen one day. As if by magic, we found a chair and squeezed closer to make room for him at the table, too. For us it was a surprise, an honor. For him, a good chance to taste genuine Neapolitan meat sauce, which is different from the kind you get with international cuisine. Karl Malden, who'd played Peppino on Broadway, also showed up for a taste.

Even though this comedy was known all over the world, and had been performed by Sir Laurence Olivier in London, its essence can't really be translated—all those dialogues, those arguments, those atmospheres. So Lina, while working on the script along with Raffaele La Capria, had shifted the time frame back from the early 1950s to 1934, right into Pozzuoli, allowing me to identify totally with my character. Actually, it wasn't hard: that world was very familiar to me, and I hadn't forgotten it. And the set designer, Enrico Job, Lina's adored husband, had reconstructed my native town just as I remembered it. Nothing remains of that world today.

My niece Alessandra was also a member of the cast, playing the part of Rosa's daughter, Giulianella. She had already played my daughter in *A Special Day*, but she had a much more important part in this movie.

One morning my sister, Maria, showed up unexpectedly on the set, saddened by a serious health-related problem. She took her daughter to one side and shared her anxiety with her. I knew nothing about it, I could see them conferring in the corner, and I didn't know why. But I was soon able to notice its effects. While shooting the lover's argument, Ale's eyes, bright from having cried for real, worked perfectly, and gave the scene its authenticity. My niece was talented, but she would soon choose another path in life.

Luckily, there was nothing wrong with Maria, and even her husband, Majid, who had been very worried, brightened up.

Saturday, Sunday and Monday was a huge success in Italy and abroad. The first time Carlo Jr. and Edoardo saw the movie they couldn't stop laughing: in Rosa they recognized many of the expressions, gestures, and lines that their own mother uses every day, and they thought it was hilarious.

But the time had come at last to shut the kitchen door behind me and go back to the big world: awaiting me was a decade to be rolled out like some long, marvelous red carpet.

STANDING OVATION

In 1963, I was asked by the Academy of Motion Pictures Arts and Sciences to deliver the Best Actor Award. Wearing a very elegant white dress designed by Emilio Schuberth, my hair teased in the style back then, I started out by reciting from the script: "It is my privilege to present the Oscar for the best performance as an actor . . ." But when I turned to the organizers backstage, I automatically switched to Italian: "*La busta, per favore . . .*" causing the audience to burst into laughter. The winner was Gregory Peck for *To Kill a Mockingbird.*

Twenty-eight years later, at the Shrine Civic Auditorium in

Los Angeles, Gregory and I had exchanged roles, but the wonderful mood in the room was exactly the same as before.

This time—it was March 25, 1991—Gregory was waiting for me at the bottom of a very long staircase, which I walked down carefully, overcome by emotion, in a glittering Valentino dress.

I had met him the evening before at the hotel. Almost thirty years had gone by since we'd last seen each other, when filming *Arabesque*. When the elevator door opened, there he was standing in front of me, as if time had never stopped. A flash, a moment that lasted an eternity. In his surprised look, in the slight hesitation he'd shown as he moved to the side to let me by, I had glimpsed a world of things he would have liked to say, but hadn't. Nor would ever say.

When he handed me my second Oscar, this one for my career, the audience stood up in a standing ovation while I tried hopelessly to hold back the tears. If anyone out there thought I was just acting they were wrong. I spoke of my gratitude, happiness, and pride. I recalled how in 1962 I had been too fear-stricken to fly out to Hollywood to get my Oscar for *Two Women*.

"Tonight I'm still scared, but I'm not alone," I concluded, as I peered into the audience searching for my family. "I want to share this special evening with the three men in my life. My husband, Carlo Ponti, without whom I wouldn't be who I am today. And my two sons, Carlo Jr. and Edoardo, who taught me to conjugate the verb 'to love' in a million ways. Thank you, America."

It had been Karl Malden, one of Hollywood's finest character actors, who had called to inform me of my prize a few weeks before. It took me completely by surprise. It was such a wonderful surprise that I had wanted my family to experience it themselves and so I'd kept the news to myself so they would discover it on their own.

"Mamma!" Edoardo shouted into the phone a few days later. "Mamma!" "An Honorary Award at the Oscars! I heard it on the radio. Why? Why didn't you tell us?"

I was laughing up my sleeve about the little prank I'd played on them. You don't get a chance to play as good a prank as this one every day!

I didn't think I'd ever experience anything as wonderful as that again. But I was wrong. In 1993 I got back up on the stage at the Academy Awards to "honor a dear friend with a towering film history"—Federico Fellini. Twelve nominations, four Oscars for Best Foreign Film, two produced by Carlo: *La strada*, in 1956, and *The Nights of Cabiria*, the following year. Sharing this privilege with me was my dear friend Marcello, who was perhaps even more excited than I was.

Federico Fellini got a long standing ovation amid tears and smiles, just as I had.

"Please-ah sit-ah down-ah, be comfortable," said the maestro with his delightful Italian accent. "If someone here has-a the right or a little bit-a the right to feel uncomfortable that's-a me!"

As I handed him the statuette, which he was very familiar with, he kissed me, and turned to his long-time friend: "*Grazie, Marcellino, grazie che sei venuto . . .*" (Thanks for coming, Marcellino).

"*Prego*, you're welcome," Marcello replied, embarrassed and amused at the same time.

They were talking as though they were on a train from Rimini to Rome thirty years before. And instead they were in Hollywood, standing before the who's who of world cinema.

The audience clearly understood, from Federico's and Marcello's gestures laden with emotion, just how deep their personal and professional relationship was. It went way back in time and had made the whole world dream.

The great Fellini, who would die just a few months later, didn't forget to mention his wife: "Thank you, Giulietta, and please, stop-a crying!"

Three years later Marcello would also leave us. The last time I saw him was in Milan. He was getting into a car on his way to the theater to rehearse *The Last Moons* by Furio Bordon. I was getting into another car, headed toward the airport. Marcello gave me a long hard look. Maybe he'd guessed we'd never see each other again.

I still find it very hard to go back to the days surrounding his death. The world shouted and talked about it, participated in it, and paid him tribute. I, instead, remained shut away in my room, shrouded in privacy. I didn't want my pain to get mixed up with that of others, I didn't want to parade my feelings for the media to lap up and exploit. I stayed by myself, trying to find a way to understand just what exactly had happened. The day of his funeral I sent a host of orchids, that their freshness might accompany him on his journey and give him the love I will always have for him.

The next decade of Italian Oscars still had some great satisfaction in store for us. In 1999 it was *Life Is Beautiful*'s turn, the film won three statuettes. And I was the one, this time wearing an Armani gown, to hand Roberto Benigni his prize for Best Foreign Language Film.

"*And the Oscar goes to . . .*" I said as I opened the envelope, "*Robbberto!!!!*" The auditorium was overwhelmed by our totally Italian celebration. As I waved the envelope in the air like some young girl, Roberto embarked on a comical obstacle race by walking across the tops of the rows of seats toward the stage. Steven Spielberg gave him a hand to prevent him from crashing down on the heads of the bejeweled stars seated there.

When the ham finally hopped up on the stage and ran toward me, our embrace was a round and spiraling one. Just like his speech, unstoppable, exhilarating, laden with brio and culture. I watched him awestruck as he talked about dives into the ocean, hailstorms, the dawning of eternity and thought about those who had lost their lives so that today we can say that life is beautiful. A kiss for Giorgio Cantarini, the little boy in the movie. And, of course, after thanking his parents in Vergaio for having given him the greatest gift of all, the gift of poverty, he dedicated his words to his wife, Nicoletta Braschi, who was shedding tears of joy.

In those years filled with prizes and acknowledgments, I reaped the fruit of all my work, the joy and sacrifices, fun, and discipline. In 1996 Carlo and I were nominated Knights Grand Cross of the Order of Merit of the Italian Republic by President Oscar Luigi Scalfaro. I've received career awards that include a César d'Honneur, Berlin's Golden Bear, and the Cecil B. DeMille Award. Each one of them is charged with my feelings about and special memories of people who appreciated me and chose me, who enlightened my life from a different perspective. I harbor a feeling of gratitude and a sense of wonder for each one of them.

In 1998, Venice, too, paid tribute to my career, awarding me with a Golden Lion, but when I received the news I was going through a particularly difficult time in my life. I felt weary, stressed, and vulnerable. Carlo and the boys as always helped me out, and they supported me by going to receive the award in my place. And they cried along with me, even as I lovingly watched them.

In those difficult months I once again poured all my love into the kitchen, which has always been my world of peace, my bulwark in the face of all the world's trials and tribulations. That's how my second cookbook, *Recipes and Memories*, was born. It was the simplest and most natural way for me to share the flavors of my existence, linking them to the episodes and encounters that had led me all the way to this moment in my life. The book was very popular, and reminded me that, at the end of the day, real success is often hidden in the domestic secret of simplicity.

"CAZZABUBBOLI"

My prizes are all right there on the shelves. Every now and again I give them a dusting, smiling inside as I do. I like to remember them all, one by one, I like to keep them in order and I like to travel in my imagination from Hollywood to Berlin, from Cannes to Venice to New York. But then I like to come back and smell the fragrance of my native land once more.

Francesca and Nunziata, the TV movie later adapted for the cinema, based on the novel by Maria Orsini Natale, tells the story of two Neapolitan pasta makers between the nineteenth and twentieth centuries. The author had sent Lina Wertmüller the manuscript before it was published, and she'd fallen in love with it. Then, as often happens in cinema, ten years went by before anything happened. And so, at the turn of the new millennium, Lina and I, accompanied by a marvelous cast, distilled its harmony in each and every frame.

Once again, the location was to our advantage. We shot part of it on the magical island of Procida, which greeted us with enthusiasm, little by little unveiling its hidden, genuine essence. Although it isn't far from Pozzuoli, I'd never seen it before and I left my heart there. In the bay of Corricella, at Punta Pizzaco, on the panoramic road overlooking Capri, in the midst of the ancient buildings surrounded by citrus groves that jut out over the water, we all breathed at a slow and natural pace, which made our work on the set sweeter and less difficult. Cinema has its tricks, and not all the scenes were shot in the Gulf of Naples, nor was all that pasta, which was at the center of the story of real pasta. The pasta that we put out to dry in the sun, were miles and miles of plastic spaghetti.

In any case, acting under the expert guidance of someone like Lina, along with her favorite actor, Giancarlo Giannini, was like being part of a family.

And the family in this story is indeed a large one. Playing Donna Francesca, I have gray hair and wear as many strings of pearls as all the children I've had. Besides my own children, I also adopt an orphan, Nunziatina, because of a vow I once made to the Virgin. She is the only one who follows in my footsteps, those of a proud, ruthless, self-made businesswoman who's made a huge fortune. Everything is going just fine until, one day, Prince Giordano Montorsi, tired of playing the role of the prince consort, wakes up from his aristocratic lethargy to try his hand at banking, with disastrous results for the fate of the family. Francesca tries to warn him when she first senses the danger. *"You were born a prince, be a prince then, let me take care of the pasta business . . ."* But her words are of no use.

This movie offered me a beautiful story, fifteen large, showy hats, which we ironically referred to as "cazzabubboli," and a character that was both strong and weak at the same time, just like me. The great monologue at the end is Lina's greatest gift to me: *"You can't die of pain, Nunziatì, but it's still bad . . ."*

However, my maternal roles didn't end there. Eight years later I was back on the screen with Rob Marshall's *Nine*, as Guido Contini's (Fellini's) "Mamma." It was an ambitious movie, adapted from the famous Broadway musical inspired by *8½*. I had accepted the part in memory of Federico, with whom, by a twist of fate, I had never managed to work, or maybe it was because I wasn't his type of actress. I had also accepted the role because I liked the idea of working with Daniel Day-Lewis, whom I believe to be the greatest actor around today.

Neither the original ideas in the script nor the excellent cast, including Penélope Cruz, Judi Dench, Nicole Kidman, and Marion Cotillard, were enough to make the movie as good as its inspiration. I will always remember a tender, moving dance with Danny who cultivates his neurotic creativity in his mother's shadow. And I will also always remember with tenderness that remarkable season of Italian cinema that I had the privilege and honor to experience firsthand.

VOICES

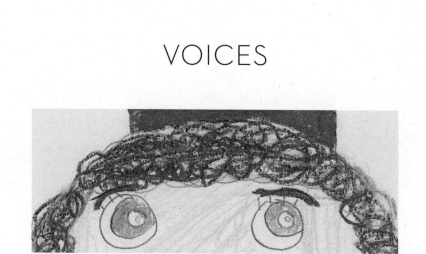

I was a mother both on and off the set, and, thanks to my son Edoardo, became both at the same time in two films. My life really is like a fairy tale that, like all fairy tales, begins and ends its chapters with great happiness as well as great sorrow.

Carlo passed away in Switzerland on January 10, 2007, at the age of ninety-four, defeated by the diabetes that in the last few weeks of his life had steadily weakened him. Edoardo and I were there to hold his hand, while his other children, Guenda-lina and Alex, and our Carlo Jr., were flying in from the United States or Rome.

I can still remember the call I got that dark winter evening from the hospital, telling us to hurry because the end was close. I can still remember an endless, hopeless night. I can remember how cold the dawn was when we said farewell before his last journey toward Magenta, where he was born and where he was to be buried.

Death is as ugly as it is normal. There's something profoundly unnatural about having to let go of someone you love so much. You turn this way and that trying to find support, knowing full well that there isn't any. And you feel completely alone, aban-doned even by words.

Then again, is there really anything left to be said when, after fifty-six years of life together, the end comes? Every morning when I wake up I struggle to believe Carlo is no longer here. I search for him in every corner of our house. I find him in our children's voices, which are identical to his, in the expressions of our grandchildren, who have meanwhile arrived to brighten my days. They complete my maternal feelings, in a way I would never have expected.

Lucia and Vittorio, Leonardo and Beatrice have made me the happiest grandmother in the world. In my treasure trove of memories I find a portrait they drew of me that makes me feel prouder than any photo could. I'm putty in their hands, I vanish completely. Not having the task of raising them I can spoil them as much as I want to, stuff them with chocolate, pamper them and hug them until they plead with me to stop. In their smiles, in their talents, I project my own happiness, my dream of a more peaceful future, of a better tomorrow. They're very lucky, and I hope they'll be able to give back to the world everything they've been given, just like their parents have done.

Today, Carlo Jr., who pursued his love of music, also thanks to his father's advice, is an orchestra conductor. When I see him up on the podium, so comfortable, confident, self-assured, my heart races and I burst with pride. He's worked with some of the greatest names, including Mehli and Zubin Mehta and Leopold Hager, and has conducted many orchestras around the world, including the Russian National Orchestra, the Simón Bolívar Symphony Orchestra, the Orchestre Philharmonique de Strasbourg, and the orchestras of both the Teatro San Carlo and the arts festival Maggio Musicale Fiorentino. And he has found his true love: the Hungarian violinist Andrea Mészáros, who shares with him the same passion for music and the raising of their two marvelous children. But the podium isn't enough for him. For some time he's been working to place his experience at the service of young people, convinced that music is a powerful instrument of individual growth and social emancipation.

Edoardo, instead, has confirmed his talent for cinema. I can still see him, a little boy playing with puppets and inventing stories and scenes while his brother accompanied him on the piano. Maybe there's some truth in the idea that a person can have a calling, and when they do it's obvious right from the start. He had always wanted to be a filmmaker, and he has pursued his ambition with intelligence and love. Sasha Alexander, his beautiful wife, is an actress, always trying to find a balance between her work in television and taking care of their children. Today, compared to my day and age, women are probably luckier, they're judged more often on the basis of what they know how to do, more than how they look. But, as opportunities grow, so do all the problems related to balancing family and work. The world is more complicated, more demanding, and women have to make more sacrifices, in proportion to the gratification. And yet, in the end, you're always back on square one, and each one of us must come to terms with oneself.

I've said it many times: my children are my best movies. And their happiness is the award that honors me the most.

"Mamma," Edoardo said to me one day as he was standing at the door to our house. Carlo was no longer with us, and Lucia, his firstborn, wasn't a year old yet. "Mamma, Sasha and I have decided to get married!"

It's no secret I've always had a soft spot for weddings, and although the one between Carlo and Andrea, first in Geneva and then in Saint Stephen's, a fabulous basilica in Budapest, had warmed my heart, it hadn't completely appeased my desire for white veils and gowns.

"How wonderful, Edoardo!" I said softly, happy with this new joy that I had given up expecting.

He looked at me quietly, as if to let me speak first.

"Where?" I asked timidly, expecting to hear the name of some Hollywood location.

"In Geneva, in the Russian church . . . Sasha's Orthodox, you know, besides, Papà really loved that church . . ."

Carlo wasn't a churchgoer, and yet he was mysteriously attracted to that small, wonderful church in the heart of the old city. Whenever he and Edoardo would go out for a walk, something they did rather frequently in the last years of his life, he'd make sure they would always walk by it. "Let's go there . . ." he'd say, almost timidly. And Edo knew that "there" meant the Église Russe. We're not the ones to choose where and how to express our soul's most sacred breath. The truth is that we're chosen.

TRIBUTES

At this point in my life and career, hiding around every corner is a party, a surprise. On May 4, 2011, Hollywood devoted a gala evening to me. Roberto Benigni said, in the video message he sent me that evening, "When I hear the name Sophia, I jump, and jump again because it's an explosion of life. Like a kiss on the cheek. It's something marvelous, and you can see my heart beating, my heart thumping, going boom boom. She is Italy, and very Italian. When she moves, when she walks, all of Italy is walking. You can see Sicily, Tuscany, Lombardy move. Then Milan, Florence, Naples, the Leaning Tower of Pisa, the Colosseum, pizza, spaghetti, Totò, De Sica, she holds all these things and all these people inside."

Words are nothing compared with the gestures, the mimicry, the comedy that's part of every single breath Roberto takes. The great comedian even sang a song that sounded a lot like "O sole mio," and that ended with a mischievous farewell: "*Grazie Sofia, amore mio, corpo inesauribile, bye bye.*" (Thanks Sofia, my love, inexhaustible body, bye bye.)

It's a good thing he got us all laughing, otherwise the tears would never have stopped flowing. That evening for me was like a third Oscar, in joy, importance, emotion. My children were there as escorts, my daughters-in-law to reassure me. Billy Crystal was master of ceremonies. John Travolta and Rob Marshall, Christian De Sica, actress Jo Champa, film executive Sid Ganis, and many other friends remembered our years together. It was all that an actress, woman, and mother could possibly wish for.

On December 12 of that same year, at the Parco della Musica auditorium in Rome, the boys and I remembered Carlo and our love for him on what would have been his ninety-ninth birthday. Sitting in the audience, watching Carlo Jr. conduct the soundtrack of our lives, with his energy and bravura, and Edoardo reading a short and moving speech in the form of a letter, for a moment there I felt the empitness his death had left us with had been filled. To the notes of the themes of *Doctor Zhivago*, *La Strada*, *Two Women*, all of which Carlo produced, and accompanied by the music of Armando Trovajoli, and Nino Rota, my nostalgia was transformed into gratitude for all the things that had led us to that point. And for an instant the four of us were together again.

Edoardo's words portrayed Carlo more sharply than any image or film clip could possibly have done. He recalled our afternoons of love listening to Tchaikovsky, Carlo's dinners with Fellini, his touching anecdotes, off-color jokes, as well as his pearls of wisdom. He remembered the delicate touch of his father's large hands that, when Edoardo was a child, made him feel safe. Then he offered us an image of Carlo seen from behind, wearing a bathrobe and slippers, his legs bare, as he would leave the house shrouded in the fog early in the morning to visit his rose garden. That garden was his pride and joy: rows of red, pink, white, and yellow roses. He tended to them with painstaking attention, strong and delicate at the same time.

"Why do you like roses so much, Papà?"

"Because roses are like dreams, the larger ones require patience and hard work."

Carlo is no longer here, but he still inspires our passions and keeps us united in his memory. The boys and I live far apart, but we love each other, we follow and chase each other around the world, we think about each other, we help each other, and we call each other. And sometimes we give each other wonderful gifts.

IN SEARCH OF TRUTH

Today, after many years of work, Edoardo is a sensitive and rigorous film director, who has turned empathy into his strong point. He loves people, he tries to understand them, to interpret their journey. This, the truth of common feelings, is what he's interested in.

Sometimes all it takes is a few hours' conversation to encourage you and show you the road.

This happened to him when he spoke with Miloš Forman, the great director of *Hair* and *Amadeus*, one afternoon a long time ago. "It doesn't matter whether the drama is dramatic or the comedy is fun," said the maestro that day, with the simplicity with which only the great are gifted. "What's important is that it's all true."

Edoardo never forgot those words, and he repeats them each time he says, "Lights! Camera! Action!"

In 2001 Edoardo had directed me in *Between Strangers*, his first feature-length movie. The film was shot in Toronto and the cast included Mira Sorvino, Malcolm McDowell, Klaus Maria Brandauer. But above all, there was Gérard Depardieu, one of the greatest actors I have ever met in my entire life. Like Alec Guinness, or Peter O'Toole, Gérard opens his mouth and a whole world comes out, with all its reliefs and all its dark-and-light sides.

Although he may be restless in daily life, on the set he is a true, courteous, and focused professional. Added to his genius and talent is a craftsman's precision. Depardieu knows his own face so well that all he has to do is move a small muscle to completely change his expression. Just as my first teacher, Pino Serpe, taught us! And then there's his rhythm . . . He has such a sense of rhythm that he doesn't need to rehearse: often the first take he does is as good as it gets.

Any other time I could have been lost in my thoughts just watching him, admiring him, acting alongside him. But this time I was preoccupied by the fact that there to direct me was my son. This was no small matter.

It wasn't at all easy on the set to strike the right balance between being a mother and an actress. Even more than usual, I felt responsible for doing my very best for Edoardo's debut; he'd devised a complex story, interweaving the lives of three women who meet by chance at the airport. But then, one morning, it became clear exactly what I was supposed to do: and it was easier than I'd thought.

It might sound funny, but it was all thanks to a dog.

That morning, we were shooting a scene in which a poodle walks from one side of the street to the other. Seemingly insignificant, it was actually an important detail, one that Edoardo was very fond of. Well, that poodle would have none of it. It would start out correctly, egged on by its trainers, but then, in the middle of the scene, it would stop dead in its tracks. And nothing could be done about it. We tried cookies, dog biscuits, shouting, pulling, a transparent leash, but nothing. That dog just froze, with all of us around it, maybe because it was scared or maybe because that's just what it felt like doing.

Its stubbornness forced us to do the scene over again many times, until we just started doing it automatically. And it was the almost mesmerizingly automatic nature of the scene that helped me to shed any worries I might have felt about being both the director's mother and an actress in his movie. I watched Edoardo patiently start over each time, completely absorbed in his role. For him, mothers, wives, families, none of these things existed. All that existed at that moment was his movie, his actors, his crew.

In that instant I realized that our relationship was of no importance on the set. Edoardo was the director, I was one of his actors. He directed and I just had to do the acting. All I had to do was listen to him and let myself go. That's how I divested myself of my maternal identity to focus on the script and my truth as an actress.

It was an important experience for both of us, and made us richer as professionals. It also strengthened our relationship and prepared us to face together another great cinematic challenge, his gift to me more than a decade later. It was the story of a mature woman who, shut inside a room, during a dramatic phone call of words, hesitation, and silence, loses the last love of her life and feels finished.

EGGPLANT PARMESAN

The first time Edoardo mentioned the role to me over the phone, he caught me by surprise.

"*The Human Voice*? You mean the one played by Anna Magnani, Ingrid Bergman, Simone Signoret? The one . . ."

"Mamma, there's no need for you to give me the whole list of names. Of course that's the one I'm talking about. *La voix humaine, The Human Voice*, by Jean Cocteau.

"How wonderful, I've been dreaming about this all my life, ever since I saw Nannarella play the part when I was a young girl!" And that's when, as usual, a war broke out inside me. Doubt hit me: "But . . . am I up to it?"

Now, however, knowing myself very well, I ironed out all the creases in this tangled-up situation, and kept only its inner heart, that enthusiasm for something new, that fear "of the first time" that causes me to act in each movie as though I were making my debut. As I worked on myself, Edoardo was thinking about production, the location, the script, the slant he wanted to give it.

The discussion that began between us is of the kind that develops around the embryo of a project that grows bigger and bigger. A discussion filled with digressions, vital and creative ones, that always accompanies the birth of a movie, and kindles the imagination, feelings.

Everything inside me had been lit, something that hadn't happened to me in a long time.

I was tempted to go and see the way the many actresses who had done the piece had interpreted it, thinking that it might have given me some ideas.

"No, Mamma, you don't want to be influenced by anyone," Edoardo said. "Every actress has her own version of it."

I obeyed, trying to say as little as possible, to hear in his voice what he expected of me.

One day he came right out and said it.

"What if it were in Neapolitan dialect?"

I couldn't believe my ears. It was such a bold idea, so poignant, an idea that was so close to me that it moved me.

Edoardo, on the other end of the line, understood my silence and said, "Yes, because a woman who is abandoned can only speak in her mother tongue, the language she spoke as a child . . ."

Erri De Luca translated the pièce by Cocteau. Both Edoardo and I loved him as a writer, and we trusted his limpid, laconic style and deep insights. We sat around a table talking with him about it, and in what seemed like no time at all he'd finished the text.

"How did you do it, Erri? How did you write it so quickly?" I asked him admiringly.

"I kept thinking about, hearing, your voice, and your voice dictated the words to me . . ." he answered with his typical straightforwardness.

Now it was up to me to interpret it the best way I could. This time, however, I realized my instinct wasn't going to be enough. We rehearsed nonstop for six weeks, almost as though we were preparing a theater performance. Careful, focused, closed in a hotel room as though it were a dressing room. And then, at last, we were ready—but is one ever really ready?—to begin.

Yes, because Edoardo had chosen to expand the "room of abandonment" to which Cocteau had deliberately confined his character, to include the city, the sea, to those subtle memories—a fragrance, a view, a touch—that, like arrows, the heart sends you when love is gone. Short flashbacks that appear swiftly and then close again instantly on the telephone cord that twists all around the room and Angela's pain. At the heart of her memories is her lover, "Signore," played by Enrico Lo Verso, who, unsurprisingly, is only seen in profile, from the back of his head, and from behind, as he kisses her passionately in times when they were still happy. A man who comes from the north and often can't even understand what she's saying in dialect. Another way of saying that he can't understand her and actually doesn't deserve her.

We shot the movie in Rome in the De Paolis studio, the one where we'd done *A Special Day*, and then later in Ostia, on the same beach as the one in *Too Bad She's Bad*, and then, finally, in Naples, between Palazzo Reale, the alleyways of the Pallonetto di Santa Lucia, the historic Sanità neighborhood, the Belvedere Sant'Antonio, in the quarter of Posillipo. We worked hard, overcoming our reluctance to explore certain things and any embarrassment. Alongside us was Carlo who helped us to choose the music, Guendalina as associate producer, Alex who put so much work into the postproduction of the DVD. Every time I turn around to look at all of us together I'm moved to tears. In life you can't avoid pain, but you can find relief for it. And in time, we became a big, very close family. By that time I'd understood that I was supposed to be an actress and not a mother, but it wasn't so easy for me to let myself go in a role as explicit as this one in front of Edoardo. When you're abandoned you feel naked, a nakedness that I had to search for inside and then act out before him, overcoming the reserve that a son usually expects from a mother.

I'm sure it was hard for him, too. As a director, he sought the truth. And knowing me well he pushed me hard until he found it. That's why, when we'd come to the end of a particularly difficult scene, I'd continue crying even after his "Cut." I kept on weeping and weeping, and I wasn't the only one. As I walked toward him I realized he was crying, too.

In the movie, unlike the original, there's another change as well, that doesn't actually express hope, but, like a typically Neapolitan counterpoint, measures the distance between desperation and the normality that has been lost. While the pain is transformed into mourning, in the other room the governess sets the table for two, and, just like any old Tuesday, she takes her eggplant Parmesan out of the oven. A favorite dish that speaks of love, and of sharing. A dish that represents Angela's strength, her determination, in spite of her downfall. The dish that has accompanied my life, and that today makes my voice even more human.

"Signò, it's eight fifteen. I'm off now . . ."

ONCE UPON A TIME

At the end of this long road is the future. Tomorrow is as still filled with dreams as yesterday and today. Going back to Naples, to my beloved city, to my people, who greet me joyfully from the balconies, made me feel like a young girl again, it made me happy. But if I were totally satisfied, then I'd feel burdened by life. Instead, living means setting new goals to strive for each and every day.

I let my mind wander, I stumble upon a project I've been

thinking about for some time now. But it's late now, I need to try to sleep a few hours. Tomorrow is Christmas Eve, my family is waiting for me.

I'm about to close the lid on my treasure trove of memories when I find myself holding two yellowing sheets of paper that are about me. Perhaps I was the one who wrote them, who knows when, who knows why. I start reading while outside the world falls fast asleep beneath the snow.

Once upon a time there was a little girl with skinny legs, big eyes, and a worried mouth.

Once upon a time there was a little girl who loved every blade of grass that ever existed, whether it was ugly or beautiful.

Once upon a time there was a little girl born inside a tangle of bitter roots in the flower of which she discovered the world—mountains to climb—treets to venture down.

Once upon a time there was a young woman who loved the whole universe, with all that was to be seen and traveled.

Once upon a time there was a woman who wanted to overcome all her fears and live in the world with big eyes and a worried mouth.

Once upon a time there was a woman who became an actress performing for others the thousands of faces she'd dreamed of but perhaps would never experience.

Once upon a time there was a woman who wanted to be a wife—it was hard and difficult to achieve.

Once upon a time there was a woman who wanted to be a mother just like every other woman and have children that were all her own.

Once upon a time there was an actress who acted in many movies—all of them mountains to be scaled. Not all mountains are like the Himalayas, and not all movies are like mountains to be scaled . . . But all of them were worth experiencing.

Once upon a time there was a bitter and wonderful life that a little girl, who has become a woman and an actress, continues to repeat to herself.

There will always be a once upon a time for every little girl who looks at the world with big eyes and a lust for life.

Epilogue

"Shhh, quiet, can't you see she's sleeping?"

"But it'll be time to eat soon . . ."

"Meatballs, meatballs, meatballs!"

"Nonna, Nonna, Nonna Sophia!"

Oh my goodness, what time is it? I must have fallen asleep. It's already morning, the sun's up, I went to bed late. The sea of memory gently carried me here, at the mercy of its capricious current.

The whispering of the wild ones, outside the half-open door, grows louder.

"Come in, *piccirilli*, my little ones, come in. What time is it?"

The first one to come forward is Lucia, with a triple series of cartwheels and somersaults. That child doesn't walk, she flies.

Nonna, it's ten o'clock!" she says smiling.

"Ten o'clock?!"

I don't think I've ever woken up so late in my whole life.

Vittorio is right behind her, with an expression so intense that it sometimes causes me pain.

"Nonna, weren't we supposed to make meatballs this morning?"

Following closely behind is Leonardo, who's holding a fine porcelain dish he stole from the table that he has decided to turn into a flying saucer.

"*Vroom, vroom*, out of my way, out of my way, here I come."

Beatrice is the last one to arrive, struggling to climb up onto my bed, which is too high for her, whispering my song in my ear: "Zoo-Be-Zoo-Be-Zoo." This child will be successful, I think to myself.

"Children, Nonna didn't get much sleep last night, let me get dressed. You wait for me in the kitchen!"

When I get there Ninni has cleared the table, set the meat on the wooden board, poured the flour into a large bowl, sliced the day-old bread. And she's rolled up the sleeves on my four little chefs, who look at me like four ponies at the starting gate.

"Let's say I prepare the meat, and you make the meatballs, is that all right?"

The children shout gleefully, their eyes shining like Christmas stars, and they get right down to work.

"No two meatballs are the same," I think to myself with amazement. "How lovely, still so completely free . . ."

"So, children, what do you want to be when you grow up?"

Leonardo pipes up with self-assurance: "A Formula Uno driver."

His sister, Lucia, sweeter than honey, whispers: "A ballet dancer."

Beatrice looks at me inquisitively:

"Grow up? Me?"

Vittorio, the most thoughtful of the bunch, comments wisely:

"I don't know, maybe a pianist. But it's still too early to decide . . ."

"And what about you, Nonna?" my wild ones shout in unison. "What do you want to be when you grow up?"

I laugh heartily.

"Me? I don't know, I have to think about it."

The Films of Sophia Loren

1950

Bluebeard's Six Wives
The Vow
Hearts at Sea
Tototarzan

1951

I Am the Capataz
White Leprosy
The Return of Pancho Villa
Milan Billionaire
Quo Vadis
Magician by Chance
The Industrialist
It Was Him! . . . Yes! Yes!
  (uncredited)
Anna

1952

I Dream of Zorro
Girls Marked Danger
The Piano Tuner Has Arrived

1953

Africa under the Seas
Aida
We'll Meet in the Gallery
Good People's Sunday
The Favorite

1954

A Day in the Lower Court
Town of Bells
Two Nights with Cleopatra
The Anatomy of Love
  (segment: "The Camera")
Neapolitan Carousel
Poverty and Nobility
Pilgrim of Love
The Gold of Naples
  (segment: "Pizza on
  Credit")
Attila
Woman of the River

1955

Too Bad She's Bad
The Sign of Venus
The Miller's Beautiful Wife
Scandal in Sorrento

1956

Lucky to Be a Woman

1957

Boy on a Dolphin
The Pride and the Passion
Legend of the Lost

1958

Desire Under the Elms
The Key
The Black Orchid
Houseboat

1959

That Kind of Woman

1960

Heller in Pink Tights
A Breath of Scandal
It Started in Naples
The Millionairess
Two Women

1961

El Cid

Madame Sans-Gêne, aka
    "Madame"

1962

Boccaccio '70
The Condemned of Altona
Five Miles to Midnight

1963

Yesterday, Today and Tomorrow

1964

The Fall of the Roman Empire
Marriage Italian Style

1965

Operation Crossbow
Lady L

1966

Judith
Arabesque

1967

A Countess from Hong Kong
More Than a Miracle

1968

Ghosts, Italian Style

1970

Sunflower
The Priest's Wife

1971

Lady Liberty

1972

Man of La Mancha

1973

The Sin

1974

The Voyage
Verdict
Brief Encounter

1975

Sex Pot

1976

The Cassandra Crossing

1977

A Special Day

1978

Angela
Blood Feud
Brass Target

1979

Firepower

1980

Sophia Loren: Her Own Story

1984

Aurora

1986

Courage

1988

The Fortunate Pilgrim

1989

Running Away

1990

Saturday, Sunday and Monday

1994

Ready to Wear (Prêt-à-Porter)

1995

Grumpier Old Men

1997

Soleil (French)

2001

Francesca and Nunziata

2002

Between Strangers

2004

Lives of the Saints
Too Much Romance . . .
 It's Time for Stuffed
 Peppers

2009

Nine

2010

My House Is Full of Mirrors

2011

Cars 2

2014

Human Voice

Index

Page numbers in *italics* refer to photography insert.

Index

Illustration and Photography Credits

Page 3 (bottom) © Archivio GBB Contrasto; Page 4 (top) © Archivio GBB Contrasto; Page 5 (center) © Archivio GBB Contrasto; Page 5 (bottom) © Mondadori/Getty; Page 6 (top) © Fedeli/Reporters Associati & Archivi; Page 6 (bottom) © Reporters Associati & Archivi; Page 7 © Vitali/Reporters Associati & Archivi; Page 10 (top) © Reporters Associati & Archivi; Page 13 (top) © Fedeli/Reporters Associati & Archivi; Page 14 © Vitali/Reporters Associati & Archivi; Page 16 (top) © Publifot/ Olycom; Page 17 © Auguste; Page 18 (top) © Pierluigi/Reporters Associati & Archivi; Page 22 © Vitali/Reporters Associati & Archivi; Page 23 © Pierluigi/Reporters Associati & Archivi; Pages 27 (center and bottom), 28, 29, 30 (top) © Pierluigi/Reporters Associati & Archivi; Pages 31, 32, 33 (top) © Reporters Associati & Archivi; Page 34 © Klaus Collignon; Page 35 © Pierluigi/Reporters Associati & Archivi; Page 36 © Tazio Secchiaroli/David Secchiaroli; Page 37 (top and center) © Reporters Associati & Archivi; Page 41 (top) © Pierluigi/Reporters Associati & Archivi; Page 41 (bottom) © Keystone/Getty Images; Page 42 (top) © Tazio Secchiaroli/David Secchiaroli; Page 42 (bottom) © Pierluigi/Reporters Associati & Archivi; Page 43 (top) © Tazio Secchiaroli/David Secchiaroli; Page 43 (bottom) © Norman Hargood; Page 44 © Photo by Jean-Claude

Deutsch/Paris Match via Getty Images; Page 45 © Keystone/ Getty Images; Page 46 (top) © Photo by Alfred Eisenstaedt/ The LIFE Picture Collection/Getty Images; Page 48 © Tazio Secchiaroli/David Secchiaroli; Page 49 © Claudio Patriarca; Page 50 (top) © Tazio Secchiaroli/David Secchiaroli; Page 51 © Photo by Jack Garofalo/Paris Match via Getty Images; Page 55 © Tazio Secchiaroli/David Secchiaroli; Page 56 © Reporters Associati & Archivi; Page 58 (top) © Photo by Kevin Winter/ DMI/The LIFE Picture Collection/Getty Images; Page 60 © Photo by Etienne George/RDA/Getty Images; Page 61 (top) © Photo by Jean-Paul Aussenard/WireImage/Getty Images; Page 61 (bottom) © Photo by Ernesto Ruscio/FilmMagic/Getty Images; Page 62 © AP Photo/Eric Draper.

Images from the Loren-Ponti family archive and documents are as follows: pages 2, 3 (top), 4 (bottom), 5 (top), 8, 9, 10 (bottom), 11, 12, 13 (bottom), 15, 16 (bottom), 18 (bottom), 19, 20, 21, 24, 25, 26, 27 (top), 30 (bottom), 33 (bottom), 37 (bottom), 38, 39, 40, 46 (bottom), 47, 50 (bottom), 52, 53, 54, 57, 58 (bottom), 59, 63, 64.

About the Author

Sophia Loren is an international film star who won an Academy Award for Best Actress for her role in *Two Women*. She has earned a record six David di Donatello awards for Best Actress, a Grammy Award, and seven special Golden Globes, including the Cecil B. DeMille Award for lifetime achievement, as well as an Honorary Academy Award in 1991. Loren lives in Europe and frequents Los Angeles where her two sons and grandchildren live.